Sr. Monica,

We continue to journey joyously despite the mountains in our lives.

Dan Siftick

D1371283

DAN SEFTICK

REAL
MOUNTAINS

A MEMOIR

Beaver's Pond
PRESS

ISBN 13: 978-1-59298-692-7
Library of Congress Catalog Number: 2016916418
Printed in the United States of America
First Printing: 2016
20 19 18 17 16   5 4 3 2 1

Book design and typesetting by Dan Pitts.

Beaver's Pond Press
7108 Ohms Lane
Edina, MN 55439–2129
(952) 829-8818
www.BeaversPondPress.com

FOR GREG

HIS WAS AN INSPIRED LIFE

CONTENTS

INTRODUCTION

I've thought about writing a book for more than twenty years. This isn't the story I wanted to tell. Initially, the writing was therapeutic. When it came time to assemble my thoughts in some coherent fashion, I was advised I should have a purpose for doing so. The reason was obvious to me—to preserve and build Greg's legacy. I want those who knew him to know him better and never forget him. I want people who didn't know him to wish they had. I don't think that's too much for a father to ask.

You're invited to explore the life of an incredible young man, Dr. Gregory Eric Seftick, my son. Greg's life was one adventure after another. He was all about experiences. He accomplished more than most people do in much longer lifetimes. He pushed himself to constantly be doing, learning, and exploring. It will always be difficult to accept that he died at the age of thirty-one in an avalanche in Grand Teton National Park the night of April 16, 2011.

So what is this book?

First of all, it's a love story. It's the story of a father's love for his son. But more than that, it's the story of a man's love for life. Greg's eagerness to spend time with his friends, welcome new people into his life, travel, climb rock and ice, and enjoy back-country skiing, mountaineering, and music were all expressions of his love for life.

This is also a personal history. It tells the history of one man's life, not in chronological detail, but through anecdotes that explain his dreams and define his character. This book isn't about me. And yet it is about me and Greg's mother, Sue; his brother, Chris; his girlfriend, Megan; his grandparents, aunts, uncles, cousins, friends, and teachers; and many others. It reflects Greg's unique ability to connect with many people on many levels—and his gift for gleaning from that connection what bound him to the other person. Forging lasting bonds wasn't a conscious effort for Greg; he seemed to do it naturally. And it made others comfortable being with him.

This is an adventure story. Greg packed a lot of life into thirty-one years. He was always planning his next trip to climb or ski. It wasn't unusual for him to visit a friend for an evening or a weekend just because he was "in the neighborhood," which to him might mean within a few hundred miles. Not many of us have the same perception of time and distance as Greg did.

This is an inspirational book. Greg's was an inspired life. He didn't preach inspiration; he lived it. His encouragement was infectious. He was so enthusiastic about the important things in his life that those things became important to his friends and family. They were inspired to embrace the things he loved, to make the most of each day, to dig deeper into their hearts.

This is a success story. Even though Greg accomplished a lot in his short life, not everything came easily to him. It may seem as if he got everything he wanted—a college education; acceptance to med school; honors as a resident; experience as a back-country skier, mountaineer, and ice and rock climber; and opportunities to nurture his inner jam-band aficionado. He had all that and more.

But he worked hard, and there were disappointments along the way. His dream of being a doctor in a small town out west never came to fruition. That he wasn't able to make that dream come true doesn't make him a failure. He was a success because, in spite of never reaching that dream, he kept dreaming and working toward it. That's an accomplishment all its own. More importantly, he plugged away with a smile on his face and learned to work through obstacles and setbacks. He never stopped living his dream. In fact, he died living his dream. How many of us will be able to make that claim?

This is also a travelogue, but not in the sense of transporting you to glamorous places or historic sights. Greg's destinations almost always included an elevation dimension and map coordinates. So if you wanted to know about a place to embark on a back-country adventure, he was the person to see. He didn't know it all, and he was just as eager to learn as to teach. It boggles my mind to think of all the adventures he might have pursued in the years ahead.

Most of this book consists of my memories, many of which were insignificant while Greg was alive. They've become more vivid and have grown in importance since his death. Now those memories are all that remain.

This book also attempts to reconstruct Greg's final days on earth, the accident that caused his and Walker's deaths, and the subsequent search and recovery details—but it doesn't explain why Greg and Walker died. There is no explanation. I've tried to find some good in this tragedy. Maybe there is none. Maybe it just is. I've also tried again and again to find one thing I could have done differently, one thing I could have said, that would have kept Greg alive. I now accept I could never influence anyone's life in that way, not even my son's.

Sue and I have been fortunate to receive so much love and support during our grief journey. We've found it remarkable how support sometimes comes from unexpected sources—people who were on the periphery of our lives or completely unknown before the avalanche—while many others we expected to be available have become invisible. Even as I appreciate those who've stepped up in unexpected ways, I continue to learn that silence isn't necessarily withdrawal. Many people don't know what to do or say in the face of a loss like ours. So even those who seem absent may actually be present in a discreet, distant, and muddled sort of way.

We've been consoled by family, friends, and acquaintances. What seems appropriate some days, isn't on another. What comforts other people, might offend me. We've been asked what to do to help. Our answers vary because nothing feels right. I finally began telling people, "If you want to help and be a comfort, come and listen." There haven't been many takers. People don't want to listen; they want to fix. This can't be fixed.

It does help to talk to others who have been through this or some other similar loss. These losses are not equal. When someone experiences the death of a spouse and tries to compare our loss to theirs, it helps, but there are differences and inconsistencies. Grief isn't competitive, it's personal. Knowing I'm not the only one in the world dealing with tragedy doesn't console me. I have come up with this analogy: When your spouse dies, you're left with a place to go but no one to go with you. When a child dies, you have someone to go with you, but nowhere to go.

We continue our grief journey. This book is part of my journey. Thank you from the bottom of my heart for walking with me through this story. Thank you for loving and supporting Sue, Chris, Megan, and everyone else touched by Greg in his brief lifetime. Please continue to travel with us. But don't get stuck here. I don't plan to. There are many other adventures awaiting us. Some Greg had already enjoyed or was planning to enjoy. Others were beyond his vision at the time. But we have our own dreams, adventures, visions, quests, and mountains to climb. They may not have been part of Greg's dream. And that's OK. Dream your own dream. Enjoy your personal adventure. Climb your mountain. I know Greg would want it that way.

MAPS

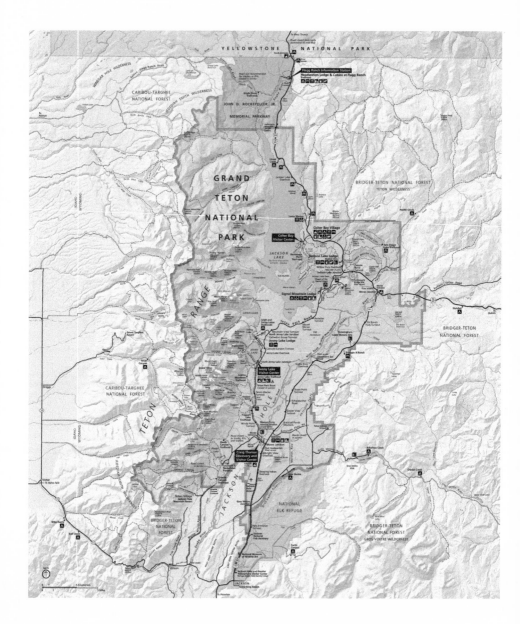

Grand Teton National Park and the surrounding area.
Source: Grand Teton National Park and Grand Teton Association.

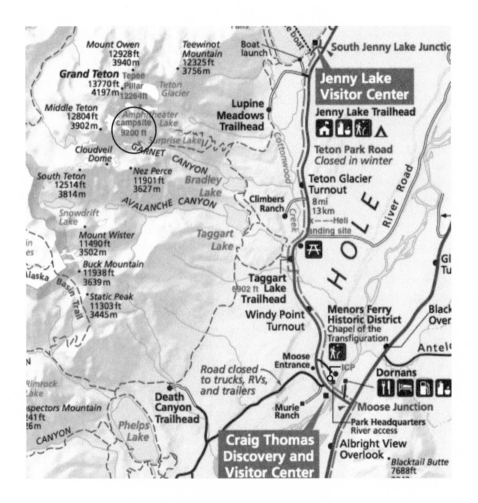

Kuhl-Seftick search area, 2011.

Source: Grand Teton National Park and Grand Teton Association.

01

The best part was my tracks were the only ones on the mountain & it really didn't look like anyone had been up there yet this year. It was my 1st time laying down the 1st set of tracks for the season on a mountain. I signed my initials GES & 6/05 on a rock in the "summit register," which was a rock pile on which people had engraved their names.

—JUNE 27, 2005, Summit of Hoback Peak, Wyoming

I stand at Greg's portal between paradises, his campsite above a ten-foot boulder the night he died. Greg considered the Teton Range one of the most beautiful places on earth. I contemplate my son's life, called here by the beauty of this place and the tragedy of his death.

The midday sun warms my face as a gentle breeze cooled by the snowpack refreshes me after the four-mile hike to Garnet Canyon. The blue sky gives the white, wispy clouds definition. The scent of pine overwhelms everything else, even the moist sensation of the melting snow. It is quiet here. A thousand thoughts crowd my mind.

I picture Greg's final hours. His gear, which was recovered with his body, included the cookstove he probably used to prepare a warm meal of ramen noodles. His last words could easily have been the conclusion of one of his long, rambling stories told through pursed lips as he took tentative sips of the steaming noodles. I imagine he drifted off to sleep after one of his hearty laughs, a big smile on his face as he contemplated the next day's climb.

I think I knew Greg well, but I realize there's so much I don't know. What I thought I knew is clouded with doubt now. My son of thirty-one years has become an enigma. He was always smiling, yet easily angered. He planned for the future, yet lived so much in the present. He was successful, yet lacked self-confidence. He was admired by his family and friends and respected by his medical colleagues, yet had a humble sense of non-accomplishment. I don't know anyone else like him.

Greg was meant for the outdoors from the start. He possessed an adventurous spirit from early childhood, and he found plenty of adventures playing on our one-acre lot. The neighborhood yards of our forty-home development in Afton, Minnesota, create an almost seamless park atmosphere. He and his brother, Chris, played baseball and soccer, dug holes, and built forts with their many childhood friends. The call of the mountains began when Greg was eleven. From then on, mountains were a consideration in all his life decisions.

The problem was, Greg was practical. He dreamed of living in the mountains, but he had other interests—music, skiing, soccer, college, and medicine—to consider. He hoped to work toward his goals, to enjoy himself, and to succeed. He thought the best place for it all to happen was in the mountains. That's how he approached life. So how did Greg's mountain dream become our nightmare? It's difficult to accept that following his heart and living his dream led to his death.

After Greg's death, I reexamined all the decisions I made that limited Greg's options or affected his choices. It is a parent's responsibility to keep his children safe. I failed. Greg is dead, and there must have been something I, as his dad, could have done to prevent it. Somewhere, sometime, somehow I missed something.

The days and weeks after Greg's death were more difficult than anything else I've endured. The stark reality was that I had to face life after Greg. It's impossible to rewrite history—and even if I came up with something I could have changed, what difference would it make? How would I know that alternate course would have kept Greg alive? Life isn't a controlled experiment. I decided to put my energy into preserving and building Greg's legacy, the positive and beautiful legacy he was creating when he died.

I was always a dreamer and a planner. My earliest dreams included having a family. Greg made that one come true. Two years later, Chris's birth rounded out our family and gave Greg a brother. But the image of my child dying was never on my radar. Parents don't think about that. At least I didn't.

Visiting Grand Teton National Park was on my list. I had hoped my wife, Sue, and I would come here with Greg and Chris someday. Standing here in Garnet Canyon, I was fulfilling a dream and living a nightmare.

It was August 2011, and Sue and I had returned to Wyoming for the first time since April—when we were there during the search for Greg and his hiking partner—to visit the actual site where Greg died. Our lives had been turned inside out and upside down from the moment Greg and his friend Walker Kuhl were overdue returning from their overnight mountaineering trip. It took seven days to find and recover their bodies. During those difficult days, I nurtured a nugget of hope that Greg and Walker would hike out with a memorable story to tell. I held on to that hope for a week—until the moment I saw the helicopter lift up over the ridgeline, the rope taut with the weight of Greg's body.

02

GREG'S TRAIL TO THE MOUNTAINS

Sitting in the tent in the Wind Rivers near Big Sandy Lake. This place is incredible. Huge granite mountains. It was a really easy hike to get here too. Only about 6 miles & maybe 500 vertical feet, tops. I can't wait. I am so excited. Tomorrow I finally get to (have to) be in charge out here. More risks & more rewards. It should be fun. We are trying this real easy (I, 5.1) climb on Haystack Pk tomorrow. Let Mike get acclimated & me adjusted to life on the sharp end. I also found out that I passed Boards, 228. I was pretty stoked. Beat the average by almost a full standard deviation.

—JULY 28, 2005, Wind River Range, Wyoming

Greg dreamed of living out west, in the mountains, since soon after he started skiing in fifth grade. He sent for trail maps from many ski areas and then mounted them on a poster board tacked to his bedroom ceiling directly above his bed. He would lie on his back, cup his hands behind his head, and think about all the places he wanted to ski.

He tried to make the move west several times in his life. Attempts to move for college, medical school, and residency didn't work out. He realized his dream for one year, though—the year between college and med school when he moved to Bozeman, Montana, to live with Chris. He took full advantage of the proximity of the mountains and loved every minute of it. But it was temporary. He wanted to live like that for the rest of his life.

His best shot at living in the mountains was after residency. He could have limited his job search to only the most desirable locations. But there was a factor that outweighed even the mountains at that point in his life. He'd met that special someone, Megan, and wanted to be close to her as she completed her final year of med school at West Virginia University (WVU) in Morgantown.

Greg received a job offer to stay in West Virginia to work as an attending physician at St. Joseph's Hospital in Buckhannon, a small town about seventy miles south of Morgantown. The hospital is affiliated with West Virginia University Hospitals, which meant Greg would begin his career in a medical system with a teaching hospital. Greg had learned during residency how much he enjoyed working with med students and younger residents.

In November 2010, Greg and Megan's relationship changed. The next month, they broke up. Greg was devastated. We worried about him. It might have seemed as if he was running away from the situation when he resigned his position to move west and play in the mountains for a while. But he was simply going back to his plan A. He wanted things with Megan to work out, but he didn't see the point of staying in West Virginia and waiting for that to happen. It wasn't an easy choice, even under the circumstances. I remember him telling me, "I only got to be happy for seven weeks." When I asked him to explain, he said, "I was in a relationship I wanted to be in, and I had my dream job." That underscored how he felt about Megan and working at St. Joe's.

Greg seemed to be leaving on good terms with Megan and his friends and colleagues at WVU and at St. Joe's. In late February 2011, he drove a very full car to Fort Wayne, Indiana, where he spent a night with his aunt Jenny and uncle Rick. The next morning, he headed for Minnesota. He spent the night with friends, and we didn't see him until the next afternoon. He seemed to be in good spirits at that point, more like the Greg we knew. That meant a lot to us. We were hoping this move would be a temporary break from work and he'd soon be looking at opportunities at Montana hospitals.

Sue was especially happy to be with Greg because she hadn't seen him since November, when he flew to Minnesota for his grandmother's birthday party. Just a couple of weeks earlier, I'd spent a few days in Morgantown helping him pack and clean his apartment. Even then we wished we were spending more time with him. Our disappointment and pain increased exponentially after Greg died, and this became the last time we saw him alive.

Greg rented an apartment in northern Montana, thirteen hundred miles from our home in Afton. That's more than a day's drive, even for Greg. He drove to Bozeman, spent a few days with Chris and friends, did some skiing and climbing, and then continued on to his new place in Columbia Falls. It wasn't much of an apartment by any standards, but especially not for a doctor. But that wasn't important to Greg. He just wanted an inexpensive headquarters to stash his gear between adventures. It was just the place for him.

Greg was on the go from the moment he arrived in Montana, skiing and climbing rock or ice. If he wasn't able to embark on an actual adventure on a given day, he researched or planned one. He was goal-oriented and driven, even more so when he was in the mountains. It was as if he had to cram as much activity as possible into the available time. I thought this would change when he moved to Columbia Falls—since opportunities to ski, climb, and hike were so close by—but it didn't seem like it from his phone calls and reports from his brother and friends.

But Greg wasn't careless. His motto was "Live to climb another day." It wasn't unusual to hear that he'd aborted his plans because of weather or other unexpected circumstances. He knew his limits. He might sometimes be frustrated because of some personal inability, but he also weighed his skills as part of his decision-making.

His adventure planning sometimes became oppressive to his friends. He would push and encourage until they finally agreed to accompany him on a road trip or day hike. Joel and Angie Menssen had a real taste of Greg's adventure enthusiasm during March and early April 2011. Greg had gotten close to him while Joel was a freshman at Montana State and Greg worked in Bozeman between college and med school. Angie became a good friend to Greg too, not just because she was Joel's wife, but because she's a special person. Greg thought the world of both of them—but what they really had going for them while he lived in Columbia Falls was that they lived nearby in Kalispell. Greg didn't know many other people in the area. In a phone conversation after Greg's death, Angie told me, "Greg was here almost every day." She asked Joel one day if Greg would be stopping by later. Joel told her, "Just figure he will, and if he doesn't come, he doesn't come." Greg usually showed up.

Greg chose Columbia Falls because of the proximity of Glacier National Park. He would phone about some line he had bagged on a certain couloir. I wish I knew how many day trips he made into Glacier in just those six weeks. Sometimes he convinced Joel or another climber to join him. Sometimes he went solo. To support his adventure habit, Greg was a regular visitor to Rocky Mountain Outfitters in Kalispell during his short time in northern Montana.

Before his final, fatal trip to Grand Teton National Park, Greg also spent a few days there in late March. I remember his call on his way home. We were concerned because it was late, and Greg indicated he would drive through to Columbia Falls without a rest stop. The next afternoon, Wednesday, March 30, he left a message that's still on our answering machine:

> Hey, it's me. Just called to say I got back from the Tetons. I slept last night like a couple hours from Columbia Falls. But I found out today that if the federal government doesn't get a budget, the park officially will be closed to all visitors, including by foot, starting on Friday, which really won't be stopping me. But I figure that since this will be the last time that I'm going to be legally accessing the park in the foreseeable future, that I should probably go and try to bag that line on the west slope of Mount Cannon, it's right off the Going-to-the-

Sun Road, just north of the—by about maybe two miles
or so—the Avalanche turn off. So do that tomorrow. I'll
talk to you guys later. Bye.

I don't know if Greg tried to ski that area on Thursday. He never
told me, and I never asked. The government's budget standoff was
resolved, so Greg wasn't rushing to get back to Glacier legally. But
there are several aspects of that message that resonate with new
meaning after his death. First, that he called to let us know that he
"got back from the Tetons." Every time I play it, I wish he'd left that
same message just one more time. Also, Greg located this route
for us by mentioning Avalanche Lake, where Sue and I had hiked in
2000. Greg knew we were familiar with this trail. And then there's
his mention of "foreseeable future." How heartbreaking now to
realize his future was so brief.

By the second week in April, Greg apparently had decided
he'd played enough. It was time to plan for the future. He had an
interview scheduled at the hospital in Libby, Montana, on April 13.
He decided to make a multipurpose road trip before he started
doctoring again, and it was to start the day after the interview. He
made plans with Walker to meet in Jackson to summit the Grand
Teton. Then he would drive on to meet his friends Jeremy and Cindy
Newman to climb at Red Rock Canyon National Conservation Area
in Nevada. Finally, he would meet Megan in Las Vegas on April 22
to celebrate her graduation from med school. Things between them
seemed to have improved—they weren't back together, but at least
things were cordial. After a few days together, he would put Megan
on a plane in Vegas and head back to Montana on April 25. Life
was good!

I expected Greg to call after his interview at the hospital in
Libby. He usually called after something significant in his life. I
also expected a call because he was on the verge of this road-trip
adventure that had him really fired up. When he hadn't called by
dinnertime on April 13, I called him. He was driving from Kalispell to

Columbia Falls. I asked about the interview, and his response was positive. The hospital had a similar number of ER visits as St. Joe's in Buckhannon. He told me about shift schedules, benefits, and the facilities. He was impressed by the plans in place to construct a new hospital. He summed up his positive impression of the place by telling me, "I think I could work there, Dad." I was very pleased.

Greg was most excited by another aspect of his day, though. The interview had ended at noon and Greg drove to Kalispell, where Angie Menssen took him clothes shopping. He wanted to look his best for Megan. To help him reach that objective, Angie created a clothing grid that matched pants with shirts and ties. When I told Sue about it later, she called the chart Garanimals for adults. Not long into our conversation, Greg had arrived home. "I'm at the apartment and need to unpack. Good-bye, Dad." It was the last time I talked to my son.

I expected to talk to Greg again before he and Walker attempted to summit the Grand, before the start of this road trip. He often called as he drove to or from some adventure. He used calls to us as a diversion, something to help him stay awake while driving. He hadn't shared his exact travel plans with me. He left Columbia Falls sometime on Thursday and drove to Bozeman, spent the night with his brother, and left for Jackson around noon on Friday. He didn't call us on either leg of the drive down. I wish he had. He met Walker at the motel in Jackson on Friday evening. It snowed that night.

The conditions on Saturday weren't the best. It was snowing again, the wind was blowing, and visibility was poor. Greg and Walker checked in at the Visitor Center in Moose. Ranger Elizabeth Maki talked with them, learned of their plans, and signed off on their back-country permit at twelve thirty that afternoon. She later informed Sue and me that the guys had discussed scaling back their plans and pursuing a less aggressive objective even before arriving at the Visitor Center. They decided they might play around the Teepe Pillar instead of trying to attain the summit. This scaled-back objective required the same approach into Garnet Canyon.

Greg and Walker were aware the avalanche conditions were rated "considerable" at the time.

The usual winter access into Garnet Canyon is from the Taggart Lake trailhead, the route Greg and Walker took—which we know because they provided this information for their permit and their cars were found in the parking lot at this trailhead. They probably set out sometime shortly after one p.m. on Saturday.

On their trek into Garnet Canyon, Greg and Walker met another group camped at the Platforms. One of the group, Brendan Hughes, remembers, "The man in front [Walker Kuhl, as I now understand] said brief words but appeared determined to move ahead. Greg came behind. Greg was also very direct in his questions. Greg was eager to get information on the snow conditions, but also seemed rushed in his attempt to keep up with his friend. I remember telling Greg that we hadn't gone higher due to the warm, wet snow on top of the pack."

Walker and Greg continued into Garnet Canyon. They set up camp in the shelter of a large boulder for protection from the snow and wind. Not knowing about their modified plans, Sue and I, Walker's family, Jeremy and Cindy, and Megan were all waiting, expectantly, to hear details of the summit of the Grand.

03

SACRED GROUND

I watched with perverse fascination as the chunks of snow broke loose, slid over the rock and snow on the side of the couloir down into the center, and then disappeared into the clouds below. I was going to ski that in a minute!

—JUNE 8, 2006, Whitetail Couloir, Beartooth Range, Montana

I wish you could see a panorama of Garnet Canyon on a perfect morning from atop that ten-foot boulder. The view east takes you over the boulder field you must traverse to gain the canyon. The dark gray rocks vary in size from barely a foot to larger than the one beneath me. They're strewn across the width of the canyon randomly, and yet their placement seems to intentionally restrict access to only those worthy of passing the test. The only way to reach this spot is over, around, and between those massive rocks, or by helicopter. Beyond the boulder field, a variety of green vegetation meets the eye. Pines grace the mouth of the canyon. Not many other trees grow above nine thousand feet. Even the scrub grass is sparse and low for late summer. As the eye searches farther, the valley comes into view. Green and blue dominate the scene. The valley floor appears lush with grass. The sky looks so much bluer than when viewed through the hazy atmosphere of a typical city day at sea level.

I focus on the details of the valley. The narrow strand of the state highway ambles along as cars and pickups with campers shuttle visitors into Grand Teton National Park and toward Yellowstone. Parallel to the road, the Snake River carries a precious cargo of cold, clear water that provides relief to thirsty wildlife and a home to the fish sought by those fly-fishing along the banks outside the park. From up here, the road and river appear to travel side by side to some unknown terminus. Taggart and Bradley Lakes, reduced to bright blue specks on a green background, disappear from view as we enter the canyon. The mountains at the far end of the valley appear distant and insignificant.

Back within the canyon, an occasional hiking group advances on the trail along the north wall. They speak quietly, perhaps out of respect for the serenity of the mountains or in deference to the significance of our mission. The canyon is littered with more boulders, not as many as the boulder field we'd already traversed and scattered randomly with enough space for foot travel. The few trees in the canyon are natural testaments to the harsh conditions and the toll taken by avalanches that lay waste to the vegetation and leave the mountain's shed rock as calling cards to mark their plunder.

A motion almost directly beneath me catches our attention. A marmot crawls into view and scampers boldly toward our gear. He is focused on his goal, but keenly aware of our presence. Any move toward him diverts his steps. He skitters away and hides, only to soon reappear from another spot and make a beeline for lunch. I have to laugh. Greg and marmots were engaged in a long-running battle.

I appreciate more of the beauty of the canyon and surrounding mountains as my gaze turns skyward. To the west, the rounded east face of Middle Teton separates the North and South Forks. A giant scar, the black dike, mars the perfect face of the mountain from near its summit to the snowpack nestled against the base at the far end of the canyon. That crevice looks small, even from this short distance from Middle. But it's massive, measuring several feet across. Its dark color contrasts with the gray-brown mountain, making it a kind of high-altitude neon sign advertising for the range.

It's summer in Grand Teton National Park. The snow at higher elevations is still melting and running down to the valley below. At first, the snowmelt travels beneath the snowpack. As it approaches Greg and Walker's campsite, it emerges from under the snow to feed Garnet Creek, which passes just to our north. The water is incredibly clear and cold. Greg thought nothing was as refreshing as filtered mountain water. The water appears to flow slowly, but experience tells me it can quickly carry away a Nalgene water bottle.

The majestic mountains of the Teton Range caress Garnet Canyon in a tender embrace. Nez Perce, Teewinot, Middle Teton, and the Grand Teton shelter the canyon, but also threaten those who visit it. The north face of Nez Perce to the south is scarred by the same boulders that lay in this canyon. Tons of snow cascaded down that face during Greg and Walker's visit in April 2011—and countless other times. The beauty here can be an attraction and a death call.

I decided I wanted to return to the park shortly after Greg and Walker were found and their bodies recovered. It seemed natural to want to stand where they died. We all have our own responses to tragedy. I may have reacted differently if the accident had happened at another place and time. But Greg's love for the Tetons drew me to Garnet Canyon.

I'm a very detail-oriented person. It was important to me to know as much about Greg's death as I could. During the search, I wanted the specifics of each day's efforts. The park staff was patient with me. They answered questions and granted as much access to the rescue operations as was permitted. Not all of my requests were granted. At times the park rangers advised it might be better not to know or see certain things. I generally listened to their advice and followed their guidance. Later I was usually happy I hadn't insisted. But there was no way I wasn't going to attain Garnet Canyon to visit this ground that's sacred to me.

I look around the canyon from a point just west of Greg's final camp. The site is nothing like I'd pictured based on the descriptions we'd heard after the recovery of Greg's body just four months ago. This has nothing to do with the heavy layer of snow and the avalanche debris blanketing the canyon. It's the location of the site that fooled me. I had pictured the protected camp area to be an outcropping along the north face of the canyon. Chris and I agreed we'd never have found the site in the middle of the canyon if we'd been looking on our own.

Two very large boulders stand at the site. The smaller one to the north is the ten-footer. The larger one approaches twenty feet. Nick Armitage, the ranger who'd picked up Walker and Greg's beacon signals, explains that the snowpack covered the smaller boulder and that Walker and Greg were camped just above the top of it, with their tent pitched on the north side of the larger boulder.

After showing us the site and explaining a little about the recovery, Nick and Chris Harder, the ranger assigned as incident commander when Greg and Walker went missing, respectfully move away and allow us time and space to think about where we are and what happened. I pray, "Dear Lord, thank you for the physical and emotional strength to be present at this place. Thank you for the gift of my sons. But how could this happen? Why Greg and Walker? Why not some useless human being, some drain on society, and not someone so young with so much to offer? I don't understand. Explain this to me! Greg, I'm honored to have been your dad. I know I wasn't perfect. There were things I wish you did differently, that I did differently. But I wouldn't trade you for anyone. I only wish you were still here."

I try to get inside Greg's mind and relive his final hours here on earth in the shadow of the Grand. Sue, Chris, and his girlfriend, Jesse, don't share their thoughts. We don't say much to each other at first.

I scramble down between the two boulders among some smaller ones and place a memorial pamphlet from Greg's funeral in a zippered snack bag on a two-foot, flat-topped rock and put a smaller rock on top to keep it from blowing away. I spread a small amount of Greg's ashes in the shadow of their campsite and pray again, "Eternal rest grant unto him, oh Lord, and let perpetual light shine upon him. May he rest in peace. Amen."

04

MOUNTAINS

The journey begins today. . . .
It was a little hard saying good-bye to people yesterday at work,
but it's always hard and this is my one and only chance to do this.

—MARCH 13, 2003, Seven-Week, 8,000-Mile Road Trip, Bozeman, Montana

Like his mother, Greg was born and raised in Minnesota. I was born and raised in Michigan. Mountains weren't an integral part of my upbringing, his mother's, or Greg's. Yet Greg was enthralled with the mountains. He came to love them. They called to him.

When Greg looked at a mountain, he not only admired it, he analyzed it. He viewed chutes, ridgelines, couloirs, and angles with access and adventure in mind. He was route-finding from the beginning. He saw details I didn't, but the majesty didn't escape him. "How can you not think about God in the mountains when you're standing among some of his best work," he once said to Sue.

Yet there was some mountain DNA in Greg. His Grandpa Seftick was born and raised in Johnstown, Pennsylvania, nestled in the Allegheny Mountains of the Appalachian Range. A good part of my dad's family remained in Pennsylvania. When I was a kid, my parents, my sister, my brother, and I made annual trips to visit our Pennsylvania aunts, uncles, and cousins. I loved to go there, looking forward to every trip. The big draw for me was being with male cousins my own age, a benefit I didn't have with my mom's side of the family in Michigan.

We'd tear around the woods and hills around my relatives' homes. There was no rock climbing, backpacking, or camping involved. But to a city kid like me, it was great to be away from crowds of people and off on our own exploring in the woods. Our kid adventures didn't compare to Greg's exploits in the mountains. But I believe there was some pull to the mountains based on that family heritage. The mountains were in Greg's blood long before he ever realized it.

After I moved to Minnesota in 1972, it became more difficult to get together with my Pennsylvania relatives because there were even more miles between us. Then I got married, Greg was born, and with other responsibilities, it became even harder to get back to Pennsylvania.

But after Greg was born, Sue and I made sure we continued our annual visits to my parents, Michael and Jane Seftick, in Michigan, influenced by those Pennsylvania trips my family took when I was a child. Our Michigan visit in October 1981 led to Greg's first trip to the mountains. Sue and I decided to extend our travels farther east to Pennsylvania, and we invited my parents to come with us. It seemed like a great idea. Dad would have another chance to visit his brothers, sisters, and extended family. Mom and Dad wouldn't have to worry about driving on their own. Sue would get to meet more of my family. I'd have a chance to reconnect with aunts, uncles, and cousins, some of whom I hadn't seen in ten years or more. And Greg would meet new family, travel with Grandma and Grandpa, and see the mountains.

We had one additional factor to consider. Sue was four months pregnant with Chris, who was due in late February 1982. The pregnancy presented no problems, though, and everything went well. So technically, Chris went on this vacation with us, and it was Greg and Chris's first road trip together!

It was another ten years before we returned to Pennsylvania when Sue, Greg, Chris, and I planned a long vacation for the summer of 1991. Things changed a lot in that time. My dad died in 1986, and my mom had a heart attack and stroke in 1987. That summer of 1991, we decided to visit Michigan as we had every year of Greg's life (and more often since Grandma was ill), and then extend our travels to Pennsylvania to visit family and places in the east that we hadn't been before.

Sue and I shared maps and brochures with Greg and Chris and invited them to each make a list of places they'd like to see. In one of the few brilliant parenting ideas of my life, I promised that each of us was guaranteed at least two things on his or her list. The trip took us as far east as Boston over seventeen days and thirty-five hundred miles. The two places we visited from Greg's list were the Baseball Hall of Fame in Cooperstown, New York, and Cedar Point, an amusement park in Sandusky, Ohio—predictable selections, considering his love of baseball and roller coasters. He and I spent hours looking at Hall of Fame displays and reading plaques long after Sue and Chris lost interest. He eagerly waited alone in line for coasters, while the rest of us stood out of the queue. Sue and I weren't interested, and Chris was too little.

That trip, driving on curving, hilly roads, tearing around with second cousins, gazing down at valleys from elevation, produced Greg's first memorable mountain experiences. At age twelve, he was creating mountain memories that weren't possible on his first Pennsylvania visit ten years earlier. But another event about six months before our trip had already planted a seed in Greg. The sixth-grade students at his school, Lake Elmo Elementary, took an annual field trip to Afton Alps, a local ski area. He was part of a split class of fifth and sixth graders. He and the other fifth graders in the class were invited on the field trip with their sixth-grade classmates.

Students who didn't know how to ski and didn't have equipment were fitted with boots, skis, and poles, given a brief lesson, and then allowed to ski under supervision. Greg loved it! Sue and I were surprised because neither of us skied, and we weren't much for winter sports in general. That didn't matter to Greg. As soon as he got home from school that day, we were pestered with requests to go skiing again. Sue and Greg, accompanied by his friend Ryan and Ryan's mom, returned to Afton one more time that season.

Next winter, Greg was ready to get back on the snow. He wanted to find his own equipment and ski more. To add to the pressure, Chris immediately felt slighted that Greg could ski and he couldn't. With skiing, the "you're not old enough" argument doesn't work. Soon they were both signed up for lessons, which we'd promised them the previous spring. Chris loved it as much as his big brother. Sue and I spent many days in the chalet, reading and watching the kids on the hill. Soon they moved on to more difficult runs that weren't visible from the windows of the chalet. Greg and Chris navigated those early years of skiing without serious injury, which in their minds was proof that they could attempt tougher runs in ski areas out west.

Greg pushed himself to advance his skiing abilities from the beginning, but always conservatively. He learned his limits and skied under control. That was my observation, anyway. Maybe that wasn't the case. Maybe he went out of control at times and was just lucky nothing serious ever happened. But that would've been out of character for Greg. He loved trying new things and pushing himself, but safety was a requirement in any activity.

Soon Greg had saved enough birthday money to purchase his own equipment and was skiing with friends and their families. I never had a desire to ski. I wish now I'd connected with Greg and Chris through their love of skiing when I was younger. I can't picture myself skiing at their level or even mountaineering as they did. But I wonder if I'd skied along with Greg from time to time, if somehow the course of events might have been altered and he would still be alive.

In March 1996 we took our only family ski vacation. We rented a condo in Park City, Utah. The guys spent their time on the mountain while Sue and I bummed around town and relaxed. Greg and Chris skied Park City, Deer Valley, and Brighton in Lower Cottonwood

Canyon. They encouraged us to take lessons. We almost did, but I was hesitant. This vacation was shortly after my bout with dermatomyositis and I hadn't completely regained my strength. Truth is, I chickened out. We enjoyed time together as a family, discussed plans at breakfast, and shared stories over dinners, all in the shadow of the Wasatch Range.

Greg was never satisfied with his skiing ability. He wanted to keep improving and experience skiing at different sites. He joined the ski club in junior high and the alpine ski team in high school. And so Greg began his short, and rather unsuccessful, career as a downhill racer. He enthusiastically adjusted his daily routine to attend even the snowiest and coldest practices and meets. Late dinners and late-night homework sessions were fine, as long as he could be on snow. He was dedicated and practiced intently, but didn't appear comfortable skiing gates. He constantly admonished himself after falls or missed gates. He wasn't satisfied with his times on good runs. We heard "I suck" more than once. Slalom skiing wasn't a rewarding experience for him—it almost seemed like a self-inflicted punishment. But he never gave up or lost his love for skiing.

The Stillwater alpine ski team made an annual training trip to Winter Park in Colorado. Greg enjoyed practicing in the Rockies. At the team's awards dinner in his senior year, he was selected as the "most improved" member of the high-school squad. He seemed surprised and pleased with this recognition. At home after the ceremony, Greg was dismissive and explained, "I had an advantage. Since I was so crappy to start, I could only get better."

After high school, he continued to race at St. Olaf College as a four-year member of the alpine ski team. St. Olaf had a strong team and always fielded a competitive squad both regionally and nationally—both the men and women competed at nationals all four years Greg was a member. He was in elite company.

As the slowest racer of the group, Greg competed infrequently, but that didn't diminish his desire to remain a part of the team. He competed in a few local races, and was rarely satisfied with his effort.

His coach at St. Olaf, Paul Wojick, was a great support to Greg and kept him on the squad. Greg felt accepted, and he stayed in touch with Paul long after his college days. In fact, I found a letter from Paul postmarked only days before Greg's death among his things.

Greg was always a very motivated individual, but he never discussed why. His lack of expertise as a racer may have led him to look for other aspects of skiing where he could differentiate himself, set himself up to succeed in ways others couldn't or didn't have a desire to do. I think that led to his interest in back-country skiing and mountaineering. That, coupled with his growing interest in climbing, seemed to take him into mountain settings away from commercial skiing.

When Greg and Chris were young, we camped as a family at various state parks. Our boys never objected when we announced a camping trip was in the works, but they never initiated the trips. Sue had more camping experience than I did, but I enjoyed the trips. Our camping style was of the "get away from it all" variety, without much planning about what we'd do each day. That wasn't Greg's style, though. He preferred being with his friends in a structured environment that included planned activities under the guidance of experienced leaders. He was a natural match for the kind of camping and outdoor activities of the Boy Scouts.

Greg's involvement in Boy Scouts contributed significantly to his mountain mentality. He worked diligently to earn badges, including his Zero Hero award for sleeping in a quinzee, a shelter hollowed out of settled snow, on a below-zero night. My only scout-camping volunteer experience with Greg wasn't a good one. Two rainy days at Tomahawk Scout Reservation in Wisconsin resulted in the cancelation of most planned activities, unhappy campers, and an early departure.

Greg enjoyed camping with his scout leaders, men who knew more about camping and the outdoors than I did. Scout leader Dale Otteson remembers Greg as "a cheerful and enthusiastic scout, someone unfazed by rain, bad food, or other circumstances. I recall a scheduled overnight camping trip on a cool, rainy weekend. Another leader and I waited at the assigned spot and Greg was the only scout to show up." The trip was canceled. A disappointed Greg asked, "Why can't we go?" Dale recalls Greg's interest in learning new things, seeing new places.

Greg got along as well with the leaders as he did with the other kids. He worked his way through the ranks, earned merit badges, and soon made First Class. He had no desire to work toward Eagle Scout. He'd accomplished his goal and was content to stay in scouts without more work or effort. When asked for an explanation, he told me, "Now that I made First Class, I'm eligible for the high-adventure trips," which had been his ambition all along.

His first high-adventure trip was to Isle Royale National Park in 1992. Although it wasn't to the mountains, it was a very different type of camping from what Greg had ever done before. After a drive to the north shore of Lake Superior and a boat ride to Isle Royale, the scouts were, for the most part, isolated. Greg was so excited. He prepared his gear and loaded his backpack. He'd just turned thirteen, but he was small for his age, maybe the smallest guy on the trip. The pack looked huge on his back, but that didn't bother Greg.

The scouts covered a good part of the island, taking day hikes from base camp and hikes from campsite to campsite. Greg enjoyed the entire trip and had a lot to talk about upon his return. We knew he'd loved it, because he was already looking forward to next year's high adventure, the Boundary Waters Canoe Area (BWCA) in northern Minnesota. That trip would involve portages, another test for Greg. He didn't grow much in the year after the Isle Royale trip and was still dwarfed by his backpack. We were concerned about how he'd manage the weight of the canoes and equipment on the portages, but the scout leaders assured us Greg would do just fine.

He returned from the BWCA trip safe and sound and ready for more. These first two high adventures were the building blocks for what was to come. He didn't know it after his BWCA trip, but his scout adventures were shaping his perspectives and preparing him to seek out the places where he thrived and enjoyed life—the mountains.

The highlight of the summer of 1995, when Greg turned sixteen, wasn't learning to drive, or entering high school, or any of the milestones most young men look forward to at that stage of their lives. Greg was going to the Philmont Scout Ranch in New Mexico. His group's scheduled trip included seven days of hiking about seventy miles in the mountains. The guys would hike from campsite to campsite with their gear, accompanied by their group leaders and Philmont guides. But the scouts themselves were responsible for the bulk of the work—managing food and water, and hauling their gear and supplies.

I watched Greg with admiration. He prepared as best he could under the guidance of the scout leaders and by his own initiative. Since he was the smallest guy going to Philmont, he loaded his backpack with rocks and hiked around the neighborhood. There was no way to acclimate himself to mountain trails and higher elevation. But he wanted to be as prepared as possible to handle what was expected of him.

At Philmont Greg discovered how much he loved mountains and the amazing opportunities they provide to experience nature. The mountains called to him from that summer until the day he died. It was such a strong pull that Greg headed to the mountains every chance he had during college, med school, and residency, and while working as an attending physician.

Greg came home from New Mexico with a huge grin on his face. He told us stories about the hikes and the camps at Philmont. We were awed by what he and the other scouts had accomplished. I doubt he'd ever physically labored as much as he did on that trip, hiking an average of ten miles each day, at elevation, on trails with elevation gain, all the while hauling his backpack. He was exhausted, but it was the kind of exhaustion he relished and strived for on future mountain trips. Immediately after he returned home, he talked about going back—which he did in the summer of 1997.

A neighboring troop scheduled to go to Philmont that summer had a couple of unfilled spots. Greg and his friend Nick St. Ores volunteered to go as assistant leaders. The troop left St. Paul for Chicago on Amtrak to catch another train to Raton, New Mexico. They arrived a day late due to a missed connection. Their route, longer and more challenging than the one Greg had done two years earlier, was adjusted to fit the shortened time. Greg enjoyed Philmont as much or more the second time. He was a couple of years older, which helped him be more comfortable.

The summer of 1998 was the beginning of mountain trail hiking for Sue and me. Doctors assured me this level of activity was acceptable after my recovery from dermatomyositis and would help build my strength. We hiked to Harney Peak in the Black Hills of South Dakota. The next year, we hiked to Blackmore Lake in Hyalite Canyon near Bozeman, Montana, as we checked out the Montana State University campus with Chris. If he had any reservations about attending Montana State, those concerns vanished after a few days in the area. We took a number of trips to Montana while Chris was in college. In fact, he liked Bozeman so much that he ended up living there after graduating with a degree in environmental science. Chris's presence provided a base for Greg when he visited, and Greg fell in love with Montana too. He returned many times in the next twelve years—whenever an opportunity arose to leave Minnesota during college and med school or West Virginia during residency. Greg and Chris were great guides and very supportive when Sue and I would join them on trails near Bozeman. They waited, encouraged, and patiently led us farther and higher than we would've ventured on our own. Sue and I grew in confidence and hiked on our own if the boys were busy. We became more comfortable in the wilderness. Sue and I soon looked forward to any chance to get outside and began to walk frequently back in Minnesota.

Greg had low self-esteem, a demon he battled for much of his life. Mountaineering was a positive, ongoing challenge that helped improve his view of himself. He began competing with himself to master successively more difficult routes and problems rather than comparing his skill level with others.

On one memorable trip to Montana, Sue and I camped overnight with Greg, Chris, and some of their friends at Mirror Lake. Greg's backpack looked at least three times as big as ours as he led the way and kept us on a good pace. The hike from the trailhead to the lake campsite was seven miles, with an elevation gain of about two thousand feet. When we arrived, we set up camp, fixed some food, relaxed, and waited for Chris and friends to arrive. We sat around the campfire with Greg as the evening light faded and soon heard some noise from up the trail. We called out and the remainder of our group approached the campsite. I thoroughly enjoyed that evening in the company of my sons and their friends.

Looking back at my life as the parent of adult children, I feel Greg and Chris had a larger impact on my life than I on theirs. This isn't normal. Parents are expected to guide, shape, and form their children. Reflecting on who I am and who my sons became—I'd say my life has been influenced by Greg and Chris much more than I influenced theirs. For example, reaching mountain summits and taking that memorable overnight backpacking hike wouldn't have happened without their influence.

The most strenuous hike Sue and I ever took with Greg was the summit of Hyalite Peak, a fifteen-mile round trip with an elevation gain of twenty-two hundred feet. I don't know if it was my lack of conditioning, my ill-preparedness to hike at altitude, the weather, the particular hike, or all of the above, but this was the only time that I actually doubted I could complete a hike with a destination. I wouldn't have finished without Greg, my motivator and cheerleader.

That was in June 2007. Greg had finished med school and was about to start his residency in July. Predictably, he headed west to visit Chris and play in the mountains as soon as school was done. Sue and I drove to Montana so the four of us could spend some time together. It was happening less frequently, so we tried to take advantage of opportunities whenever we could. Greg wanted to get us "up on top of something" and thought we should summit Hyalite. We decided to give it a try under his guidance.

It was a day hike. No extra gear was required, just food, water, and clothes for the attempted summit. The weather wasn't the best—cloudy skies and a low ceiling that obscured the 10,303-foot summit. Sue, Greg, and I parked at the Grotto Falls Trailhead and started out. "Our goal is to summit, but first let's get to the lake about five and a half miles in. We'll reevaluate how we feel and check the weather before deciding to summit or not," Greg told us. I knew he had no intention of letting us quit at the lake, though.

As we ate lunch at the lake, I didn't feel too bad. But I realized the more difficult part of the hike still lay ahead, even though we'd already covered the bulk of the distance. Greg led us away from the lake and back to the trail. The summit was obscured by fog, mist, and clouds. We continued under Greg's encouragement. "You're doing great. Just a little more to go." (I knew that was a lie.) "Just take one hundred steps and rest again. If that's too many for one spurt, do fifty, or twenty, or five! Just keep putting one foot in front of the other."

He didn't complain at my frequent requests for breathers. Soon we'd made our way through the switchbacks and gained the ridgeline. The low clouds obscured our view of the summit above and the lake below. We were socked in. We continued slowly along the ridgeline and Greg kept repeating, "We're getting close, we're almost there now." After about ten minutes, I couldn't continue. I had nothing left. I sat down and announced, "You go on without me. I'm done." Greg encouraged me. Sue was worried about leaving me behind. Finally, I just laid down on the ground. Greg told me not to move, but I couldn't get lost unless I rolled down either side of the ridge. Sue and Greg left me and I remained on the ground, extremely content and relaxed.

Ten minutes later, Greg bounded down the trail. "Dad, you have to go on. It's not even a hundred yards. Mom is at the summit. You'll be disappointed if you stop here." He was right about that. I got up and actually felt pretty good. That little lie-down was just what I needed.

We got to the summit and reconnected with Sue, who stood a hundred and eighty degrees opposite the trail, looking for us in the fog. She hadn't paid attention when Greg left to walk back to me, was disoriented, and didn't know from which direction we'd come. Fortunately, it all worked out, and there we were together on the summit of Hyalite Peak. And we couldn't see a thing! We took some pictures and signed the summit log. Greg found the page he'd signed on an earlier ascent and added today's date. We headed down.

I was exhausted when we reached the trailhead as the sun set. But Greg was right about the importance of attaining the summit. I was pleased to have finally made it "up on top of something," and I'll never forget it. I always thought I'd get back to the summit of Hyalite Peak to enjoy the view with Greg on a beautiful, sunny day. If I do get back there, it won't be with him. But he'll still be my biggest cheerleader. I can just imagine him waiting for me at the summit with a long-winded monologue about everything visible in Hyalite Canyon and all the surrounding peaks.

Sue and I looked forward to going to Montana to visit Chris and to hike in the mountains as much as Greg did. Like Greg, I felt I was wasting precious time if we weren't hiking each day. "Let's do something today," I would tell everyone. "There will be time to rest when I return home and go back to work!" I looked forward to my favorite hikes and trails. I could have hiked to Lava Lake and Grotto Falls every visit and it would have never gotten old. We achieved a perfect blend of enjoying known commodities and exploring new trails for the first time.

Greg provided a glowing example of how to love the outdoors, the wilderness, everything about nature. He also showed me how to live life to the fullest, to enjoy every minute of every day. He did this by teaching me to adjust to situations as they came up.

Greg taught me to be more flexible, especially on vacation. If something didn't work out, there were other options. He taught me I didn't need to force the issue. Part of that perspective came from his understanding of nature, the role weather can play. Safety in the wilderness was always important to Greg.

A good example of this flexibility was during a trip Sue and I took to California in 2010 for our thirty-fifth wedding anniversary. We both wanted to see San Francisco and much more. We had a difficult time deciding where to visit. Our solution was to select three different areas and get a taste of each. After enjoying two days in downtown San Francisco, we drove north over the Golden Gate Bridge to Sonoma Valley with a stop at Muir Woods. Then it was on to Yosemite National Park.

Yosemite was even more beautiful than in pictures! We hiked at May Lake off the Tioga Road the first day and drove into the valley and enjoyed Bridalveil Falls, Half Dome, El Capitan, and the famous Ahwahnee Hotel the next.

While there we frequently connected with other tourists and the conversation usually included, "What have you seen? Where are you going next?" We were advised to visit sites for which we unfortunately had no time on this quick trip. The beauty of the Glacier Point overlook was mentioned several times.

We planned to leave Yosemite in late afternoon to drive to our motel in San Jose and a flight home early the next morning. We got in the car to leave Yosemite at about five p.m. Sue asked if I planned to drive to Glacier Point, usually about an hour drive. We noticed "Road Construction" signs on the route, so we decided not to stop at the overlook on our way to San Jose.

As we approached the Glacier Point turnoff, though, I pulled into the turn lane. "Sue, we're so close, and who knows if we'll ever be here again. We should go, even if it means arriving at the motel late. Besides, if it were Greg or Chris, they'd definitely go."

It was worth the drive. The view was amazing! We spent only a little time before we left to finish the drive to our motel. It was well after dark by the time we arrived, much later than planned. We both thought it was worth our time to change plans for this little diversion. I know our sons' influence played the biggest part in the decision to make that left turn. While not the sort of thing Greg would consider significant, that moment of spontaneity reflected his encouragement to be flexible. While not as adventuresome as Greg's back-country skiing or climbing, that last-minute addition to our last vacation day represented a change in my attitude from the comfort of a defined, rigid schedule. With that apparently small decision, I felt myself move more in line with Greg's quest for a "constantly changing horizon."

Greg never told me if he had a favorite summit or mountaineering adventure. I suspect they were all favorites for different reasons. One that particularly impressed me was his summit of Mount Rainier with Chris and their friend Ian. I know he was stoked to make the attempt, but it's extremely difficult. Greg admitted they wouldn't have made it without Ian. Greg led for a while, but he was postholing and making slow progress. Then the guys put on their skis and skins and Ian broke trail. The pace improved considerably.

A framed picture of Greg and Chris on the summit of Mount Rainier hangs in our dining room—a gift from the guys for Christmas 2010, Greg's last Christmas. We have it hanging with a framed print of *Wildcat*, the painting of Grand Teton and Garnet Canyon that Allison McGree did after Greg died. I refer to that corner as the Agony and the Ecstasy; the two images stand as symbols of the tragedy and triumph of Greg's mountaineering.

05

OUR RETURN TO GARNET CANYON

Entering the valley was almost magical. It made the work of getting here somewhat worth it. Seeing Half Dome and the falls are just incredible. . . . everything is super-sized here. All the trees are enormous. The cliffs and waterfalls reach the sky.

—MARCH 31, 2003, Yosemite National Park, California

Winter 2010/11 is an unusual season, and the snowpack is exceptionally deep in Grand Teton National Park (GTNP). About six hundred inches of snow fall by mid-April, compared to a season average of four hundred inches. The unusually large snowpack takes longer to melt. The park rangers initially advise that we'll probably be able to reach Garnet Canyon by mid- to late July. When I contact Ranger Terry Roper in July, though, she reports, "There's still a lot of snow. In mid-August the trail will be clear."

My call to Terry four weeks later brings a favorable response. Rangers Chris Harder, Scott Guenther, the operations manager, and Nick Armitage, the field operations manager, tell Terry this is a good time for us to return to the park. Sue and I quickly make plans, inform family and friends, pack, and hit the road.

We leave home at six a.m. on Sunday, August 21, heading for Buffalo, Wyoming, in the foothills of the Bighorn Mountains. Our two-day drive covers about eight hundred miles of interstate driving the first day and three hundred fifty miles through the mountains the second. Doubts about our ability to handle the emotional impact of this visit haunt me, but I'm determined to reach the site of Greg's death in the canyon.

In a single-lane construction zone near Rapid City, South Dakota, I notice a deer running through the median. I point it out to Sue, and we watch as the car two vehicles ahead nails the poor animal. We stop to see if we can help. The driver is a young man with a child in the car. They're both OK, but the car's radiator is demolished and coolant spews on the interstate shoulder. Although I sympathize with the driver, I'm glad it isn't us. We don't need another problem.

We rise early Monday morning and drive out of Buffalo on US Route 16 and ascend into the Bighorn Mountains. At an elevation of 9,666 feet, we pass through the Powder River Pass and head down into Ten Sleep Canyon and the town of Ten Sleep. My thoughts turn to Greg. How many mountain passes and little towns had his many road trips included? Had he ever driven this road?

Sue and I take the route through Yellowstone National Park, hoping to connect with Bonnie Whitman, a park ranger who served as one of our family advocates. We enter through the east entrance. Sue and I had entered Yellowstone here only once before, on our honeymoon. We reminisce and reflect on the vast difference in emotions between visits—the first so full of expectation and hope, this time filled with sorrow. Responding to our phone message, Bonnie tells us, "I won't be available today, but I'll be at Old Faithful tomorrow." We arrange to meet Bonnie for lunch at noon on Tuesday, and then we coordinate our schedule with Chris, our son, who's meeting us for the memorial hike.

The Teton Range finally comes into view as Sue and I drive into Grand Teton National Park from Yellowstone. "You beautiful mountains," I think. "You damn beautiful mountains!"

We arrive at the Moose Visitor Center and ask a ranger at the information desk if she'll contact Elizabeth Maki or Terry Roper. "Elizabeth is right in the back office," she replies. "Let me tell her you're here."

Family advocates were tactically and emotionally important during the search for Greg and Walker. They kept us informed, tended to details, and supported us. Our family was fortunate to work with three rangers. Elizabeth Maki made the initial phone call to inform us Greg was overdue. She met us at the airport and introduced us to Bonnie Whitman. A previously scheduled vacation took Elizabeth away from the park during the remainder of the search. A couple of days later, Bonnie was called back to Yellowstone. At about the same time, Terry Roper, who'd been working with Walker's family, was assigned to work with us. This personnel shuffling wasn't a problem. We got to know three incredible, compassionate people who were involved in the search and in our emotional responses every step of the way.

Now Elizabeth greets us with hugs and words of welcome and sympathy, letting us know we're among people who mourn Greg's and Walker's deaths along with us. We pick up maps and information on hiking trails. Elizabeth loans us her can of bear spray. Sue feels more comfortable having it along for the hike on the Taggart Lake Trail that we're planning to take this evening, a route similar to the one Walker and Greg followed in April. We've been driving for two solid days, and we need some exercise. We also need to acclimate to the altitude for the more difficult hike to Garnet Canyon.

I intentionally park across the lot from where Walker and Greg had parked their cars. Sue knows what I'm doing. Our one-mile hike to Taggart Lake provides time and an appropriate setting to think about our son's journey to the site of his death. We know the hike to Garnet Canyon will be difficult, but I already know the physical effort will be minor compared to the emotional impact.

Tuesday morning is sunny and cool, and goes according to plan. Sue and I arrive at Old Faithful and within a short while Chris and Jesse, his girlfriend, appear. Sue and I are happy to be with

Chris again. It's only been two months since our last visit, but being physically present with my son means so much more than before Greg's death. Bonnie walks over from her office to join us. We all enjoy a pleasant outdoor lunch. We'd only been with Bonnie for a couple of days during the search, and we've only known her for four months. Yet we're sharing very personal emotions.

After our lunch with Bonnie, we drive to Jenny Lake. Chris and Jesse walk around the area while Sue and I go to the ranger station to look for Ron Johnson, another member of the search crew. We met Ron in 2003 while visiting Grand Teton National Park with Sue's mom and stepdad, Dorothy and Mike Drazich, from Proctor, Minnesota. Ron has connections to Proctor, and he was Greg's avalanche course instructor earlier that year. To our disappointment, Ron isn't there. Instead, we're surprised to find Nick Armitage. He and Chris Harder will lead us to the site of Greg's and Walker's deaths the next day. Sue and I leave the planning to the two rangers, and hike along Jenny Lake to Inspiration Point to prepare for tomorrow's hike to Garnet Canyon.

That evening we eat in Jackson at Bubba's Barbecue, a large, family-style restaurant that serves a variety of ribs and barbecued entrées. I had reviewed Greg's credit card statement after his death to check for suspicious charges, but I was also looking for clues. The final charge on his statement was from Bubba's, dated April 16. As I enjoy some tasty ribs, I wonder, "What did Greg eat here? Where did they sit?"

Wednesday dawns cool, clear, and calm. Chris wants to get an early start since the forecast high is in the eighties. The car thermometer reads thirty-five degrees as Sue and I drive to the trailhead. The heat won't be a problem at the start of the hike. We're fifteen minutes behind Chris's desired departure time as he, Jesse, Sue, and I hike onto the trail at seven fifteen. "There are southeast-facing switchbacks in the bowl approaching the canyon. The sun is hot there, so it would be good to be through there by ten," Chris tells us.

The first part of the trail has cell reception. Upon reaching a designated point, Chris plans to call Nick Armitage and Chris Harder, who calculate that they can reach the boulder field about the same time we do if they coordinate their departure from the ranger station.

As we leave the parking lot, I call Greg's girlfriend, Megan Webb, and my brother, Rick. I leave messages with both to let them know our location. They'll be traveling with us, even if they aren't physically present.

I peel off a layer as perspiration soaks the shirt under my backpack; it's mile three, and nine a.m. approaches. We hike through an open area and navigate some switchbacks. Neither Sue nor I think they're too bad. At the three-mile mark we reach a fork in the trail. The right fork goes to Surprise Lake and Amphitheater Lake. We take the left fork toward Garnet Canyon.

Soon we're nearing the mouth of the canyon. I ask Chris about the switchbacks he'd warned us about. "Those were the ones we passed a while back," he explains. Sue and I look at each other with some surprise. We've hiked tougher trails.

Our rest and water stops become more frequent. At the designated point, Chris sends word of our position to the rangers. We're making good progress, and Sue and I aren't feeling too tired. But at this rest, we remove our packs and shed a layer of clothing. The packs aren't heavy, just bulky. Mountain hikes are the only times we carry packs, so we're unaccustomed to the feel of them.

My emotions shift between the pleasure of being in this beautiful place and the heartbreak of why we're here. One minute I'm enjoying a spectacular view with warm sun beaming on my face and a gentle breeze cooling me as I perspire—the next, I'm aware of the pain of knowing my son is dead and I'll never enjoy another mountain hike with him. The conflicting feelings weigh heavily on me, but also motivate me to continue.

At eleven a.m. we arrive at the boulder field. The hike to this point hasn't been too hard. Sue and I both think previous hikes in

Montana to summit Hyalite Peak with Greg and Mount Blackmore with Chris were more difficult. But the boulder field isn't what I'm expecting. I imagined a trail ending at a rockslide of one- or two-foot boulders covering the ground. I thought that there wouldn't be a trail, but that a person could scramble through, on all fours if necessary. But these boulders are larger than I anticipated, some as big as cars. There's no clear way through. We'll have to navigate our own way.

Nick and Chris Harder arrive as Sue and I follow Chris and Jesse unsuccessfully into the boulder field. Ranger Harder hikes ahead while Nick leads us through the field. The crossing isn't strenuous, but it's tenuous and not without mishap. At one point I plant my lead foot on a three-foot boulder with a flat face that slopes at a forty-five-degree angle. As I raise my back foot, my plant foot slips. I put out my right hand to catch myself and jam the ring finger. By evening, it will be swollen and sore. We proceed under Nick's lead without needing to backtrack. Crossing the boulder field is slow going for Sue and me, largely because it requires more flexibility than a typical hike. Sometimes a long stretch is the only way to reach the next boulder. Our backpacks add an extra dimension of discomfort and restriction. Sue later admits she doesn't think she could have made it without Nick to lend a hand to pull her up or get her down from boulder to boulder. She's also restricted because she carries a hiking pole in one hand. At times it provides stability and balance, but sometimes it just gets in the way. We finally make it through. Or so we think.

We descend to an actual trail and wend our way for a few hundred feet before coming face-to-face with another boulder field, a smaller version of the one we've just traversed. Soon we're on another dirt trail. It takes us over thirty minutes to navigate the five hundred feet of boulder fields.

The winter's heavy snows created another problem. Though it's August, snow is still melting and producing a lot of runoff. An unanticipated stream of snowmelt passes between us and our destination. The stream is too wide to jump over and too deep to step through, a lot like my grief. To reach the campsite, we continue up into the canyon, above the sacred ground, until we come to snowpack. Here the stream flows beneath the snow. We gingerly make our way over the slippery snow bridge and double back on the other side of the stream. Nick and Chris Harder point out the campsite. We arrive, exactly four months—to the day—after Greg's and Walker's bodies were airlifted out of this canyon.

As Nick wanders toward the campsite alone, I follow. I ask him more specific questions about the search, their camp, and the recovery of their bodies. Nick graciously answers all my questions. He understands that these details are essential for me to process Greg's death and help me deal with my sorrow. Nick and Chris Harder explain the depth of the avalanche debris at the boulders during the search. Only a very small portion of the large boulder was visible, they tell us. The avalanche's debris field had covered much of the canyon, maybe an area of two hundred by three hundred yards. It was a massive slide.

Too soon, it's time to head back. I don't want to leave! I feel so connected to Greg here. I can see why he loved this place. I try to picture his last vision of earth. Our clear, warm August afternoon is quite different from that April evening of falling and blowing snow. I can see for miles. Greg's visibility would have been very limited. I take some comfort knowing Greg died here rather than on a street corner in downtown Minneapolis.

Nick leaves us to hike farther up the canyon. We follow Chris Harder back through the boulder field. Once we're back on the main trail, he moves ahead at a quicker pace and we take our time. After thirty minutes, Jesse and Chris pick up their pace and leave Sue and me to make our way down. I'm having more trouble than usual on the descent. Today my legs are sore, beyond the familiar tired feeling I've experienced on other hikes. The scramble through the boulder field was different from anything I've ever done. The stretching and bending did a number on me. We press on, slowly.

We arrive at the trailhead parking lot in about three hours. I call Megan and Rick to update them. I'm so happy we reached the canyon to visit the campsite. So many emotions rush through me, all of them distorted by fatigue. I want to thank Greg for exposing me to the Tetons and, at the same time, cuss him out for ever discovering these mountains. I want to tell him about our hike. I'm overwhelmed, and nothing feels real. It's just not possible that Greg and Walker are dead.

We drive to the Climber's Ranch to retrieve the remainder of Greg's things from Chris Harder. It's everything that wasn't brought off the mountain when Greg's and Walker's bodies were recovered. Among the gear is Greg's climbing helmet. There's no mistaking it. He listed climbs in black marker, the exceptional and memorable ones were on one side and the ones that sucked on the other. Greg wasn't rating the routes, just the way the day's events had gone. We load the gear into Chris's car and drive back to Jackson for dinner with Terry Roper, Nick Armitage and his fiancée, and Chris Harder and his wife.

On Thursday Sue and I return to the national park to look for Elizabeth since she hadn't joined us for dinner the previous evening. The three of us enjoy cool lemonades at nearby Dornan's, where we sit on the restaurant's roof patio and discuss the search. The Grand rises majestically over my shoulder. I turn frequently to view its beauty. Elizabeth tells us how torn she was to leave during the search for a planned visit to her sister. She was invested in the search for Walker and Greg, and told us she'd frequently checked the Internet for updates. Her sister even commented to Elizabeth that she wasn't mentally present at times.

Our discussion turns to Walker and Greg's decision-making process the day they'd stopped at the Visitor Center for their back-country permits. Elizabeth assured us Greg and Walker had made good choices. Their deaths were a tragic accident that resulted from some very unusual events. This made the tragedy harder to accept. What's the point of setting goals, working toward those goals, applying yourself in school, and trying to do a job to the best of your ability when it can all be randomly taken from you? It's my grief screaming out, my emotions overwhelming logic. I want an answer to an unanswerable question.

Sue becomes concerned we're taking too much of Elizabeth's time. "Do you need to get back to the office?"

"I'll find something in my job description this visit falls under," she tells us.

"But aren't you missing the ice-cream social for the park staff?" Sue presses.

"I can have ice cream anytime, but you're in the park just for the day."

We talk a little longer, then finally head back to the Visitor Center to see Ranger Scott Guenther, who's just returned from his back-country assignment. We thank him for his part in the search. He apologizes that he wasn't available to hike with us to Garnet Canyon. We talk about details of the search and the site, as we had with other staff. It's helpful to see Scott, even for only a brief visit.

Sue and I are amazed by the compassion shown by the staff at Grand Teton National Park. They're affected by this tragedy too, and are comfortable sharing their feelings with us. We expected a cordial welcome, but we're surprised to be thanked time and time again for coming back to the park. The rangers tell us our visit helps them heal. They're dealing with the deaths of two young men they didn't know, by the pain of two families torn apart because a son and brother were taken from them much too soon. I learn that Greg's death is touching many more people than I imagined, a fact that would be borne out again and again in the weeks ahead.

After our visit with Scott, Sue and I decide to take a short, late-afternoon hike to Phelps Lake. In less than an hour we're at the overlook, gazing through the dense pine growth down to the blue waters of the lake, which is perfectly calm except for the ripples created by a moose wading near the far shore. A mother, hiking stick in hand, with two preteen children at her side, approaches from the opposite direction. "If you keep going," she warns us, "watch out for a bear. It's been traveling parallel to the trail, almost tracking us for a half mile." We decide to turn back. Sue feels more comfortable with that choice, since we already returned Elizabeth's can of bear spray.

Back in Jackson, we walk through the square to Café Genevieve for a nice, quiet dinner, just the two of us. We talk about our visit so far and our conversations with the rangers. Sue and I agree about the sentiment I'd expressed to more than one of them, "We're so glad we've met you, but we wish we could have figured out a different way to do it."

Early the next morning, we pack and leave for home. We drive north through the park. As we pass the Moose turnoff, the Tetons loom majestically on our left. The bright sun illuminates the entire east face of the range on that cool, still morning. Soon we're directly in line with Garnet Canyon. "Good-bye, Greg," we both blurt through the tears running down our cheeks. The tears finally stop ten miles later, near Moran Junction.

Neither of us want to leave! I'd thought the campsite visit would be the biggest emotional challenge. That was hard, but leaving is even more difficult. I feel as if I'm abandoning Greg. I feel connected to him here. Maybe his spirit resides here. How had it all come to this? Why did our lives take this turn? My faith is being tested. I still believe and trust in God, but right now I need an explanation, something to hold on to. I don't get one.

But I know Greg loved the Tetons. He thought they were among the most beautiful mountains he'd seen. They were paradise to him. So maybe it did make sense that he should leave this life in a paradise and move directly into the paradise of the next life. That comforts me.

06

INTO THE WILD

This adventure was very important to me because it showed me, as Chris McCandless had in Into the Wild, *that happiness is all around us. . . . It's up to us to go out there and get out of our unhappy, safe, daily lives and take the risks that are necessary to find happiness. . . . The last 7 weeks were more fun than I could imagine, and it was basically a solitary experience.*

—MAY 3, 2003, Reflection on a Seven-Week Road Trip, Bozeman, Montana

Books were always important to Greg—which is good, because there was no way to avoid textbooks through his twenty-six years of education, which included a program for four-year-olds with speech issues and a second year of kindergarten.

He loved to read and be read to as a boy. While I read Little Golden Books to young Greg at times, Sue spent many hours with him over books as a young child. Even late into his elementary-school days, the two of them often read books together, such as *The Chronicles of Narnia* series. His favorite books were adventure stories—no surprise there. Gary Paulsen books followed Childcraft books with stories that featured Davy Crockett and Daniel Boone. Greg envied the pioneers. He'd even lament, "There are no more frontiers left!" He was destined to explore, if not the wilderness, then maybe space, the depths of the ocean, or the human body.

In addition to all the assigned reading Greg worked his way through over the years, he loved to read magazines and study maps. Skiing and climbing books and videos comprised his collection of "ski porn." Especially in his post-college years, searching through published literature for his next adventure in the mountains was a source of relaxation and a way for Greg to wind down. His mind was definitely still working and analyzing, but in a different vein. Sometimes just seeing pictures of a route he wanted to climb or ski gave him a rush—and that was all the motivation he needed to get back to the matter at hand, whatever it was.

With all that going on, Greg had little time for what might be called pleasure reading. Although he accumulated a fair-sized *Calvin and Hobbes* collection, he seldom read a book unrelated to his studies or interests. Occasionally, though, Greg found a book that would really resonate with him. Jon Krakauer's *Into the Wild* was one of those. Greg loved that book. He was mesmerized by the main figure, Chris McCandless. For him, the travels and nomadic lifestyle portrayed in the book were idyllic. They matched his vision.

Greg didn't want to give up his entire life to live off the land, travel, and enjoy nature and the great outdoors. But he sure wanted to try it for a short while. Like so many of Greg's dreams, he didn't just think about it, he pursued it. In the spring of 2003, Greg took some time off from his job at Spring Meadows, a senior-living community in Bozeman, and set out on a seven-week journey across the western United States. He visited several national parks. He skied in Colorado—at nationally known resorts and the back-country ski area in Silverton. This had to have been his favorite. Back-country skiers require a high level of skill. There are no lifts or established runs. A helicopter drops you somewhere on the mountain to enjoy a private day of skiing. During that trip, Greg also spent time in New Mexico, Arizona, and California. He traveled to Oregon and Washington, visiting friends and interviewing for med school. It was the trip of a lifetime.

Greg told me *Into the Wild* had a great impact on his vision of life and was part of the motivation for this adventure. He bought a copy for me as a present from him and Chris on my birthday in 2003. I've read the book and seen the movie, and I can relate to the attraction of the kind of immersive adventure Chris McCandless attempted. It's not something I'd try, at least not to that degree, but I see how it appealed to Greg.

That copy of *Into the Wild* is now a treasured possession. But the book was only half the gift. Greg included a letter. It was probably the most philosophical dissertation I ever heard from him. In it, he explains the attraction of such a nomadic adventure and shares his vision of an ideal existence.

Dad,

I hope you enjoy this book as much as I did. I doubt that it will have the impact on your life that it has had on mine, simply because more things in your life are already established. It gets harder and harder to change things the more commitments you have, so I guess I (and Chris) am giving you this not to change you but as an aid to understanding me. I don't think I have ever read a book where I identified more with the protagonist. This book showed me that I don't have to be content with a cookie cutter-type experience for life. I can "think outside the box" and do what I want, even if society actively discourages me from seeking out an experience. This book was ultimately what gave me the courage to embark on my adventure. That experience (I am obviously just guessing here) is something that years from now I will look back on as being something that revolutionized my perspective and defined my life. It showed me the fulfillment to be found in a more nomadic existence. A "constantly changing horizon" (to quote Mr. McCandless) is exciting and when that change is between different parts of the western U.S. (where God has done some of his finest work, in my opinion), it is even better. The opportunity, at least temporarily, to surround yourself with the indescribable beauty intrinsically brings happiness and fulfillment. Happiness does not only come from human relationships. God puts it all around us in the natural world. It is simply up to us to find it. My trip (and thus, this book) have shown me the importance of being able to take a couple continuous months off to be on my own. Thus family practice is probably out, but my love of a "constantly changing horizon" is pushing me into something like emergency medicine. Therefore, I hope you find this book as entertaining as Chris and I found it, and even if it does not change you personally at all, I hope it helps you in understanding me. Happy (belated) birthday.

Love, Greg

I envied that Greg found such profound inspiration in a book. Even more, I admired him for recognizing the inspiration, adopting it in his own life, and following through on changes that would allow him to live his dream. He was clearly impressed with the short life of Chris McCandless. So much so that he lived a modified version of McCandless's approach for a few weeks. He experienced the joys and disappointments of those constantly changing horizons he sought—and like Chris McCandless, Greg's search for adventure eventually resulted in his death. Sadly, Greg's dream became our nightmare.

Greg was twenty-three years old when he wrote the letter he gave me with *Into the Wild*. He hadn't yet been accepted to med school. Yet his vision of the future was clear—even down to his specialty of choice. Only the how and where were in question, not the final achievement. I still marvel at his vision and focus.

Late in his journey alone through the western United States, Greg pursued one other Chris McCandless–inspired adventure, a seven-day solo hike in the Bitterroots. In that week, he saw only one other human being, another backpacker hiking out as Greg was hiking in. He told me he found it a humbling and invigorating experience. He would've been ecstatic after completing the adventure, except he returned to find his car had been broken into and many of his possessions stolen. Greg was amused at the items the thief took and those that were left in the car. His packed suitcase and music collection, dozens of CDs, were taken. But his suit, tie, and dress shoes for a med-school interview were left behind. "The thief had no use for dress clothes, just underwear. Or maybe they weren't his size," he said in his call the night he emerged to find his damaged car. He seemed too tired to be upset. "I never thought my first phone call after returning to civilization would be 911."

There is more to that story, though, than Greg returning to a break-in. The local sheriff had come across Greg's car earlier in the week. The sheriff called Sue's parents because his phone book on the front seat of the car was open to their names. Eventually I talked with the sheriff, who was concerned Greg had been in harm's way. I assured him that Greg planned to hike and camp for several days. The sheriff offered to organize a search for Greg to make certain he hadn't been injured, or worse, by whoever broke into the car. He was pursuing the worst-case scenario—that Greg had been attacked and then the car was ransacked. I was making some assumptions when I told the sheriff I didn't think a search was necessary. My opinion was based largely on the fact that the driver's-side window was broken. The only reason that would have happened was to gain entry, which meant the car was locked and Greg and the keys were gone. My assessment proved correct.

In the end, the car was repaired and the clothes replaced, and Greg had his interview. Sue and I helped Greg with the insurance forms. The settlement didn't cover the cost of everything taken, but his main disappointment about the whole episode was that he wasn't accepted to the med school in Washington.

The search for a constantly changing horizon continued to resonate in Greg's future. He often amazed me and tired me just with descriptions of his travels and adventures. I don't know how long he might have pursued that vision, but I don't think he was hell-bent on running this dream into oblivion. Oh, he would've continued to enjoy back-country adventures until health or age prohibited. But his constant need to go, go, go had diminished. About seven years after his Bitterroot solo trek, Greg indicated after one of his road trips that he could see himself settling down a little and moving on to the next phase of his life. Again, he impressed me with his insight and a willingness to change. I wonder where he'd be now.

07

*On the traverses I had to cross multiple spots where I was really
exposed for a while. Did a bit of praying. Lots of signs of avalanches
on the way up. Big ones that haven't slid in at least probably 20 years,
judging from the size of the trees in the debris. Even more unnerving than
that though, were the few that I saw that looked recent. . . . it doesn't take
much snow to bury you, and if I get buried, it is for good.*

—APRIL 15, 2003, Seven-Day Solo Trek, Bitterroot Range, Montana

Too easily we become nonchalant about life. Healthy, young, and
not-so-young individuals don't routinely consider that we might be
doing something for the last time. And yet, we're regularly confronted
with reminders that life can and does change in an instant. Or with
a phone call.

I remember my sister's call at four forty on the afternoon of New
Year's Day in 1986. Our father had a heart attack, she told me.
Just forty-five minutes later a second call informed us he was dead
at age sixty-six. I expected to bury my father, but not this soon. I
felt like a cannonball had passed through my gut. I was only thirty-
seven, and my dad was dead. Life changed with a phone call.

In 1994, I experienced a persistent bout of flu-like symptoms. It
devastated our family when I was diagnosed with dermatomyositis, an
autoimmune disease that affects the muscles and skin. We'd never
heard of the condition. It took me two days to learn to pronounce

it correctly. I was in the hospital for two months, remained unable to take solid or liquid food by mouth for six months, and was out of work for almost a year. Our lives changed the moment I received the diagnosis.

Sue and I always insisted Greg or Chris call with their itinerary when going into the mountains and again when they came out, especially on solo trips. They were loyal to this request, most of the time.

We knew that the normal procedure for the summit attempt Walker and Greg planned that April weekend involved a partial ascent the first day before setting up camp. Then on day two, rising before sunrise to continue the climb, attaining the summit, and descending. The early start on the second day was critical to ensure everyone was off the mountain before midday, the time of peak avalanche danger.

As of Sunday morning, April 17, Sue and I believe Greg and Walker still plan to summit. We don't know they've scaled back their goal. I'm imagining their progress in the hours before noon. As I've done so often before, I'm traveling vicariously through my son.

By late Sunday afternoon, Sue and I anticipate a phone call from Greg to let us know he's out of the national park. The phone doesn't ring. As the evening grows late, we call Greg, but it goes straight to voice mail. He doesn't return our call by bedtime. Sue expresses her concern. I try to remain calm for her, but I'm worried despite my internal rationalizations.

On Monday, April 18, Sue goes to work, and I wait at home for Greg's call. I wait all day. I wonder why Greg hasn't called, but I keep busy and don't allow myself to consider the possibility that anything terrible has happened. We call Greg again Monday evening after Sue gets home from work. Same result. Sue is very concerned. Unable to suppress the negative thoughts racing through my mind, I now share her fears.

An unspoken tension hangs in the air. We don't discuss possible scenarios. We just go about our chores and evening rituals. We keep our distance from each other, not wanting to say the wrong thing or fuel any emotions. We call Chris to see if he's heard from Greg. He answers immediately, and tells us he hasn't heard from his brother. We find out later this was a true statement, but not the whole story. Chris knows Walker and Greg are late coming out of the canyon. He decides he isn't going to be the one to tell us.

The evening wears on. No word from Greg. I'm very apprehensive by now. I try to convince myself he got distracted or lost his phone—or some other kind of absentmindedness is playing out. At nine forty-five the phone rings, the ring that indicates a long-distance call. It rings again. I pick up the phone and look at the caller ID: NPS. National Park Service. Believe it or not, I don't panic. My first thought is to wonder why Greg is calling from a Park Service phone. I answer with a hello. It isn't Greg's voice at the other end. The voice is female. My chest tightens. My heart beats harder and faster than ever before. Time stops.

The caller identifies herself as Elizabeth Maki, a ranger with the National Park Service in Grand Teton National Park. She asks if I'm related to Greg. I confirm that he's my son. Elizabeth says she wants to make sure she is speaking with the right person. She apologizes for calling so late and taking so long to contact us. Even though our name isn't a common one, the park staff had difficulty tracking us down since Greg listed Montana as home on his back-country permit.

By this time Sue is right by my shoulder, mouthing questions with a frightened expression on her face. Elizabeth informs me that Walker and Greg are late out from the back country. The alarm was raised when Walker's employer called his emergency contact, his girlfriend, Erica Logue, on Monday morning because he hadn't shown up at work. Erica then called the park to ask about his and Greg's situation. A ranger checked the back-country permit log and was dispatched to the parking area at the trailhead to look for Walker's and Greg's vehicles. The cars were still in the lot. A search-and-rescue (SAR) group was organized, equipped, and sent into Garnet Canyon. The approach on skis takes about three hours, leaving little search time for the rangers before dark. They looked for signs of distress along the route to the canyon and in the canyon itself, both on foot and by air with brief helicopter reconnaissance flights, as time permitted. Elizabeth reports that the SAR team had accomplished this objective without seeing any sign of Greg and Walker.

Elizabeth is calm and reassures us that they may have had some minor mishap and are unable to ski out. The weather has been snowy and windy, she tells us. It's possible that they hunkered down for a while to avoid storms and would still exit the canyon on their own. Either she's very convincing or I'm very naïve, because I really believe this might happen. Maybe it's just denial on my part. I refuse to admit the situation is dire.

We talk about search plans and options. "Additional SAR personnel will return to the canyon tomorrow. A helicopter will transport personnel to the search area to minimize access time and increase search time," she tells me. The SAR team will be fresh when they arrive in Garnet Canyon on Tuesday morning. "The helicopter will fly multiple reconnaissance flights in and around the Grand as time and weather allows." SAR would search in the area Greg and Walker had indicated on their permit and in surrounding areas. This would cover possibilities such as injury or being lost. Elizabeth promises she'll contact us as soon as anything develops. I'm too numb to say anything but "Thank you."

I hang up the phone and turn to Sue. I hold her and relay in detail everything Elizabeth told me. We cry, trembling in each other's arms. What are we supposed to do now?

We call Chris to fill him in on the situation. He already knows Greg and Walker are overdue. Though there was confusion about an emergency contact for Greg in the initial stages of the search, the news of Walker's situation was quickly communicated by park personnel to his parents and Erica. The news spread quickly among his circle of friends. This group overlaps with people who know Greg as well. That's how Chris found out. When we ask why he hadn't called us, he says there was no way he wanted to be the one to give us this news. Also, he believed the guys would turn up before nightfall on Monday. I understand how hard it would have been for Chris to make that call, but I wish he had.

We stay up late into the night, praying, worrying, trying to figure out how we can help, and wondering what to do next. We finally go to bed, but just lie still, as if encased in a womb of fear. We're both emotionally and physically drained, but sleep eludes us.

08

FAMILY

I was the only one skiing that day. I remember being mad at my parents when I was younger & went to Beartooth Pass in late June & they told me there would not be any skiing there. Of course there was snow & we saw people skiing.

—JULY 14, 2010, Beartooth Mountains, Montana

My aspirations as a young man were simple. I had no profound goals, no great heights I was seeking to attain. My plans for the future were in line with the goals of most of my peers growing up during the 1960s—a decent job doing something I enjoyed, a house, a wife, and a family.

Greg's birth in 1979 was the start of fulfilling that last part. I was thirty-one years old, and felt I had everything in the world I wanted. My marriage to Sue had made us a couple, and Greg's birth made us a family. I remember sharing that observation with others when Greg was a baby.

Becoming a family was a significant milestone in my life. My parents stressed the value of love, respect, and simply being present to each other in everyday life. Sundays were synonymous with visits to my grandparents. We celebrated holidays, and birthdays with aunts, uncles, and cousins. All were a big part of my childhood.

Family has always been important to me. I thought ours was typical, like everyone else's.

Sue's experience was similar. Her father's death when she was only fifteen was a heartbreaking loss for her. But her mother made sure the family remained intact and in touch. Grandparents, aunts, and uncles included her in every event, just as always. Her appreciation of and strong feeling for family was part of what attracted me to her.

We brought that shared sense of family into our marriage and built on it after Greg and Chris were born. We took many pictures of them as young boys with their grandparents. Sue and I maintained relationships with our siblings and tried to give the boys opportunities to see their aunts and uncles frequently to develop their own relationships. Looking back, we weren't together as much as I would've liked. Since our families lived in other cities, we couldn't enjoy a weekly Sunday dinner or count on frequent gatherings to build traditions. We planned trips to Detroit to see my family and visited Sue's family in Duluth a few times a year.

Greg seemed more at ease with adults than other children, not a surprise since he had no cousins his age. He spent much of his early family time with adults, and they made Greg the center of attention. Greg grew close to his grandparents, built lasting relationships with aunts, uncles, and cousins, and maintained contact with extended family into adulthood.

We made at least three drives to Michigan every two years, an annual summer visit and alternate Christmases, even when the boys were babies. I can only remember flying twice. The first time was Chris's first Christmas at age eleven months. That was a hassle, even in the days before airport security became so complex. In addition to diapers, clothes, and toys, Greg and Chris always traveled with their "friends," their stuffed animals. It began with each boy bringing one favorite friend, but eventually they'd pack an entire suitcase of stuffed animals. In the moment, it was irritating, but now I cherish those memories.

Many of our family and friends didn't attempt to travel—driving or flying—with young children. We never gave it a second thought. Greg was a good traveler. He slept readily and was easily entertained. The travel dynamics got a little more tense and complicated once Chris was born, but we still made it every summer. Greg did have a problem with car sickness for a brief period of time. After a couple of incidents and cleanups, we discovered that postponing breakfast until later in the morning and avoiding Egg McMuffins and butter on toast and rolls were helpful strategies.

Sue and I expected that having two children of the same sex close in age would have advantages and also create problems. Greg and Chris didn't disappoint us. From the start, they had different personalities—Greg, precise and calculating, and Chris, spontaneous and carefree. Sue and I thought our sons might go through their entire lives without using their given names. They were usually "moron" and "idiot" to each other.

They argued a lot during their elementary school years. One day Chris strategically rigged up an ice-cream bucket full of water above Greg's bedroom door. The bucket and water hit their mark as Greg opened the door. Most of the water landed on the floor, much to our dismay. But Greg was wet enough to plot revenge. A few nights later, as Chris lay sleeping in his bed, Greg snuck in and tied his arms to the bedposts. Sue and I were awakened during the night by blood-curdling screams. Chris was frantically attempting to get free. This act bordered on the edges of safety, so we declared the issue closed, and it was.

Soon the brotherly relationship matured, and Greg looked out for Chris. Chris now fondly remembers when Greg gave him the "hoops" lecture. Chris was adamantly refusing to perform some required task, and we sentenced him to sit at the kitchen table until completion. Greg advised Chris, "Hey, you've just got to learn to jump through the hoops. Get through the first hoop put in front of you, then the next one, and pretty soon you're free to do pretty much anything you want." Chris's argumentative, combative brother had become a mentor.

When we visited Detroit, we stayed at my parents' house. Grandma and Grandpa were thrilled to host their young grandkids. They were together infrequently and looked forward to seeing each other. After my dad died—a loss Greg felt keenly—Mom sold the house and lived with my sister. But even in the later years when we stayed in a motel, we spent most of our time with Grandma.

No matter the situation, Greg always enjoyed visiting Michigan. From the early trips as a baby until the last while in med school, he was ready to go. Grandma and Grandpa, Aunt Jan, and all the aunts, uncles, and cousins wanted to see all of us, and they always planned something special for Greg when he visited.

Our most difficult Detroit trip was for my mom's funeral in July 1994. I was still weak after battling my myositis. I couldn't drive, and Sue didn't think she could drive all seven hundred miles herself. It was the only other time we flew out. I was a burden rather than a help on that trip. I didn't even know if I could manage the travel to Michigan. Greg pushed the wheelchair for me at the airports in Minneapolis and Detroit. He had a lot of unwanted responsibility on that trip.

It was a very emotional time for him too. Greg had a close relationship with Grandpa Seftick, but he was only six when my dad died. With Grandma it was different. Greg was the first grandchild. He was special for that reason alone. The births of other grandchildren couldn't take away that distinction. Greg was heartbroken when she died. He spent a lot of time standing near her coffin at the funeral home during the visitation. I don't know if he couldn't believe she was dead, if he was trying to make sense of death at age fifteen, or if he just couldn't bear to say good-bye. We never talked about that time. I wish we had.

During our family visits, Greg always had plenty to talk about and stories to tell. He had willing ears available with his grandparents and other adults present. Greg was comfortable with and enjoyed each side of our extended family equally. During his med-school and residency years, he took advantage of opportunities to see family on his personal travels—often visiting Uncle Rick and Aunt Jenny, my brother and sister-in-law in Fort Wayne, Indiana. His visit in late February 2011, as he was relocating to Montana, was the last time Rick and Jenny saw Greg. They would've missed that opportunity if they weren't so inviting and if Greg wasn't comfortable and eager to visit.

Greg also relished the opportunity to have friends and family visit him. He couldn't offer luxurious accommodations to guests, but he was eager to have the pleasure of their company. His Morgantown apartment, his first without a roommate, was the only place he lived that handled a couple of visitors comfortably. Sue made a deal with Greg when we helped him move. We bought a futon for his apartment with the understanding that we could stay with him during visits. His random residency work schedule often meant an empty apartment when we were in town.

Other family visited Greg in Morgantown. Sue's sister, Barb, and her family stopped to see him as they returned from Boston. Our neighbors Helen and Eldo, who are like family to us, stopped also. They didn't stay overnight, but Greg appreciated the extra effort that went into their visits. He worked around schedules to hike, have a meal, or show off the beauty of the local nature to those who came to see him.

In early 2008, toward the end of Greg's intern year, Sue and I were invited to our niece Hannah's graduation open house in Indiana. We asked Sue's mom and another niece, Kaity, to ride along. The four of us first drove to Morgantown to see Greg before the graduation. Greg could accommodate two guests in his one-bedroom apartment, but four of us? Greg gave up his bed, and his grandma slept in his room. Sue and I were on the futon. Kaity slept on the floor under the table in the dining area in a makeshift fort she built. I don't recall what Greg did those few nights. Maybe he worked. Maybe he crashed with a friend. He might have slept in the bathtub for all I know! But he welcomed our visit. He made sacrifices and adjustments because family was important to him.

I've always been proud that Greg and Chris accepted and cherished their families. At gatherings, Greg often surprised me by visiting with members with whom he had little in common— or so it seemed to me. There the two of them would be, talking about something, Greg listening intently. When I'd ask him about it later, he made it seem like no big deal. "We were just having a conversation." Over the years, people have mentioned that Greg gave the impression they were the only person in the room when they conversed with him. They remembered that, and gravitated toward him when the opportunity arose.

Greg supported his family because he knew his family supported him. In a June 19, 2005, journal entry, Greg wrote, "Everyone in my family is so good to me and supportive. I am lucky to have them." I hope this recognition was an inspiration to him and helped him through the tough spots during his life.

More proof that family was important to Greg were all the greeting cards. Sue and I always sent cards for significant events. Greg and Chris picked up on the tradition by marking birthdays and holidays by sending cards. After Greg's death, I found a bag with two cards among his possessions—a birthday card for me and a Mother's Day card for Sue. I read that birthday card often. I like to believe Greg bought it because of the sentiment:

Dad,

No one has to tell me how lucky I am to have you, because I've known for a long time.

When I think back over the years and remember everything you've done for me, I realize how wonderful you are. You've taught me so much about life and love and giving, and those are lessons I'll never forget. You showed me how to stand on my own in the world, and for that I'll always be grateful. So many things that have added to my happiness have been gifts from you. Maybe having a dad like you has spoiled me a bit, but don't ever think I don't appreciate and love you, because I do . . . with all my heart.

Happy Birthday, Dad.

I wish he could have handed it to me personally, but I'm grateful I found it. It's a precious remembrance of my son.

While being a husband and a dad was high on my list of life's ambitions, that wasn't the case for Greg. His family was important to him, but for many years he didn't see himself settling down with a wife, a home, and, maybe eventually, children. But that changed. I don't know if the change was spurred by Megan, or if he changed and allowed Megan to enter his life. Greg's biggest obstacle to marriage appeared to be his lack of openness to relationships. I think he avoided relationships because he feared rejection—and avoiding relationships was his strategy for avoiding rejection. It worked for a while, until his friends started getting married. Then he saw that his buddies were still enjoying life like before and even looked happy married to some pretty amazing women.

During his July 2010 road trip, he ended his journal with some musings. He talked about "not being as young as I used to be," and a month being too long to be away. He missed Megan and couldn't "wait to see her in ten days." Greg was changing. Greg was letting himself change. The seed of the importance of family planted in Greg from early childhood was sprouting. He recognized the shift and referred to himself as a "completely different person."

In fact, he was a different person. He wrote, "Life sure is a long, strange trip." Greg's trip was long in miles; he covered a lot of ground. Looking back now, though, I'd say the strange part of his life was the next nine months, the final nine months of his too short life.

09

TRADITIONS

I looked up & saw sunlight. After a bit more Class 3, I was on the summit. . . . I was so stoked. The mountain looked big & intimidating from the bottom, but I had done it! My first Class 5 route. And I had done it in perfect style, no gear/rope, on-sight, ground-up, free-solo first ascent. I could not have been happier or more fulfilled. I took some pics & followed the very easy ridge back to the trail. Got back around 7:30–8:00. Not bad for 16–18 miles & about 5,000 vertical ft. of climbing.

—SEPTEMBER 4, 2005, Spanish Peaks, Montana

Traditions were important in my family and in Sue's when we were young. We incorporated some of those traditions into our family after Greg and Chris were born because we treasured them and hoped to continue them. We couldn't include them all, in part because of the greater distance from our parents.

Greg never balked at traditions. I expected there would come a time in his teenage years when he would resist our attempts to maintain the status quo. He never did. This was particularly true for traditions that included grandparents, aunts, uncles, and cousins. Both Greg and Chris inquired about holiday plans if Sue and I failed to bring them up in a timely manner. We were surprised by that, but grateful.

Most of our family traditions centered on holidays, particularly Christmas. We realized we had a dilemma to resolve shortly after our wedding: Where would we spend Christmas? Not only were families important to us, but each had Christmas customs we hoped to maintain—most connected to our families' ethnic backgrounds. We proposed a plan that both our families accepted: Rather than try to visit everyone each Christmas, we'd alternate between Detroit and Duluth. It worked well, and reduced our holiday stress level significantly, so we made it a new tradition.

Sue and I combined our Christmas traditions connected to location, worship, food, gifts, and decorations. And we introduced our traditions to each other's families. The drawback to our plan was that we never developed our own Christmas traditions at home. It bothered Sue and me more than Greg and Chris.

After a death, survivors usually find things they regret doing or not doing while the deceased was alive. One of my biggest regrets was how we handled Greg's last Christmas. As a first-year attending, he was low man on the totem pole. I assumed he'd have to work on Christmas, and we never discussed our plans with him. Our holiday rotation schedule put us in Detroit in 2010. As a ski patroller at Big Sky Resort south of Bozeman, Chris expected to work during the extremely busy Christmas week. So Sue and I decided to stay home alone in Minnesota. Just before Christmas, Greg told us, rather casually, that he was going to New Jersey to visit friends. Sue and I were devastated. How could we have let this happen? It was a lonely Christmas at home. We talked to Greg on the evening of Christmas Day. He sounded down, but dismissed our apologies and downplayed the significance of the day. That was Greg. We knew he was depressed.

Our family's Easter traditions began with colored eggs on Good Friday evening after dinner. Early Easter morning at Grandma and Grandpa Drazich's house, we hid baskets for Greg and Chris while they slept. There were only a limited number of hiding places because we didn't want them ransacking every room in the house. One year we hid Greg's basket in the oven, and he quickly found it. The next year we hid it in the exact same place. We should have known better. That was the first place he looked. He pulled his Easter basket out of the oven, turned around and looked at us, and exclaimed, "That Easter bunny has no imagination!"

For Halloween, Greg loved picking out costumes and trick-or-treating in the neighborhood. Sue made most of the boys' costumes when they were young. At four months old, Greg wore a purple Minnesota Vikings jersey over a heavy jacket and a "football helmet" cut and taped together from a diaper box. I spelled "Coach" on my jacket with pieces of masking tape. Greg thrashed around and cried as I carried him to the house next door. He definitely wasn't having as much fun as I was, so we returned home after that one stop. Most of Greg's costume requests were quite original—a bowling pin, a Civil War soldier, and an award-winning clown costume.

I find particular irony in the pair of costumes Greg and Chris selected the year Greg dressed as Superman and Chris as a doctor. Though he'd become one, Greg never wanted to dress up as a doctor for Halloween. And I consider Chris more of a Superman type with his recent skydiving and parasailing activities. That Halloween, it was if they were trying out a sibling role reversal—not that they, or we, realized it at the time.

Our most memorable Halloween in Afton was 1991, the Halloween Blizzard. Just a few days earlier, the Minnesota Twins won their second World Series in four years. Baseball, celebrations, victory parades, and the residual excitement were on most young boys' minds at the time. It started to snow on the afternoon of October 31. Greg and Chris came home from school already anxious for candy. Costumes weren't much of an issue since the weather called for winter jackets that would cover them anyway—and the candy givers probably couldn't see out the front door far enough to decipher whatever costume elements weren't covered.

I got home from work and was given the duty of escorting Greg and Chris while Sue stayed home to distribute candy. By the time we finished dinner, at least four inches of snow blanketed the ground, and it was still coming down. We got in our van and headed to the Pedersons' house to pick up Chris and Greg's friends Ryan and Heidi. It was only a mile north, but the roads weren't plowed.

I drove the kids through the Pedersons' neighborhood first. The van didn't have enough traction to climb the little hill east of their home. I backed up, turned around, and went the opposite direction. We made it through their neighborhood and headed home to visit our neighbors. Finally, we took Ryan and Heidi home and returned to our house. The boys were jubilant! They had more candy than they dreamed possible because few trick-or-treaters were out and our neighbors were giving away candy by the handful!

All trick-or-treating activities were preceded—a day or two before Halloween—by the main tradition, pumpkin carving. Greg and Chris were the designers, and I provided the manual labor. We used knives, spoons, and a hole saw. The early designs were simple, usually consisting of eyes, a nose, and a mouth with teeth on a symmetrical face. Later efforts were more creative, with eyebrows, mustaches, and ears added. In retrospect, I'm surprised Greg wasn't more interested in cleaning out the pumpkins. It would have been a strong indicator of his future in medicine. Maybe he knew he'd never be a surgeon. Or maybe he didn't plan to operate on vegetables! The pumpkin-carving tradition carried on after Greg and Chris left home. My most prized design was produced the year Greg died. I scraped "Wildcat"—Greg's nickname—into the pumpkin, not all the way through, but deep enough that the candle inside lit the letters and made them visible from a distance.

Over the years, several food traditions developed outside the ethnic dishes that were part of our holiday traditions. Now those foods each maintain a special place in our hearts as we remember Greg.

One of those food traditions developed at Afton's Fourth of July parades—which have been held annually since 1979, the year Greg was born. The first one we attended was in 1982. Greg had just turned three, and Chris wasn't quite six months old. We took the boys to the parade because I was riding in it as a member of the Afton City Council. Greg was very excited when he saw me ride by in the convertible. The festivities in the town park after the parade included a dunk tank, and I agreed to take a shift. Greg laughed every time he dunked me. He couldn't throw straight, far, or hard enough to hit the target, but the kid running the tank dunked me each time Greg threw. Then it was time for ice cream. Selma's, the oldest ice-cream parlor in Minnesota, has been in Afton since 1913. We each cooled off with a cone at "our bench." Soon after we moved to Afton, Sue and I aimlessly wandered from Selma's with our ice cream to a bench on a point on the St. Croix River. We adopted it and returned frequently. The bench has never been occupied when we've stopped. The parade, ice cream from Selma's, and the bench became a Fourth of July and extended birthday (since Greg's was July 2) tradition for us.

Sue gave me raspberry bushes soon after we bought our house. They continue to thrive and produce berries, though some years yield better than others. We've often had more berries than we could eat or use. Greg loved our raspberries. He and our neighbor Joanna picked their own when they were preschoolers. Sue packed raspberries for Greg and Chris for school lunch. Greg told us one day at lunch he passed the container of homegrown berries around to his friends sitting at the table with him. One of them asked if he knew how much they cost. "They're from our yard. They're free!" he told them. After that his friends would ask Greg if he had berries for lunch.

Some attempts to revive old family customs didn't take hold. Sue wanted Greg and Chris to taste homemade doughnuts like her grandma made when she was a child. They were eager to help, so the three of them took on the project. At ages five and three, the boys were definitely entertained, but not necessarily helpful. The doughnuts were excellent, but Sue wasn't convinced they were worth the effort and massive cleanup that followed. She'd already accomplished her goal of letting the kids experience these superior-tasting treats and opted for inferior store bought pastries in the future.

Then there were the pancakes. Sue called them Swedish pancakes when she was growing up. We called them skinny pancakes in Detroit when my mom made them. But they were the same. Plain pancakes similar to crepes made one at a time in a large skillet. Just eggs, flour, and milk that, combined, became a tradition in our home. Greg and Chris both loved them. They asked for them regularly, and skinny pancakes became a breakfast staple whenever their friends slept over.

This next tradition began as a Christmas cookie. Chocolate mint sticks are multilayered bars made in a nine-by-thirteen pan. While "chocolate mint sticks" is the name of the recipe, in our house, they've always been known as mint brownies or grasshoppers. The bottom layer is a rich, mint-flavored brownie. Next comes a layer of peppermint frosting that's topped with a layer of bitter chocolate. Sue is the only one on my side of the family to make these, so we often brought them to Detroit. We packaged leftover mint brownies for Greg as he returned for January term in college. During residency, his birthday care package always included them. Megan had the privilege of sharing them with Greg. Now, Chris, Megan, and Kathleen (the boys' cousin and my godchild) are each treated to mint brownies, a.k.a. grasshoppers, on their birthdays. I benefit from this tradition because when she makes them to send, Sue packs the prime pieces, but keeps the edges. Guess who eats most of these?

For years I've made salsa with homegrown tomatoes and jalapeño peppers. I started out following a recipe, then modified it to various degrees of hotness. By college, Greg had developed a taste for spicy food. One year I made really hot salsa with habaneros from the garden. I kept some of the master batch, but diluted the rest with tomatoes to make a milder salsa. I offered Greg the undiluted hot stuff when he was home from St. Olaf. I warned him it was strong. He heaped a tortilla chip with salsa and chomped down. He ate another, then another, as his face got red and perspiration formed on his forehead. I asked him how it was. "It's good," he responded in a weak, raspy voice. He could barely talk! Greg had given me the ultimate compliment.

Then there's a tradition that has gained importance and grown since Greg's death: blackberry brandy. Not just any blackberry brandy will do. The tradition has evolved to one specific brand—Leroux. My grandfather, dad, and uncles were "shot and a beer" drinkers. My cousins and I enjoyed a beer with the older generation, but I never acquired a taste for whiskey. During one visit, my cousin offered me a beer and poured me a shot of blackberry brandy. Brandy wasn't entirely foreign to our family. My aunt kept a bottle of apricot brandy on hand for medicinal purposes and sometimes informed me on the phone, "I think I'll have a little brandy. I have a scratchy throat." The blackberry brandy my cousin shared was milder than Grandpa's preferred whiskey, but I wasn't impressed with the taste.

I began sampling different brands. One label at the liquor store caught my eye: "Jezynowka—Made specially to the Polish taste." The taste was pleasant, and it went down so easily. This was the smoothest blackberry brandy I had ever tried. From then on, I bought only Jezynowka, for myself, trips to Michigan, and holiday gatherings. Soon the entire family was exposed to Jezynowka. Greg and Chris enjoyed toasts with their aunts, uncles, and cousins. The tradition flourished within our family, but didn't take hold with friends until after Greg died. Now Jezynowka is on hand for toasts to Greg's memory whether we're home, at Chris's, or on a trail. I was surprised to find Jezynowka bottles lined up during a memorial for Greg in Bozeman in June after he died. There were at least fifty people there—and we made the largest blackberry brandy toast I've ever witnessed.

One of my family's traditions has been to regularly toast our dearly departed—either at a large event or individually in private. In either case, it's customary to leave an overturned shot glass on the table for the one no longer with us. More and more family have died over the years. Now a single shot glass represents all our loved ones, but especially Greg.

Greg's death has resulted in the creation of new traditions. On the twenty-fourth of each month, at eleven a.m. mountain time, I go out to sit on Greg's lift chair in our yard. Chris bought a Bridger

Bowl dual chair as a gift for his brother when the runs there were upgraded. I acquired it after Greg's death and wouldn't give it up. My brother-in-law Bob and nephew Brady helped me build a stand for it one Labor Day. At the designated time, I pour myself a shot, an overturned glass on the chair next to me, and look west. I picture the helicopter as it rose out of Garnet Canyon with Greg and Walker on their final descent with tears in my eyes.

The night of April 16 is now a sacred time for our family. In memory and honor of Greg and Walker, we invite our family and friends to light candles at sunset. This annual remembrance, called Greg's Night of Light, keeps the memory of two extraordinary young men alive. Candles have been lit on all seven continents. Phone calls, messages, visits, and pictures of candle displays—some simple, some elaborate—make a difficult day tolerable. Together we bring light to the darkness in our hearts.

Fulfilling these old and new traditions comforts me by reminding me of happy memories of Greg. I wish he still shared the traditions with me in body, but I know he's there in spirit.

10

THE SEARCH BEGINS

I love early mornings in the mountains. I get one tomorrow since we are climbing Teewinot. The ranger I talked to said snow conditions were variable, so we will see what we find up there. I am pretty stoked though, and hopefully conditions are good so we can summit.

—JUNE 4, 2007, Garnet Canyon, Grand Teton National Park, Wyoming

I hope for a call with positive news early Tuesday morning. It doesn't come. I sense Greg and Walker aren't coming out of Garnet Canyon on their own—they'll need help from the SAR team. I still believe everything will be OK. The wait continues.

It's such a helpless feeling. Though Greg is thirty-one years old, I'm his father and I should be able to help him, to fix this problem. But there's nothing I can do.

Later that morning we're faced with the additional decision of informing people. Who do we tell, and how much do we tell them? We have to tell Greg's immediate family. And Megan. She certainly should know about the situation. Chris, Sue, and I can't face this alone. Any extra prayers will help. None of these are calls we want to make, but we feel we should.

We're uncertain about so many things. Where should we be? Should we stay home or fly to Jackson? I even imagine the illogical scenario that if we book flights, maybe Greg will be found immediately, so it would be worth it to waste the effort and money for plane reservations.

I want advice. David Francis is the first person to come to mind. David has been a friend for fifteen years. His son, Jon, played soccer with Chris on a team David coached. He's head of the Jon Francis Foundation, an organization founded in honor of and named for Jon after he tragically died hiking in Idaho's Sawtooth Range. Jon went missing on a solo hike. It took a year to recover his body.

I call David and explain the situation. I tell him Greg and Walker are in Grand Teton National Park. David reassures me that the park's SAR team is top-notch. He says this search will be nothing like Jon's. Their family had to coordinate and fund much of the effort. "If I could pick a place to go missing, it would be in a national park," he tells me. That's reassuring, but it doesn't solve anything or help find Greg.

David and I talk for fifteen minutes. During our conversation, he decisively answers my location question. "Dan, you need to be out there. You need to be in Jackson."

Soon Elizabeth calls with an update. "There are no signs of Walker, Greg, or any of their gear." She tells us more about the search and weather conditions and asks, "What are your plans?"

We tell her we're flying to Jackson.

"Walker's family will be arriving tomorrow," she informs us.

Sue and I make our flight reservations and then call Elizabeth to tell her we'll be arriving in Jackson shortly after noon on Wednesday, April 20.

Unknown to us, word is spreading in predictable and unexpected ways. Sue and I know the news would be shared among Walker's and Greg's many friends. Without our prompting, our close relatives make calls to extended family. Good thing, because after a few initial phone conversations it's emotionally impossible for us to reason what other calls we should make. When we do think of someone to phone, it's increasingly difficult to repeat the terrible news.

Late Tuesday I haven't even considered Greg's larger trip itinerary—he should have hooked up with Jeremy and Cindy Newman in Vegas on Monday. They learn Greg is missing in a roundabout way, thanks to his network of friends. The source of the news for his friends and colleagues is Judy Kraycar, administrative assistant in the Department of Emergency Medicine at West Virginia University Hospitals. "I received a call from either an NBC or ABC reporter. They had tracked him down as doing a residency at WVU," Judy tells us later. "I was in shock when they told me he was missing. I remember people asking me if I was OK as I walked down the hallway. I was probably white as a ghost." Judy is like a professional mom to most residents, guiding them through paperwork mazes. But every year, one resident stands out for her. Among his cohort, that resident was Greg. What an awful way to learn the fate of a good friend.

Judy spreads the news, which eventually reaches Cindy. "I called Greg on Sunday night and the phone went straight to his voice mail," Cindy recalled later. "I didn't think too much of it, just envisioned Greg driving south through an area with no cell reception. I pushed away the fleeting voice in the back of my head that made me worry he'd run into trouble on his adventure. Then on Monday, I didn't hear from Greg and was a little peeved, thinking maybe he was flaking out on us. On Tuesday, I got a call from my friend—the wife of one of Greg's residency classmates. She told me Greg was missing in the mountains."

Sue and I stay close to the phone and hold out hope that SAR will find Greg. Elizabeth, who we learn is serving officially as our family advocate, calls Tuesday evening to report more of the same. No sign of Greg or Walker. She shares more details about the scope of the search, the resources used, and the areas covered. Elizabeth tells about the plans for Wednesday's search. At least the weather will cooperate for a full-blown effort. All SAR resources will be on the mountain and in the air. We can only pray and hope.

11

FRIENDS

I started reflecting on this whole alone thing, since it has now been about 4 days since I've seen anyone. . . . Being alone has been rather fun for the most part, and it is definitely convenient that I can do whatever I want, whenever I want, but it lacks in two respects. Humor and laughing have definitely been very lacking over the last five days. Even though there can be a lot of quiet time with another human, there is also bound to be a minute or two of laughter (or there isn't much point in hanging out w/ that person).

—APRIL 15, 2003, Seven-Day Solo Trek, Bitterroot Range, Montana

Friends are blessings—they support us, encourage us, and help us have fun. A neighbor and good friend of mine frequently told me, "To have friends you have to be a friend." Very true. Who wants to spend time with someone who enters a relationship only for his or her own selfish purposes? Friendship is a two-way street; you have to be there for each other.

Greg's friends were a solid influence on him throughout school. Education was important to Sue and me, so we were pleased that Greg was always motivated to study and get good grades. His friends were of the same mind. He hung out with some very good students. During his school years, the peer pressure he experienced was always positive. That made a bigger difference than anything we said.

Greg had a wealth of friends, very good ones. Greg made friends because he was willing to be a friend. But the most amazing thing to me about Greg was how he maintained his friendships. I don't mean that he kept in touch with every past friend. He didn't. But he kept in touch with more people on a regular basis than I can imagine doing.

Many of his friends have maintained contact with me since his death, which is a great support. It keeps Greg alive to me. Some have told me Greg influenced their lives. They acquired some characteristic or interest of his. They also had an impact on his life. His friends helped him become the man he was.

Not only was Greg able to make and keep friends, he introduced his friends to each other, expanding his friendships into a web that transcended time and place. Greg's friendships often had their origin in a specific interest. He had friends who loved the same music he did, liked to ski, enjoyed rock and ice climbing, or participated in a sport he enjoyed. He also formed friendships at various stages of his life—elementary school, high school, college, med school, and residency. Greg was an organizer. He enjoyed many activities, but he wanted to share the experience.

When he had free time, Greg would usually plan an adventure of some kind. He constantly attempted to make optimum use of his time. He couldn't sit. His boundless energy for mountains and music led to his nickname, Wildcat. Greg would plan to attend a concert or go climbing. The word would spread, and soon a group would be put together and the adventure was on. If Greg had his eyes on a concert, his group of invitees wasn't limited to people who happened to like this type of music. He'd mention his plans to individuals from different parts of his life—and soon a diverse group was assembled. A friend from residency soon became friends with Greg's high-school classmate or college roommate. That's how friends from different times in his past got to know each other and formed their own friendships. This was no small accomplishment because he and his friends led busy lives. They all worked diligently and advanced in their studies and careers. But like Greg, they all respected the importance of a balanced life with time for work and time for play.

Greg seemed to be at the center of this web of friends. After his death, a friend remarked, "I don't know what we'll do now, don't know what will happen to us. Greg was the glue that held us together." Greg was formally recognized scholastically, medically, even athletically, at times in his life, but to me this acknowledgment was the ultimate testimony. It's fairly common to hear people talk about how they want to be remembered, and being well liked is a top response. If that was a goal of Greg's, he achieved it.

Sometimes his commitment to friends came at the expense of sleep. He functioned well and was full of energy on little sleep. I called him on a day off as he drove from Morgantown to central Pennsylvania, a several-hour drive, to meet some friends at a concert. To Greg the drive was nothing. Two days later he was off somewhere else. When I commented about his schedule and suggested he might want to give it a rest, he responded, "I'm fine, Dad." I joked, "I'm not worried about you, but you might want to give the car a break."

During one of the many times Greg passed through Bozeman, he called Joel, a friend living in Billings, about one hundred and fifty miles away. Greg asked if he had plans for dinner. Joel was free. Greg said, "I'll stop by. I'm in the neighborhood." Joel asked where he was, and Greg told him he was in Bozeman. Joel said, "That's two hours away, not really in the neighborhood." Greg said, "Yeah, what's your point?" Distance wasn't a significant factor to Greg when it came to friends. If there was time enough to get there and get it done, the plans were made. There aren't too many people who would do that on a regular basis for their friends. Greg did.

Since his death, several people close to Greg have shared stories and commented about what a good friend he was. The stories and the comments led me to reflect on various characteristics in Greg's personality. Where did these come from? How did they develop? As I think back on his life and his friendships, there are two tendencies that may have influenced Greg to be such a good friend and inspired him to be proactive in his approach to life.

When he was very young, Greg was quiet around children his own age. There weren't many kids in our neighborhood when Greg was a preschooler. He didn't have cousins his age. He was shy, and since he was exposed to more situations with adults than with kids, he was more comfortable among adults. Family members and neighbors all thought he was a great kid because he was very talkative in social situations. He just didn't have many opportunities to interact with other children. That changed when Greg went to school, developed friendships, and made more friends in the extended neighborhood. But I wonder if this early peer isolation may have later prompted him to be the initiator in friendships.

The second factor is more personal and more disturbing. Greg might have heard me speak in a way that influenced how he approached life. I always thought I would die young. I don't know why I felt that way and have no idea where that fatalism came from—even now when too many years have passed for it to be true. Greg seemed to approach life as if he wouldn't live long either. For him, it proved true. He didn't do things recklessly, though. He wasn't intent on proving himself right. But his belief inspired him to fill each day with the people and the activities most important to him. He wasn't going to waste any time because he didn't know how much time he had.

Greg lived a short, but an inspired, life. He influenced his friends in many ways, just as his friends had a deep and meaningful impact on his life. They paid tribute to their departed friend in meaningful ways.

The WVU Department of Emergency Medicine honored Greg and dedicated the residents' lounge to him at a ceremony on October 6, 2011, in the auditorium in the Health Sciences Building. Sue and I; Chris; Megan; my sister, Jan; family from Pennsylvania; and two of Greg's fellow residents, Jon Hanowell and A.J. Monseau, were part of the sixty to seventy people present. Current residents, individuals Greg had interviewed and mentored; attending physicians; administrative staff, including Judy Kraycar; and Dr. Robert Blake,

Greg's supervisor from St. Joe's in Buckhannon, also attended. Dr. Hollynn Larrabee and her husband, Ron Cunningham, were largely responsible for making this happen and played prominent roles in the function. Speakers included department head Dr. Todd Crocco, Dr. Blake, and Dr. Larrabee. Jon Hanowell and I also said a few words. I presented a print of Chris's friend Allison McGree's painting *Wildcat*—a tribute to Greg that shows Grand Teton and Garnet Canyon—to the department to be hung in the lounge. The department unveiled a picture of Greg and his big smile that would also stay in the lounge. They gave a copy of the photo to Sue and me.

The picture comes with a great story. Residents practice procedures on mannequins. Some are designed to be impossible to resolve to teach young doctors they won't always be successful and to assess their response to failure. Greg was told to intubate a dummy, not knowing it contained an airway blockage that couldn't be circumvented. Dr. Larrabee returned from her office to find Greg leaning on the bedrail. "Greg, get going," she prompted.

"What do you want me to do?" he asked.

"The intubation," she insisted.

"What do you want me to do next?"

"You weren't supposed to be able to do that."

Greg smiled.

"You realize you've ruined the entire exercise for the morning."

Greg grinned, and she snapped his picture. He had performed the impossible intubation.

The most touching moment and the highlight of the event for me was the proclamation. The significance of the dedication didn't hit home until Dr. Crocco declared the lounge would "from this day forward, forever be known as the 'Gregory E. Seftick, MD, Resident Lounge.'" Forever is a long time. A plaque on the wall outside the lounge reads:

West Virginia University Department of Emergency
Medicine

Gregory E. Seftick, MD

Resident Lounge

Dedicated October 2011,

in memory of

a doctor, an adventurer,

and a good friend.

Montani Semper Liberi

The final line is the West Virginia state motto: "Mountaineers are
forever free," an accurate reflection of Greg's spirit and love of the
mountains.

Our copy of Dr. Larrabee's picture of Greg sits on an easel in
our dining room. She told us the size of the print was intentional
"because Greg was bigger than life." He greets me every morning
with his big grin. He welcomes visitors to our home in the same way.

Since Greg's death, three of his friends have told us they
don't know if they'd have completed med school or residency
and become doctors without him. That was nice to hear. I believe
these people would be doctors today without any influence from
Greg—and I imagine he would too. But maybe he provided support
or encouragement when it was most helpful. There were times he
needed and received that same type of support. It's like a web, a
network, of pulling each other up, over, and through. It's something
friends do for friends. It's great to know Greg was a part of such
a network of friends. I know they were important to him. And it's
gratifying to learn how important he was to them. They influenced
each other, and now Greg's spirit lives on in their hearts. I hope we
all leave a similar legacy.

12

WALKER AND GREG

I called Walker and he said we could crash with him so we were off to
Missoula to climb Blodgett Canyon the next day. . . .
Walker suggested Shoshone Spire, an 8 pitch 5.8+ Grade III route.

—MAY 29, 2007, Bitterroot Range, Montana

Regrets were part of every day following Greg's death. Some centered on things I'd done, but the majority concerned things left undone. These regrets didn't haunt me or deepen my sorrow. I rationalized it was impossible to do everything in thirty-one short years. But occasionally an unexpected memory led to some tangential thought that made me realize what I'd missed or would be missing now that Greg was dead.

I take some comfort in knowing Greg died instantly, that he didn't suffer, and that he didn't die alone. That comfort was tempered by the knowledge that because Greg didn't die alone, this tragedy extended to another family and group of friends, some overlapping with Greg's.

I never met Walker. This is a big regret for me. I should've known the man who died with my son. Still, based on how Greg described him, I considered him to be a good, trustworthy man. Sue and I heard stories about him and his abilities in the wilderness. We felt reassured when we learned Greg was with him—confident that together Walker and Greg would make good decisions. I don't know why this feeling of comfort developed, but it did. Sue and I both felt the same way. After Greg died, Sue mentioned she wasn't worried about Greg that weekend because he was with Walker. "I always worried about Greg when he was in the mountains," she told me. "But I didn't this weekend, and look what happened."

Walker and Greg met through Joel Menssen, a mutual friend. Walker and Joel graduated together from Flathead High School in Kalispell, Montana. Greg met Joel the year he lived in Bozeman. As a freshman at Montana State, Joel frequently visited Chris and Greg in their basement apartment. They became good friends.

The next summer, Greg moved back to Minnesota to begin med school. He eagerly planned a trip west at Christmas break. He and a high-school friend, Mike Danaher, encountered heavy snow during their drive, which delayed their arrival in Bozeman.

According to Joel, "After entrenching myself firmly on the couch the previous year, I was a logical candidate to take over Greg's spot at the house. So when Walker came to Bozeman that winter to go ice climbing, we already had the fireplace roaring when Greg and Mike showed up from their icy interstate adventure. It was very cold, so I'm sure we were drinking Black Butte Porter. I couldn't have asked for better company. You know you're in a special place when four single men in their twenties would rather sit around the fire and tell stories on New Year's Eve than tear it up at the bars in a college town. It was probably the most chill evening Walker and Greg spent together."

At one point, Sue and I met Joel and his parents, Anita and Paul, and learned about their Minnesota connections. They both grew up and graduated from high school in Hutchinson, a city seventy-five miles from St. Paul and home to a large 3M plant, where I spent many days early in my career and where both Anita's and Paul's fathers worked. They returned annually to visit family in the area. The Menssens were supportive of both Chris and Greg. Anita has long referred to herself as "Greg and Chris's Montana mom," and she truly is. Greg stayed with Anita and Paul during a rotation in Kalispell. Chris spent Christmas 2005 with them after graduating from MSU.

Our sons often shared stories with us over the phone and during visits. These tales included not only their own adventures, but also their friends' exploits—sometimes we knew the friend in the tale and sometimes we didn't. Stories about Walker were our introduction to him. Everything we heard about him was positive. His Montana background and his mountain experience inspired confidence in his abilities. After high school, Walker served in the military and earned a college degree following his discharge. Most important to Greg, he loved spending time in the mountains. His military background and discipline to complete his education solidified our positive opinions.

Greg would often try to round up people to ski or climb with him on his frequent road trips west. If he wasn't doing something, he was planning something. He could be persistent. He felt at a disadvantage because he had to pack all his mountain activities into the few weeks he could visit, whereas the guys living in Montana weren't under pressure because the mountains were available to them all the time. Greg typically sought a partner for an adventure—sometimes maybe only a reluctantly willing one. That meant he might call friends he didn't see very often or do things with frequently. Walker fell into that category.

I don't recall a specific road trip that Greg took with Walker, but Joel recalls one very special occasion. "Walker, Greg, Zac Fawcett, and I all climbed and skied a big unnamed peak in the Taylor-Hilgard portion of the Lee Metcalf Wilderness for my bachelor party. It involved several small stream crossings and many miles of hiking before we reached the snowline where we set up camp. The next day we all skinned [climbing skins are strips attached to the bottom of skis to ascend back-country slopes] up to a knife-edge ridge that topped out a little over nine thousand feet. Wet slides were coming down all over the place because it was mid-May. At dusk, we were all shocked to see a huge shadow moving down the creek toward us, I mean like twelve feet tall and fifty feet long. We were really freaked out for a minute or two until we realized it was a tree being sent down to the beaver dam we were camped next to."

It didn't surprise us that Greg and Walker planned to meet in the Tetons that April weekend in 2011, the first episode Greg planned for his road trip. In his usual style, Greg packed that trip as full as possible. He provided us with more itinerary details than usual, and we felt fairly well informed. He and Walker would meet in Jackson, start up the trail Saturday, and attempt to summit the Grand on Sunday. Walker would return home to Salt Lake City for work on Monday. Greg would go on to climb at Red Rock with Cindy and Jeremy Newman, and finally meet Megan in Vegas. I don't know which piece of the plan solidified first and which elements were added.

"Looking back, Greg and Walker did very little in the mountains together," Joel reflected later. "It's a little strange, considering Greg and Walker were such great friends of mine, but I don't know— outside of that first New Year's Eve together and that one ski trip— that they ever did any climbing or skiing together. Walker was in the army up until about the time Greg started residency, so they weren't often in close proximity."

As we flew to Jackson during the search, Sue and I were both very concerned that Walker's parents would be angry with us, blame us for their son's death. We met Richard and Marylane in Jackson, and shared our fear for our sons as the search continued. At some point, I mentioned our concern that they'd be angry with us. They told us they'd had the same concern, that we'd be angry with them. They've been caring, supportive friends in the face of the circumstances that brought us together.

A parent's grief is said to be the greatest grief. There's no greater loss than the death of a child. I won't argue that assessment. Then I think of Greg's and Walker's friends. Their deaths were probably the first among their circles of friends. So their friends were also navigating new ground. Loss and grief eventually happen to all of us, but there's always a "first" death. I think of Greg's friends and pray for them as they face their grief, this real mountain of emotion they must scale.

I think of those who knew both Walker and Greg. How hard is it to grieve the deaths of two friends? I think particularly of Joel, the mutual friend who introduced Walker and Greg. I know his pain is different from mine, maybe even more difficult in some ways.

Then I get selfish and wonder why my son had to be the first to die. Why can't Greg be the one grieving?

13

ON THE PLANE

Summiting Rainier would be intense since it is so much higher than everything else. That is one thing that I have to do sometime. It would be cool since it's all glacier travel too.

—APRIL 25, 2003, Mount Rainier National Park, Washington

Sue and I arrive at the Minneapolis–St. Paul Airport before six a.m. on Wednesday, April 20. It feels unnatural to be here. The uncertainty of Greg's situation and all the possible negative outcomes weigh heavily on my mind. Being at the airport with excited travelers anxious to catch a flight to vacation or visit family only makes me feel worse. I want to tell everyone the mission of our trip—to quell their euphoria, to elicit their sympathy, and to make everyone feel as scared and concerned as Sue and I.

The first leg of our journey, a flight to Salt Lake City, departs on time. We arrive, make a few calls during our layover, and try to remain calm. We call Elizabeth Maki, who tells us there are no new developments in the search.

The Salt Lake City airport is crowded. Many others gather in the gate area to board the plane to Jackson. But I feel so alone. I am emotionally drained, empty, as is Sue—and I feel guilty. I am the husband and father, the man of the family, but my son is missing and my wife sits next to me, uncomforted. I have nothing to offer to give her hope. My mind drifts from the reality of the situation to denial, anger, despair, and pain. At times, it seems as if I'm not actually here. My body is in the Salt Lake City Airport, but mentally, emotionally, and spiritually I'm elsewhere. I don't know where. Maybe with Greg. Maybe I sense he needs me.

Soon we board the plane for the forty-five-minute flight to Jackson. As we approach the airport, the Tetons rise majestically in the west. I wish the area were more familiar so I could pinpoint the exact location of Garnet Canyon. Nonetheless, my eyes scan the area, looking for some sign of my son. There is none.

Elizabeth had arranged to meet us in a secure area of the airport. She'll be leaving Jackson on the same plane in which we arrive for a previously scheduled vacation to visit her sister in California. Chris, Jesse, and their good friend Brandon are at the airport with Elizabeth and her replacement, Bonnie Whitman. Bonnie, a ranger from nearby Yellowstone National Park, will be on loan during the search to serve as our family advocate in Elizabeth's absence.

It's a somber reception. I find it especially difficult to look Chris in the eyes and not be overwhelmed with despair. After a lot of hugs all around, Elizabeth briefs us on the current search efforts, our motel arrangements, and rental-car needs. Sue and I ride back to Grand Teton National Park with Bonnie and defer the rental-car decision.

We're taken to the Incident Command Post and introduced to some of the rangers involved in the Kuhl-Seftick Search, as it had been designated. We meet Chris Harder, the incident commander, and Scott Guenther, the operations chief. A few others are around as well, mostly in communications or support capacities. Chris and Scott review topographical maps and point out the approach to Garnet Canyon and Grand Teton. They describe the terrain and detail areas already searched on foot or by air. We learn that a helicopter from Hillsboro Aviation is in Jackson on contract for the winter with the Teton County Sheriff's Office for search and rescue. The helicopter transports personnel to the canyon and flies reconnaissance. It's a lot of information to absorb, especially since we have so little experience with the technical aspects of a search-and-rescue operation and essentially no knowledge of the terrain and topography in the park. We ask a lot of questions, trying to understand more about the area, get a clue about what might have happened to Walker and Greg, and learn how the search effort will proceed. After the introductions and briefing, we head to the Teton Park Road staging area, the SAR team's logistical headquarters and helicopter access site.

I squint as the sun reflects off the snow-covered Tetons. My face feels warm in the coolness of early spring at over six thousand feet elevation. Inside, I shiver with fear despite my winter coat, gloves, and stocking cap. This is our first opportunity to view the Grand and specifically locate Garnet Canyon, Greg and Walker's likely first-night destination. It's obvious why Greg loved this place so much. In that moment, though, the beauty is overshadowed by the tragedy at hand and the potential outcomes we face. None are good, but some are better than others. I feel the best-case scenario at this point is finding Walker and Greg alive, even seriously injured. I believe there's a good possibility for this, even after three days. The worst outcome is finding Greg dead. My perspective would change before the search was over.

We meet more of the SAR crew at the heli staging area. The rangers point out the location of Garnet Canyon and the approach Walker and Greg would have taken, which helps orient me. But so much still escapes us. For one thing, only the mouth of the canyon and the far end at the base of Middle Teton are visible from the Teton Park Road. The area where Greg and Walker most likely camped for the night is hidden behind a slight rise at the canyon entrance. The SAR team isn't in sight either. We'd learned from Elizabeth that Walker and Greg originally planned to summit the Grand and ski out, but they'd discussed scaling back their plans to play around Teepe Pillar. The Pillars are on the north side of the canyon, just off the upper bowl. Also nearby is Disappointment Peak. The area has been inspected visually by air on both the canyon and far sides. There is no reason to expect Greg to be up on that ridgeline, but the heli did a flyover on both sides to be thorough.

All I can do is stare at the Tetons and hope and pray.

A second piece of evidence places Walker and Greg in the search area, a call from a back-country group of four who'd seen two mountaineers on Saturday afternoon. One of the group was Brendan Hughes, whom we'd meet by chance in the summer of 2012. Hughes was fairly certain Walker and Greg passed through their camp in the Platforms. "I received a call from one of the guys when we were back in town saying that the two men we'd seen passing camp hadn't returned. They said that the park rangers wanted me to call, in case I knew anything about their intended route, et cetera." The report is important because it verifies Walker and Greg's location and provides some idea of how much farther they might have traveled in poor conditions, before stopping to set up camp for the night. This information gives SAR more confidence that the correct area is being searched. There are no guarantees, but it's better than having nothing to go on.

It's difficult for me to be up here, so close to Greg, and not able to do a thing to help. I want to be involved, but know I couldn't. I want to be in Garnet Canyon and witness the activity, but know I would just be in the way. Chris and his friends had discussed offering their services immediately upon learning Walker and Greg were missing, but decided that wasn't a good idea, despite their varied levels of back-country experience. The people in the park are very qualified. Other resources have been called in to improve efficiency and increase the chance for success. There is nothing we can do. As David Francis assured me, we are in good hands. My place is here beside my wife and my son.

Sue and I decide to rent a car. After Bonnie takes us back to the airport to pick it up, we drive into Jackson, and check in at the motel. Elizabeth and Terry Roper, the park's family advocate for Walker's family, had made arrangements for us to stay at the same place.

At the motel, we meet Walker's family—his parents, Richard Kuhl and Marylane Pannel; his sister, Kendra; and his girlfriend, Erica Logue. We get acquainted and share our perspectives on the situation. I listen intently to what everyone says and how they say it. I hope to get some clue about others' thoughts on Greg and Walker's chances for survival. I had tried the same approach with the SAR team, but they were hard to read. Their comments were guarded and noncommittal. Somehow this conversation makes me less hopeful. The Kuhls are better acquainted with the mountains and more aware of what could happen. They live in Montana, and Richard had worked as a ranger. I sense they feel there is little chance of survival by this time. I am naïve and in denial. I refuse to believe this is already a recovery rather than a rescue operation. I want to shout, "They could still be alive!" Sue and Chris say nothing that reveals their expectations.

After we pick up some food, we head for the Incident Command Post for the day's debriefing. I'm extremely anxious—fearful of receiving bad news, but more concerned about the search being abandoned without finding our sons. The SAR crew is in the conference room when we arrive. They'd already met to discuss the day's activities. Family couldn't be present during that initial phase of the debriefing because SAR personnel need to candidly discuss details of the search. They don't want to say the wrong thing in front of the families. Scott Guenther gives a brief summary of the day's events and then invites our families to speak. Richard Kuhl introduces Walker's family and thanks the men and women involved in the search for all their hard work. He remarks that it's obvious all are emotionally involved in the effort to find Walker and Greg and that we appreciate their compassion and respect. He says above all they should work safely because the last thing we want is someone to get hurt during the search and add more sorrow to an already tragic situation.

Then I introduce Greg's family—Sue, Chris, Jesse, Brandon, and myself. I don't have much to add. I express our thanks and reiterate that SAR safety is top priority. My few words seem inadequate and meaningless. There isn't much more to say to this exhausted team of dedicated people.

These strangers are putting their lives on the line for Walker and Greg, two young men most of them have never met. The compassion in the room is palpable—it's apparent we're all of the same heart. These mountains are their playgrounds, just as they were Greg's and Walker's. Every one of these women and men know accidents happen, that nature is in charge no matter how carefully the mountains are approached and how many precautions are taken. They're searching Garnet Canyon because Walker and Greg are each "one of them."

I still hope they will be found alive, and the SAR team doesn't give me any reason to think otherwise. I don't know if that's their intention—or if I'm too naïve to know different, and I'm just hearing what I want to hear. But I do get a sense of comfort from hearing the remarks from the searchers and seeing the looks on their faces. They're doing their best.

During our short time in Jackson earlier that day, someone had mentioned that avalanches had been heard in the area of Garnet Canyon, but their occurrence wasn't explicitly connected to Greg and Walker's timeline in the park. It is one tragic fact I keep out of the search picture until much later.

It's difficult to understand why I'm still hopeful they'll be found alive. Numerous flights to Garnet Canyon, around the Grand, and over adjacent ridgelines turn up no signs of Greg and Walker. Three days of searching on foot, visual observations, searching for beacon signals, and probing have yielded no evidence of the guys or their camp and equipment. Things don't look good. In addition, the weather isn't cooperating. Snow and low ceilings scuttle search efforts on Thursday and Friday. The next SAR search will be Saturday. It will be a big, well-organized, concerted effort. But that's three days away. If Greg and Walker are alive and are to be rescued, they'll have to come off that mountain on their own. How is that possible? I'm not sure how, but I hold on to hope even in light of these circumstances.

At Wednesday's briefing, we're told that probing was done to locate bodies. That should clue me in that the effort has shifted from rescue to recovery. Looking back, I think Walker's family picks up on it. I don't. Maybe denial, the first stage of grief, has already planted itself firmly in my psyche. At the time, I only know I'm in uncharted emotional waters, in a place I've never been before. I'm somewhere I never want to be again, and I hope no other parent has to experience.

14

I feel like I definitely accomplished the goal I put in my first journal of "dramatically increasing the amount & variety of terrain which I feel comfortable moving over." All in all, it was a fantastic summer. I can't wait to graduate so that I have an extended time to get in good physical & mental shape to continue expanding the size of the world that I can visit.

— SEPTEMBER 8, 2005, Orthopedics Rotation, Duluth, Minnesota

Friends come in all shapes and sizes. Tall and short, thin and round, old and young. Some of our closest and most loyal friends even have four legs. Our adopted Lhasa mix, Lady, was a valued canine pal to our whole family. Each of us had a special relationship and connection with her, but Greg trusted Lady and relied upon her for more than the rest of us.

There were other animals in our house when Greg and Chris were kids. We never had a menagerie, but there was usually a critter around. Our various pets over the years included a parakeet, hamsters, goldfish, an anole, and Lady. Chris was the main driving force behind adopting Lady. The summer he was ten, he got it in his head that we should have a dog. He brought home a couple of strays for a day or two. Sue and I finally agreed to visit the animal shelter and check what dogs were available. The first visit was unproductive. We returned a week later and then several more times, but found nothing promising. After one visit through the kennels, a volunteer offered to show Sue, Chris, and Greg the dogs inside, the ones not yet eligible for adoption. All the dogs barked and barked, but one. She looked so scared. The volunteer told them the dog would be adoptable the next morning. They returned home and excitedly told me about her. We went back early the next day and brought her home.

That quiet dog didn't stay quiet for long. Once she settled in, she barked at everything. She turned out to be very protective. At the animal shelter she didn't feel at home or attached to anything. But once she decided our house was her home, she was in charge.

At first Lady slept in the basement at night. We were convinced we'd never let her sleep in any of the beds. But during my illness and hospitalization in 1994, she was allowed to sleep upstairs on the floor. Before long, she was in a bed, usually Greg's. This led to a somewhat raucous morning routine. When we'd wake the boys for school, we had a problem at Greg's room. All we had to do was walk down the hall and stand outside the door to his room, and Lady growled. A slight rap on the door and she was barking up a storm. Our objective was accomplished, though. Greg was definitely awake.

Lady not only assumed control of the house, but the yard too. She would hop up on the seat of a bench by the front window, then up on the back of the bench on her way to her destination, the windowsill. Sue even put a piece of carpet on the sill for her to sit on. From this perch, Lady had a view of her domain. The doorbell might as well have been broken. Lady's barking alerted us to anyone approaching by foot or car. She was on the lookout for nonhuman invaders too. Any squirrel who dared to skitter through the yard aroused her ire. We all egged her on, telling her, "Go get 'em! Don't let that mean squirrel run around in your yard." Lady was always ready for a walk through the neighborhood. She must have felt she was inspecting her entire kingdom.

Greg and Chris didn't walk Lady very often—our efforts on that front were futile. They were busy with other things. They did take her on trails when we visited the mountains. We met others with dogs on the trails, but they were usually big dogs. Lady impressed a lot of people with her spunk. We hiked with her to Grotto Falls in Hyalite Canyon, a ten-mile round trip, on a warm Montana day. Upon arriving at our destination, Lady found a way behind the main waterfall and sat in the mist, enjoying the cooling effect of the spray. Lady started out fine on the hike back. Then she started slowing down and finally just stopped. I carried her the rest of the way; it was one time I was grateful she weighed only ten pounds.

As much as Lady loved to walk, she loved to ride in the car even more. All you had to say was "Lady, car," and she was at the front door, tail wagging wildly. Anytime Lady saw all four of us getting ready to go out the door, she expected to come along. When it was obvious she wasn't included, her tail dropped and she put on her sad face, inflicting a guilt trip on us all.

Greg and Chris loved to tease her. As we prepared to leave, Greg would tell Lady, "I'm sorry you have to stay home, Lady," in a very sad voice. We closed the door, went to the car, got in, and started backing out. Lady observed this from her spot in the window. Suddenly we stopped the car, Greg ran back to the house, opened the door, and exclaimed, "I was just joking, Lady. You can come too." She was out the door in a flash and flew to the car. We made sure the rear car door was open because she'd leap straight onto the back seat. She never held a grudge about the teasing; she was just happy to be included.

Lady loved all of us, but especially Greg and Chris. She watched out for them and protected them from everything and everyone, including their parents. She even found them in a new residence in a strange city and state. Sue, Lady, and I arrived in Bozeman after sunset on our first visit to the boys' new apartment in the fall of 2002. We put the leash on Lady and opened the car door. She pulled us to the correct house and around back to the patio door on the lower level. There were the guys, on the couch, screaming, "Lady! Hi, girl!" as she walked up to the screen door.

Lady loved to eat. She wasn't fat, but she ate as much as we let her. Greg and Chris exposed her to table food, and soon she was begging. And she knew who was susceptible to her pleas!

Not long after we got her, we noticed some food missing from the table. We naïvely thought she couldn't jump on a kitchen chair and then onto the table when the chairs were pushed in. One evening after dinner we set a trap. We left a few pieces of meat on a plate on the table. Then we all got up from the table and went outside, leaving Lady in the house alone. We went around to the side and looked through the kitchen window. Lady got up on a chair, squeezed her head between the chair back and table, and proceeded to eat the meat. We exclaimed, "Lady, what are you doing?" She was surprised, but finished the meat before she scampered down from the chair. From then on we were careful where we left food.

Desserts were among her favorite heists, like the great *krumkake* feast. Sue made a big batch of *krumkake*, a Norwegian waffle cookie, for her church's craft and bake sale. She neatly packaged these delicious pastries on paper plates inside plastic bags, with six or twelve to a package, and placed them on the dining room table. The chairs were pushed in tight so Lady couldn't get at them. Or so we thought! We left Lady home alone to run an errand. We returned to find crumbs, an empty paper plate and a plastic bag torn open on the dining room floor. Lady came when called. We asked her what had happened. She slowly turned, head down, and walked into the other room. Somehow she'd again managed to get on a chair and then up on the table. She only disturbed one package, but wisely selected one with a full dozen.

Lady was always the queen of her domain, but she sometimes had to share the house with another pet. One of her buddies was a parakeet Chris kept in a cage on a nightstand in his bedroom at just the perfect height for Lady. She stood with her front paws on the top, so fascinated by that bird. She didn't bother it, bark at it, or touch the cage, just stood on her back paws and observed.

The parakeet devised a way to tease Lady—or so it seemed—just like we had with the car ride and the food on the table. When Lady came to the birdcage, the bird would jump up on the top rung and move to the very back of the cage as far from Lady as possible. There the bird stayed until Lady finally got bored from the inactivity, her fascination diminished, and turned to walk away. The bird would hop down to the front of the cage and give a little peep. When Lady heard the noise, she turned around and returned to her original position. The parakeet was quickly up on the top perch at the back of the cage again. This repeated for several sequences. The bird didn't live very long. We speculated maybe it was afraid of Lady and the constant exposure had frightened her to death.

Greg took good care of all his pets. He gave them names and interacted with them. Greg's interest in baseball and the Minnesota Twins meant his pets, even the goldfish, often had sports-related names. Two I remember were Kirby Pucker and Gary Gilletti, inspired by Twins stars Kirby Puckett and Gary Gaetti. Don't blame Greg for those puns. I actually concocted those names. He obviously couldn't play with the fish like he did with Lady, but he felt bad when they died. He definitely had a caring, compassionate nature with animals. He was that way with friends and family too, even at a very young age. I believe his empathy with patients as a doctor stemmed, at least in part, from his pet experiences.

The only pet besides Lady with whom Greg had a really long relationship was a green anole, a small American chameleon. This guy was named Chuckie, after one of Greg's favorite Twins players at the time, Chuck Knoblauch.

Chuckie came to us via the elementary school after a completed experiment. In either fifth or sixth grade, the class had half a dozen anoles. At the end of the school year, the students were invited to take one home. Greg asked for permission, and we agreed. We got a cage for Chuckie with a hot rock and climbing branches. The entire assembly went in Greg's room.

Chuckie ate crickets. Every week or so, Sue or I stopped at the pet store to purchase a dozen. Apparently, the tasty ones are young and don't chirp. As they matured, they began to make noise. At that point, they were no longer appetizing to Chuckie.

Chuckie had a very distinctive characteristic. His tail had a bend near the very tip. This wasn't just a curve, but a sharp bend, like a kink in the tail. I don't know if this was the result of an accident or some genetic defect, but it was there from the time Greg brought him home. We thought Chuckie would only live for a number of months. Turned out that Greg and Chuckie shared a room for five years.

One day after school we heard a shout from Greg's room. "Chuckie's gone!" We looked everywhere in the bedroom, pretty much tore the room apart. We looked all around the house. We didn't know how long he was gone and had no idea how he had escaped. Greg was frantic.

Chuckie had entered Greg's life about the same time as something else very important, skiing. A couple of days after Chuckie's escape, Greg was in bed looking up at his ski-run collage, now sagging under the weight of many added brochures and the heat and humidity of summer months. Suddenly he hollered, "I found Chuckie!" We came to his bedroom and he said, "Chuckie's behind the collage." After some gentle removal of paper from the ceiling and coaxing and reaching, we recovered Chuckie.

One of the first indications that Lady was slowing down was her inability to jump on the bench to access her throne in the front window. I thought it might just be old age or something that came with it, like arthritis. Then other symptoms showed up. A visit to the vet indicated problems with her adrenal gland, which affected her cortisol levels. An ultrasound showed abnormalities in her gall bladder. This didn't sound good, but it was not an immediate death sentence either.

The morning of June 8, 2004, was warm and humid. Lady was at the foot of our bed, just barely able to move. She had thrown up on the bedroom floor during the night. That in itself wasn't alarming. She'd done that occasionally before. But this morning she was obviously hurting. I tried to get her to follow me to the door. She did, but it was a real effort for her. When I opened the outside door, she just lay there. I picked her up and put her on the grass outside. No response.

The vet told us to bring her right in. They took samples to run tests and did an ultrasound. We were told the test results would be available soon. I failed to ask the right questions. I assumed we'd be waiting hours; I didn't think this was by any means the end for Lady. Leaving Lady at the vet, I went to work. Sue called Greg. He was a first-year med student at the time, living near the University of Minnesota campus.

The call from the vet came quickly, about thirty minutes after I'd left their office. Sue and I returned to the clinic to find Greg already there. He was with Lady, holding her paw, stroking her back, and talking gently to her. The tests showed Lady's gall bladder had burst. She was full of infection. We were told surgery was an option, but it would have to be done at the University of Minnesota. It would be expensive and came with no guarantee of success at age thirteen. It was time to put our sweet friend to sleep.

The vet explained the procedure and said, "Take all the time you want with Lady." The three of us (since Chris was in Bozeman) comforted Lady. "We love you, girl. You're such a good dog," we told her. Greg asked Sue and I if he could have time alone with Lady. We left the room.

Greg came out into the waiting area after about five minutes. He never told us what he said to Lady, and I never asked. The three of us went back in and were there while Lady took her last breath. We all cried.

We brought Lady home and put her in the small baby quilt from her kennel, a quilt she slept on for many years. Greg picked a spot in the high grass in the back of our yard for a grave. We started to dig. It was late morning by now, humid and warm. Greg didn't say much. He just dug and dug. The sweat poured off him. He was exhausted physically and hurting emotionally. When Greg was satisfied the grave was proper, we laid Lady to rest.

I had hoped this day wouldn't come this quickly. Greg was heartbroken. There were no words to comfort him. He lost a valued friend, a confidante. It was a big loss to all of us, but most of all to Greg. For him, Lady was unconditional love in every way possible. It was something he often seemed to require. Lady never let him down. I loved Lady too, but I don't think I had a real idea of the pain Greg felt until now. It isn't right to compare Lady's death to Greg's, but after Greg died, I think I have a better understanding of how Greg felt the day Lady died.

15

*I was about the only guy in shorts and sandals under my gown,
but whatever. I don't have to impress anyone with my attire
(until interviewing for jobs). The whole experience was weird because
it was like attending the funeral for Greg the student.*

—MAY 9, 2007, U of MN Medical School Graduation, Minneapolis, Minnesota

*I have never done anything like this—even in Bozeman I was moving in
with people I knew. Here I don't know anyone and am a complete unknown.
I guess that means I can reinvent myself however I want since I won't have
people's prior expectations locking me into a role,
but it is also scary to be moving to a place all by my lonesome.*

—JUNE 14, 2007, Morgantown, West Virginia

*He was born in the summer of his 27th year,
Coming home to a place he'd never been before.*

—JOHN DENVER, "Rocky Mountain High"

Greg started his medical residency at age twenty-seven. It wasn't in
Colorado, or anywhere near the Rockies. He moved to West Virginia,
the Mountaineer State. He thrived there. He gained knowledge and
grew in wisdom and maturity. He became part of a supportive program
with an exceptional group of people whom he admired and who

respected him. He became part of the WVU family, and Morgantown became home in "a place he'd never been before."

Greg's interest in medicine began years earlier. He was intrigued with first aid as a Cub Scout. In 1988, Chris took a nasty spill on his bike after skidding on some sand on the road and losing control. His chin split wide open. Nine-year-old Greg was right there to check things out. We took Chris to the ER to have the wound cleaned and have his chin and the inside of his mouth stitched. Greg inspected the doctor's work when Chris returned home.

But Greg's first interest wasn't medicine—it was garbage. I recall Greg, at age two or three, eagerly watching for the garbage truck. His eyes were big as saucers as our trash was dumped into the back of the truck. There was pure joy on his giddy face on the lucky days he watched the garbage being crushed. Sue and I often played garbageman with Greg on the living room floor. Wads of paper were strategically put at each "house" as Greg drove one of his many toy garbage trucks, picked up the trash, and crushed it with a whirring, grinding noise, just like the real thing.

Greg did well in most aspects of elementary school. His speech and language skills improved in the years after kindergarten, when he'd struggled with that. He had an easy time with math and science and loved to read. His interest in science led him to participate in the annual science fair, where his first project was titled "Phases of the Moon." He depicted the lunar cycle in drawings with explanations on a large piece of poster board. I had little to offer in the way of ideas or artistic ability. He did the best he could with his own skills. The same was true in Cub Scouts and the annual pinewood derby and sailboat regatta.

In March 1994, when I was diagnosed with dermatomyositis, Sue was essentially a single parent with the added burden of a husband to worry about and hospital visits to fit into a schedule full of kids' activities and part-time work as a food scientist involved in nutrition studies at the University of Minnesota's Nutrition Coordinating Center. Underlying it all was the uncertainty of the final outcome of my illness. Even the doctors had little to go on since each case is different. My condition was stable, but my future was still uncertain. We didn't know how much strength I would regain, or if I might even die.

Many family and friends stepped up to help at this time, some did not. We also received help from unexpected sources. This pattern repeated after Greg's death. I had learned the first time that it's important to accept help from any source, and it's unproductive to analyze why others we expected to help didn't.

Chris and Greg responded differently to my illness. Greg was in denial. He refused to admit that I was sick. He seemed to approach each day with indifference, a sure sign of his discomfort since he generally took things very seriously. Chris was angry. Sue had a hard time convincing him to visit me in the hospital. "Why does Dad have to be sick?" he asked. "None of my friends' dads are sick." Understandably, both of our boys were stressed by the circumstances, and they were a handful for Sue during my illness. Greg actually got into some serious trouble while I was hospitalized. Sue stopped for a quick visit at the hospital on her way home from work, leaving the boys home unsupervised for an hour after school. Greg overreacted to some taunting and took out his anger on Chris's friend. His parents pressed charges. We had to hire a lawyer, and Greg appeared in juvenile court. In the end, he was required to perform twenty-five hours of community service as restitution, which he completed at Sue's church.

Greg didn't object to hospital visits because he could watch sports on cable. ESPN carried hockey, soccer, and baseball, and Greg took advantage of the opportunity to watch. He also was curious about the medical activity in my room. He looked at the equipment, checked the pump settings, and inspected the IV bags on the rack. His attention would shift away from the TV whenever medical personnel arrived. He questioned Sue and me and the nurses he got to know about my condition and treatment.

His attention intensified when a doctor entered the room. He listened intently as the doctor addressed my most recent lab results, discussed a medication change, noted changes in my condition, and interacted with nurses, therapists, and other hospital personnel. It was obvious Greg was interested in what was going on. This was the first time I thought Greg might pursue a career in medicine. Sometimes I wonder if my long hospital stay was the reason he selected medicine as a profession. I never asked. He never told me.

Greg observed the doctors' bedside manner. We discussed doctor-patient dynamics. For the most part, I remember our assessments matched very closely. Many different doctors from various specialties attended to me. Many of them were new to me. Some I only saw once. Greg was able to read them quickly.

Greg took the Myers-Briggs skills test in high school. I expected the results would point to an interest in science, maybe even medicine. I was surprised when he came home from school upset and angry. "What's wrong, Greg?"

"That stupid test," he said. "My skills indicate I'm best suited to be a drywall installer!"

It took some discussion to convince him these results didn't confine him to a life of manual labor. It's hilarious to think back on it now, but he was genuinely distressed at the time.

During high school Greg volunteered at Lakeview Hospital in Stillwater. His initial assignment was the surgical waiting area, signing people in and out as they waited for someone in surgery. He became acquainted with the staff, and they learned of his interest in medicine. In his second year of volunteering, he inquired about other opportunities and was sometimes assigned to the ER. Even at this suburban Level 3 Trauma Center, Greg was drawn in by the pace, activity, and variety of cases. His interests began to focus on the emergency department. The intensity of that interest would ebb and flow during college and med school, but it never went away.

Greg's first job at age fifteen was at Afton Alps Ski Area as a ski instructor for young kids. Greg looked at the job as being a glorified babysitter, but it provided an opportunity to be outdoors, ski, and share his love of skiing with others. He discovered something about himself here: He liked to teach.

Greg's college selection process was stressful for him and for us. Sue accompanied Greg to Northfield, Minnesota, to tour the campuses of St. Olaf and Carleton Colleges. She realized she was biased toward St. Olaf and carefully attempted to restrain her comments so as not to influence Greg. At the end of the day, Sue was surprised that she was more impressed with Carleton. Not Greg. He was definitely drawn to St. Olaf.

His application list was eventually whittled to six—University of Minnesota–Morris, Concordia (Moorhead, Minnesota), St. Olaf College, Washington University (St. Louis), Colorado College (Colorado Springs), and Johns Hopkins (Baltimore). Wash U and Hopkins had such strong reputations for medicine that Greg was willing to be stuck in a big city to attend there. He was accepted at five, snubbed only by Hopkins. He eliminated Concordia and Morris. He decided against Wash U because he wouldn't know anyone else attending there. His heart was set on Colorado College, but the tuition was several thousand dollars higher and we couldn't get them to throw in any scholarship money.

Sue pointed out to Greg, "You can make quite a few ski trips for $7,500 a year."

I put it to him this way. "Greg, if you can tell me what we get for the additional $7,500, we'll figure out a way to make it happen."

He thought long and hard. He worked every conceivable angle. After a couple of days, he came to me and reported, "Dad, I got nothing."

It turned out that the remaining option, St. Olaf, was a good fit for Greg—and not just because it was less expensive.

Greg continued his volunteer work while he was at St. Olaf. He was assigned to visit a gentleman in a Northfield nursing home. I wish

I could remember his name. This was a different situation for Greg, not a one and done, but a weekly meeting that led to a relationship and a real friendship through conversation and card playing. Greg enjoyed it, but it created a dilemma for him. He knew he liked many aspects of an ER setting. In that situation, though, long-term doctor-patient relationships don't develop. Greg was good with that. But this gentleman became a friend, someone he genuinely cared about, and Greg caught a glimpse of the appeal of other specialties in which doctors get to know their patients more. Greg returned to the nursing home to visit the older gentleman even after he stopped volunteering. Greg's gift of a caring and nurturing attitude served him well during his specialty rotations in med school and residency. He was a great fit in the ER, yet with a good bedside manner.

At the start of his senior year of college, Greg informed us that after graduation he'd take a year off from his studies, move west, and look for a job to gain experience in the medical field. He didn't want the pressure of studying for the MCAT during his final year of college. He'd study after graduation and take the test in the fall. Typical Greg. He had everything planned out.

During the summer after graduation, Greg studied hard to prepare for the MCAT, but as usual, he wasn't feeling confident. He scored poorly on online practice tests, but he kept at it. He also took an EMT-B class to become certified as a basic emergency medical technician. He hoped to find a job in the medical field, possibly as a paramedic, near Bozeman. He enjoyed and did well in the EMT training.

Greg faced the MCAT with definite objectives. "I'll probably get a 30 [out of 45 points max]. If I'm lucky, 31. The absolute highest score I expect is 32." The scores came. He couldn't believe it: 34. He was ecstatic! We were proud.

Now that the MCAT was done, it was on to Bozeman for a year of work, fun, and med-school applications. Mostly it was a year of fun.

Greg worked at Spring Meadows, a nursing home in Bozeman. It wasn't exactly what he wanted, but he earned enough to cover expenses. He was able to climb and ski in the mountains, and he worked on med-school applications. He thought his year in Bozeman would also make him a Montana resident and qualify him for the WWAMI program in Washington. Since there are no med schools in Wyoming, Alaska, Montana, and Idaho, residents of these states are treated as in-state students in Washington. Greg wasn't considered a Montana resident for the program, though, and he wasn't accepted in Washington. He was accepted at the University of Minnesota—and Sue and I were thrilled that he was accepted anywhere on his first attempt. Greg seemed disappointed initially. He had nothing against the prestigious U of MN, except it was located in a very flat state. Soon Greg acknowledged he was excited to be accepted.

Med school begins with two extremely difficult months of anatomy. Greg got through it, but more importantly, realized he had an ability and passion for learning at a higher level than he'd experienced up to that point. Greg also willingly offered guidance and encouragement in support of his classmates.

During one visit home, Greg agonized about all there was to remember and how he wasn't doing as well as he hoped. I mistakenly stated, "Anatomy must be difficult because the program wants to weed out those who won't make it all the way through."

"That's not how it works in med school, Dad. Once an individual is accepted, they want you to succeed and finish. The weeding occurs during application. After that, the school will do everything it can to help you graduate. It doesn't look good for a med school to lose students during the program. They want everyone accepted to become a doctor."

Medicine, music, and mountains were Greg's passions. He could focus on each with laser intensity. In his mind, there were parallels and common themes in all three, but especially mountains and medicine. Greg was skilled at drawing attention to these parallels. I came across his answer to an essay question on treating immigrant, non-English-speaking ER patients in a first-year test.

In this instance, after discussing the patient's knowledge of our medical system and their incredulity of Western medicine, I would recommend a simple treatment . . . one must offer treatment under the real and immediate context in which it is being issued. If you are backpacking with someone and they fall and receive a massive laceration on their leg, one could argue that it is discriminatory to attempt to cauterize the wound with a hot knife, wrap it in torn up T-shirts, and then get them walking back to civilization. Someone in a similar situation would receive anesthetic and stitches if they were close to a hospital. However, a hospital is not part of the reality one is working within in that situation.

The comment along this paragraph reads, "Interesting analogy."

The classwork, reading load, and memorization in the first two years were grueling. The third and fourth years involved more hands-on work in hospitals and clinics. Greg guided his rotations to be just that, hands on. He spent time in an ER in Seward, Alaska, where he stitched up his first patient. He did a surgery rotation in Duluth, where it was just the surgeon and Greg in the operating room. Greg wanted to be taught and work with his hands, not just observe in a setting where many levels of students and residents participated.

As much as Greg felt a strong attraction to surgery, he realized it wasn't for him. The big drawback is the surgeon's lifestyle. Their days start early and continue without a set end time. There are patients to see, consults to do, and charts to complete after the final surgery of the day. Phone calls need to be answered all through the night. Greg was amazed the Duluth surgeon he learned from could maintain any semblance of a family life with his wife and children. But his biggest question was, "How do you make any significant road trips?"

It was inspiring to see how Greg applied himself to his third- and fourth-year rotations. I was pleased with his development and spoke of his progress often, probably too often. Sue and I definitely sounded like proud parents. Greg continued to nurture his other interests amid all the demands of med school. He kept close contact with his friends and family. The next road trip to the mountains was always on the drawing board. He balanced them all, prioritized, and disregarded anything and anyone superficial.

Sue and I observed Greg's ability to listen during Christmas 2006, his last spent with his Detroit family. He sat with my aunt Sally— then eighty-five years old and showing early signs of dementia— looked her in the eye, and blocked out all the other conversations in the room. Greg lovingly heard her stories and answered her questions. It's a simple, beautiful memory I cherish. I imagine it was also a glimpse into the kind of focus Greg invested in his patients.

He'd already talked about specializing in emergency medicine, but during these four years he became aware of other exciting and rewarding opportunities available on the periphery of medicine. He found his niche in wilderness medicine. He joined the Wilderness Medicine Society early in med school and became active in the group. He thoroughly enjoyed the topics discussed and the people who shared his love of the outdoors.

The residency application process was next. The nearest program he considered was about a thousand miles away. The mountains still called to Greg. He laughed when an attending would ask, "Where else are you applying for residency besides here?" He had no intention of staying in Minnesota. No way some twist of fate would cause him to land here again!

Greg asked me to proofread his personal statement for his residency applications. In it, he compares medicine with rock climbing. It seems unorthodox, but applicants look for ways to set themselves apart. The final paragraph reads, "Another aspect that drew me to climbing and emergency medicine is the autonomy of decision-making in stressful situations." But he also acknowledges:

"Stabilizing a critical patient also requires teamwork." One point we debated was shifting his perspective in: "There is a beauty and simplicity to life and death situations, as one can truly determine what is essential. All thoughts and actions are directed toward one common goal, not dying." I encouraged him to conclude with "staying alive" rather than "not dying." He refused.

He received interview invitations from only seven programs. He accepted six, one in Texas, two in California, and three in the east. He felt strongest about Loma Linda, California, and Morgantown, West Virginia. He laughed about an exchange during the West Virginia interview. He was lured east when the interviewer countered Greg's love for the Rockies by saying, "We have mountains here." Greg responded, "But they aren't real mountains. Real mountains don't have trees at the summit."

By this time, Greg's residency criteria had evolved. Location was important, but he was considering each program's offerings, the facilities, staff, and how he thought he would fit in based on interactions with the interviewers. After much agonizing, contemplation, and adjusting, Greg submitted his rankings and waited for Match Day, the day on which medical students across the United States are paired with residencies.

I was in Detroit with my aunt that Thursday in March 2007, when Greg called. I heard the excitement and joy in his voice. "Guess where I matched," he said.

Since he was so happy, I assumed he was finally headed west, so I guessed California.

"No. Guess again," he insisted.

Now I had no idea, and I told him so.

"Morgantown!" he announced.

"Really," I said, trying to hide the disappointment I felt for him.

"Yep," was his response.

I asked hesitantly, "Are you all right with that?"

"Yeah," he said. "I think it's going to be good."

And it was an excellent match for him in many ways. He couldn't imagine any other place being as good a fit. Thinking back, Greg knew all along he wanted to match there, but he just couldn't admit to himself that going west, his dream for years, wasn't in the cards. I was impressed he allowed himself to be happy with the outcome.

Sue and I were so proud of Greg at his med-school graduation. That young boy who lamented the lack of frontiers after being read storybooks about Daniel Boone had found his field to explore and conquer. He looked impressive in his robe with all the accoutrements—but on that rainy day in early May, he was wearing shorts and sandals under his regalia.

"Is this appropriate attire for a med-school graduation?" we asked.

"Well, they told us to wear comfortable clothes. I find this very comfortable." We continue to chuckle at the picture of Greg receiving his diploma, bare legs and sandals in plain view.

After medical school, Greg began his residency with trepidation. But he seemed to change more during those three years than during any other phase of his life. He matured, mellowed, and found himself. He became more comfortable in his own skin, more accepting of his limitations. There were still outbursts of anger at seemingly trivial problems beyond his control, but not as frequently. Greg occasionally got down on himself. Maybe we didn't hear about these moments once Megan was in his life and bore the brunt of his disappointments. One aspect of Greg's personality that didn't change was his humility. He downplayed any accomplishment as insignificant.

During one of our frequent conversations about life in Morgantown, I asked Greg how things were going.

"Good," he said.

"Really?" I pressed.

"Yes. Even better than I expected."

That response was music to my ears.

Toward the end of his intern year, a new residency director was brought in. The change worked out well for Greg. He connected with Dr. Hollynn Larrabee. He spoke about her guidance and support.

The two formed a solid friendship and a deep trust. Sue and I didn't meet Dr. Larrabee until the residency banquet in June 2010. We were immediately impressed. She's been a supportive friend to us since Greg's death. The tributes to Greg at WVU wouldn't have materialized without her involvement. She let us know Greg had become an excellent physician and was respected by his colleagues.

Early in his residency, Greg displayed his knowledge and skills to us. Sue was home alone while I was in Michigan. She awoke at three a.m. with intense chest pain. She called the nurse line, and they advised that someone should drive her to the ER. Our neighbor kindly answered her call for help. An EKG, blood work, and other tests were all negative for cardiac issues. Sue called Greg later that morning to inform him and seek his advice. He listened, asked a couple of questions about the ER visit, and asked Sue if she was itchy, a question not raised at the hospital. Sue admitted she had some irritation. Greg said, "You have shingles." Two days later Greg's thousand-mile diagnosis was confirmed when Sue followed up with her primary care physician.

Greg liked his monthly changes of assignments, though some more than others. Working with the helicopter medical team was among his favorites. The adrenaline rush from incidents involving this crew was right up his alley. He experienced traumas in a new way. Greg enjoyed the company of the flight crew even after they put his stomach to the test on his maiden flight—probably standard procedure to humble the hotshot residents. Greg may not have needed this grounding, but he laughed about it afterward.

During a phone conversation at the end of June 2009 as his second year of residency concluded, I remarked, "Two years of residency complete already."

"That means a very important night is coming up," he said.

"When is that?"

"The night of June 30."

"What's so special about that night?"

"It's somehow magical."

"What are you talking about?"

"Well, on the last day of the second year of residency, we're treated like we don't know anything. But when we come to the hospital the next day as a third-year, we're supposed to know everything!" I don't know if this was Greg's private observation or a common perception among residents, but he thought it was pretty funny.

Early in 2010 Greg mentioned he was meeting with the staff at WVU to discuss future plans. "What do you expect to hear?" I asked.

"They'll ask, 'Where do you think you want to apply for jobs?'" When I asked him to explain further, Greg told me the question would imply there wouldn't be a job offer to stay in the WVU hospital system.

The tone of his voice reflected disappointment, which surprised me because I was sure he didn't want to settle more permanently anywhere in the eastern part of the United States. "As third-year residents, we'll continue to learn and develop our skills, and also share what we've already learned with the younger residents," he explained. "I'm enjoying the teaching aspect of this phase of my training. I've been told I could definitely fit into a teaching hospital. Immediately after residency is the best time to try that. Within the medical community, it's easier to move from an academic setting into a purely clinical one than the other way around. So it makes sense for me to look for work somewhere that includes an academic program."

Greg was learning what was important to him, accepting himself, developing a new level of comfort with his abilities and perception of what he could and could not do. This development was obvious to us as parents and encouraging to observe.

We talked again shortly after Greg's meeting with the WVU staff. "How did it go?" I asked.

"Not like I expected," he said. "Instead of asking where I planned to apply for jobs, they asked, 'What will it take to get you to stay here?' I was surprised. I guess they were offering me a job!"

Sue and I eagerly attended the residency banquet in mid-June 2010. We were introduced to many of the faculty, most of whom

Greg spoke about with admiration and respect. We met Greg's fellow residents, putting faces to names we'd been hearing about from him. We were proud parents at the dinner, happy for Greg—for what he'd accomplished and who he'd become.

During the ceremony, the residency directors presented the Resident Excellence in Teaching Award. Dr. Joe Minardi prefaced the presentation of the award by saying this resident had med students and residents following him around all the time because they knew they'd learn something. He described the recipient as a person with a knack for sharing information. Then Greg's name was announced.

I was surprised, to say the least. We had a new understanding of why Greg was interested in the academic side of medicine. He didn't just enjoy it; he was exceptional at it!

Greg returned to the table after receiving the award. I leaned toward him, congratulated him, and said, "I didn't expect that."

"I didn't either." He was grinning from ear to ear. Sue and I were bursting with pride.

To me, this was the most significant recognition Greg ever received. The Excellence in Teaching Award was the culmination of his hard work, tied everything he'd done together, and represented not only teaching excellence but also a newfound maturity. We had no idea, of course, that this would be the final recognition given to Greg during his life. I often wonder what more he could have accomplished. Sue and I still discuss his potential to grow as a doctor, a teacher, a humanitarian, and a person.

During the banquet we heard numerous mentions about the WVU family. The camaraderie, respect, and sense of family among all were apparent. What a great atmosphere in which to be taught. What a great place to become an ER doc.

After the banquet, we attended a party at the home of the department head, Dr. Todd Crocco. It was a casual event consisting of staff, residents, and their families. We met more of Greg's colleagues, many of whom had good things to say about Greg. Sue and I introduced ourselves to our host and thanked him for everything he had done for Greg. He told us Greg was an intelligent man, that Greg impressed him with his ability to absorb and retain information. His remarks caught me off guard, and made me very proud again.

Greg thrived at WVU, and he loved it here. His girlfriend, Megan, once described residency as "the place where Greg blossomed." He was now a real doctor, not a "practice doctor," as he liked to refer to himself. Dr. Seftick! A first for our family. It sounded so good.

After his death we received a book of memories from Greg's WVU family. Dr. Larrabee included the final paragraph of Greg's residency evaluation:

> Greg is an incredibly talented physician who has mastered the art of medicine. He is compassionate, thorough, efficient, and thoughtful as a care provider. He is the resident I would want to care for me or my family member if we were ill. Excellent self-insight. Greg is an exceptional teacher and is encouraged to find a way to incorporate this into future practice. We are very proud of you as a graduate of this program.

Greg began working at St. Joseph's Hospital in Buckhannon, West Virginia, part of the WVU system. He kept his Morgantown apartment and commuted seventy miles for his twelve-hour shifts. The commute didn't bother him, but an apartment in Buckhannon was available for doctors in case weather or fatigue made travel difficult. St. Joe's seemed to suit Greg just fine. He had good things to say about the other ER docs and the support staff. At the time, we had no way of knowing how colleagues and patients perceived his work, but we found out through the numerous cards and notes they sent after Greg's death. He was described as "kind, skilled, enthusiastic, thorough, and conscientious about his patients." One writer offered a common sentiment: "I'd gladly let him treat me and my family because he had become so good."

Dr. Larrabee summarized her opinion of Greg as a doctor. She had gotten a call as one of his references. She answered several questions and finally told the caller, "Just hire Greg. That's all you need to know: You should hire him."

In November 2010, Greg resigned as an attending at the hospital after his relationship with Megan changed. I suggested he stay with WVU and continue to work at St. Joe's, maybe even move to Buckhannon. I learned later that Greg never resigned his position. He was reclassified from full time to per diem. The department expected Greg would come back.

Once he decided to go, there was no stopping him from moving west to pursue his mountain dream. At the time, I feared he was running from something instead of toward it.

16

WAITING

*The Tetons were awesome on my way, with storm clouds behind them,
the sun shining only on the core of the range, & more storms moving in.*

—JUNE 27, 2005, Grand Teton National Park, Wyoming

On Thursday morning, we don't awake to an all-out blizzard, or to
deep snowdrifts in the motel parking lot. Only a few wind-driven flakes
fall from a gray sky and settle onto the lightly snow-dusted pavement
outside our Jackson motel. Maybe the search can continue today,
I think hopefully. Quickly I remind myself that weather changes with
elevation in the mountains. Visibility is definitely poor. The search
can't resume anyway. No plans or resources are in place for today
or Friday—though the weather clears enough for the helicopter to fly
avalanche-control explosive missions in preparation for the big push
on Saturday. As much as we want the SAR team looking for Greg
and Walker, we know in our hearts postponing the search was the
right call. Greg and Walker will have to walk off the mountain on their
own if they are to be found today. We'll be waiting until Saturday.

We're all emotionally drained. But I don't sleep. I'm awake early,
and I mindlessly sort through Greg's possessions, try to organize my

thoughts, and pray: "Bring Greg back to us. Please return Walker to his family, safe and sound. Is that realistic to hope for, to pray for? Since the search has to be suspended, bring Greg and Walker out on their own, no matter their conditions. Please, Lord, give us good weather for Saturday. Keep the SAR team safe. Give me strength!"

I want to formulate some sort of plan for the day, but my mind drifts from one thought to another. Finally, Sue and the others are up and about. I wander out to the parking lot to see what the Kuhls have in mind. They're going for breakfast, but I'm not hungry. Chris, Jesse, and Brandon had gone to the grocery store the previous afternoon and delivered bagels and fruit to Sue and me. We decide to stay at the motel and just eat some of the food in the room.

Later that morning, we head for the Incident Command Post in the park. We talk with some of the team and decide it might be a good chance to get into the cars to go through Walker's and Greg's things and make preparations to move the cars out of the parking lot.

At first I feel very uneasy about this. It almost seems like a sign we're giving up. Then I have one of my backward, foolish ideas: Maybe this is just what we need to do to help the guys show up. As soon as the cars are out of the lot, I picture Greg and Walker coming off the trail, walking into the parking lot, and shouting, "Someone stole the cars!" Imagining that helps me accept the idea, just to have them come out of the canyon and see their expressions.

The rangers have to break in to Greg's Buick Rendezvous since he has the keys with him. We don't want to take everything out of the car, because the wind is creating snow swirls on the pavement around the cars, eliminating most bare spots to set gear and luggage. Our shoes crunch as we walk in the parking lot. We search through a backpack, close a car door, open it again, and set off the car alarm. We repeat the sequence numerous times. It gets to be a joke every time it happens. It's a sign of how incoherent we all are.

We open one of Greg's suitcases, and right on top is the clothing grid Angie Menssen created. He told me how impressed he was with her simple chart. The fact he brought it with him and has it readily accessible proves how much he values it.

We take only a few items from Greg's car because we don't have room in our luggage for much more than we brought with us. For the most part, things are replaced as we found them. After it's rekeyed, Chris will drive the Rendezvous back to Bozeman and go through Greg's stuff at home.

Sue and I head back to the motel. Chris, Jesse, and Brandon join us there, and we make dinner plans with the Kuhls. I haven't eaten much since Monday and have no appetite now. But I don't want to be by myself either, so I join the group for dinner at the Merry Piglets Mexican Grill. I don't remember much about the evening except the restaurant is noisy and people are too happy. I don't want a beer or glass of wine. Nothing appeals to me. I eat a little, try to visit politely, yet wish I was somewhere else by myself. Later, when I'm alone, I wish other people are with me. Nothing seems right. This uncertainty accompanies me for months and still overcomes me at times.

One thing we discuss that evening is the approaching crossroads in the search. Saturday is still looking good for an all-out effort. But if that day's search doesn't lead to Walker and Greg, the effort will be scaled back. Sue and I aren't sure what that means yet, and SAR may not have planned that far ahead. We just know Saturday needs to be a productive day.

The park staff has gained a good sense of our families by this time. Both Walker's and Greg's cars are now in our hands. We can't help in the search effort. The business stuff is done. There isn't much to do but wait. We can wait at home as easily as in Jackson. Richard and Marylane decide their family will leave Jackson on Friday. Chris, Jesse, and Brandon make similar plans. Sue and I have a return flight booked for Monday, so we decide to stick with our original plans. I want to be in Teton during the Saturday search effort. We'll be here alone.

The weather on Friday morning looks pretty good. I wish the search could resume. We join the Kuhls for breakfast at the Bunnery. I still don't eat much, but we linger for a while, then head back to the motel. Everyone loads their cars to depart, except Sue and me. It's an eerie feeling. I know why I want Chris to stay—as support for us. But I don't want Walker's family to leave either. We've only known each other two days, but I feel an emotional connection, a bond because of our terrible situation. No family should have to endure a tragedy like this, but if I do have to face it, I want to be with people who understand what I'm up against.

The cars leave the parking lot. Sue and I are alone. We're alone in Jackson, Wyoming, on the outskirts of Grand Teton National Park, and Greg and Walker are alone in there somewhere. I feel so near, yet so terribly far from my son.

In the afternoon, we drive into the park and stop at the Taggart Lake Trailhead. I don't know why I came here or what I expect to find, but I know this is where I want to be. The weather at this elevation isn't as good as in town. A concerted search really isn't possible today. The biggest challenge would be shuttling SAR personnel to Garnet Canyon. Flying conditions could deteriorate quickly if the clouds descend to ninety-two hundred feet, the elevation of the canyon. The staff made the right call. The last thing we want during the search are injuries to the SAR people.

We walk along the closed section of the Teton Park Road. It helps knowing I'm as close as I can be to where Greg was last seen. Somehow I still hope to see Greg and Walker alive. I look at the mountains as we walk. I admire the beauty of the majestic snow-covered peaks, the very majesty that attracted Greg to them. As I admire them, I search, looking foolishly, hopefully for some sign of my son and his friend. I don't want to give up hope. But time is running out.

I reflect on Greg's earlier brush with death. One night in February 2005, after a day of second-year classes and studying in med school, Greg waited for the bus back to campus to meet friends at a bar. At the bus stop, someone approached Greg and asked the time, and when Greg looked back after glancing at his cell phone, he saw a gun pointed at him. Greg surrendered his wallet, and the worthless piece of shit ran off. Greg returned to his apartment, called 911, canceled his credit cards, and called us, very upset. I feel the same sense of unease now as I did then.

When we return to the parking lot, I walk toward the trailhead and step onto the snow. I think about Greg and Walker as they left the parking lot last Saturday, expecting to return to their cars the next day and back to their lives and everything they have planned. I feel connected to them as I stand on the trail they took to their unknown fate. Terror grips my heart as I think about what we might still find—yet I also feel reassured that this is a good place for me to be now and for them just six days ago. It feels right to be here. I don't want to leave.

That evening, Sue insists we eat a decent meal for dinner, something that will include a salad and vegetables. I want fish since it's Good Friday. The server at Giovanni's Italian Restaurant arrives at our table and very politely and cheerfully tells us about the dinner specials and offers to take our drink order. We decline drinks. She returns, still cheerful, to take our orders. Our dinners are brought to the table, and the server soon checks back with us. We're rather quiet, but she keeps returning, smiling, trying to make our dining experience enjoyable. Finally, Sue says, "Everything is very good. We realize we aren't the most pleasant of customers, but our son is one of the two young men missing in Garnet Canyon." The server is shocked and expresses her sympathy. After we finish our meal, she brings boxes for our leftovers and the check. When she returns with our credit card, she also brings a tiramisu to go. "The manager thought you might enjoy it later in the motel room." It's another example of how the entire community is aware of the search for Walker and Greg and sympathetic to our situation.

We're relieved to not be burdened by the need to handle the media. We know it would only add to the emotional stress of the terrible tragedy we're living. We decline requests to talk with TV and newspaper reporters. Back in Minnesota, David Francis fields media requests and answers questions on our behalf. Jackie Skaggs, Grand Teton National Park's spokesperson, issues daily press releases. We watch news reports and read articles in St. Paul's *Pioneer Press* online.

We talk to David on Friday and tell him Chris and Walker's family have left. He doesn't want us to be alone. He contacts his daughter, Jocelyn Plass, in Stanley, Idaho, and she immediately drives to Jackson to be with us as a representative of the Jon Francis Foundation. Sue and I are grateful to have company, especially someone who has been through a search for a loved family member. First thing Saturday morning, Jocelyn arrives at our motel with her children, Audrey and Charlie. As a group, we head for the Incident Command Post.

17

TRUE LOVE

I was awakened the next a.m. by my alarm.
I hit the snooze button once & then was awakened by what I thought was my
alarm. It was actually Megan calling me, the best wake-up call
I could have gotten. It was so good to hear her voice again.

—JULY 14, 2010, Kalispell, Montana

Looking for someone to love is a waste of time. That's not how it works. Love more often finds you than you find it. But you have to be open to love, to think of yourself as lovable. Greg finally learned to see himself as lovable during residency. The shift was obvious to me, but only because we were so much alike that way. Like father, like son.

As a young man, about the time I'd resolved myself to the fact that nobody was right for me, when I wasn't even looking, it happened. I was on a solo road trip to the Upper Peninsula of Michigan, on to Duluth, Minnesota, and then into Canada around Lake Superior in September 1970. The trip was my focus. I wasn't looking for that someone special. Yet there she was. I met Sue on a blind date during that trip. That proved to me that there are no directions to find love, to fall in love.

Watching Greg grow up, mature, and leave home, I often saw myself in him. Apparently I wasn't alone in seeing the parallels. Over the years, friends commented about how Greg took after me. "He looks like you," they'd say, and "he's good in science like you." Both true. In addition, I saw a young man lacking skills when it came to young women. Like me, Greg was socially inept. Like me, he feared rejection. If I could have erased one attribute he inherited from me, it would have been this fear.

Neither Greg nor I dated much in high school. Neither of us went to our high-school proms. That didn't bother me, and there was no indication it bothered him. It wasn't that he didn't like girls. I know he did. I know he was interested in some of the young women who were his classmates.

Greg didn't like to lose or come up short. It's another way we were alike—we both avoided situations that were likely to bring defeat or rejection. Sue and I worked with him on that attitude continuously in high school. We were never able to help him adopt a more adventurous and forgiving (of himself) attitude. He eventually accomplished that on his own when he started climbing and back-country skiing.

The first indication Sue and I had of Greg's interest in a woman was a surprise. It happened during med school. The three of us were in Proctor with Sue's family for Christmas 2005. We were staying in a motel since not everyone would fit at Grandma's house. Greg was on his cell phone talking to someone, smiling, laughing, and enjoying the conversation. We learned it was a young lady on the line with him, but he didn't elaborate. There were more conversations that day and the next. I was definitely surprised because Greg hadn't mentioned her to us at all.

Sometime during the holidays, Greg informed us he and this young lady were corresponding and he planned to visit her somewhere out east. He didn't provide any details of how long this had been going on and acted as if this were nothing new for him. He casually mentioned they'd met at a conference. That's all I learned about the relationship until he returned from his visit the next month.

Greg said nothing until we asked how things went. He was surprisingly calm when he told us it was pretty much a disaster. He'd gone out with a set of expectations and the young woman had a very different set of expectations. I never figured out what that meant. Greg never spoke of her again. We felt badly for him, but we knew these things happened. The positive side of the whole ordeal was Greg accepted the outcome and didn't criticize himself for it, at least not in front of Sue and me.

When Greg finished med school and prepared to move to Morgantown for his residency, he was flying solo. He easily selected an apartment with modest living accommodations. "All I need is AC and one of those magic dish-cleaning boxes [i.e., a dishwasher]," he said. Sue and I moved some of his things to West Virginia in our van. I observed other young people entering other units in Greg's building. We met a couple who lived across from Greg. They were a little younger than Sue and I and very friendly. They assured us they'd keep an eye on him and help him feel comfortable in his first days in Morgantown. It was reassuring to know there were friendly people around and tenants Greg's age nearby.

I was concerned for him now that he was so far from family and friends. He was definitely on his own. He had that encouraging history of making and keeping friends, but it didn't seem as if he'd made many new connections in recent years. His best and closest friends when he completed med school seemed to be friends from high school and college. Had he lost his touch?

Sue and I made another drive to visit and deliver more of his things in October 2007. He seemed happy and comfortable. We learned he was finding places to do things and people who shared his interests. We left with a good feeling.

Our conversations with Greg usually focused on play rather than work. New names would pop up, several more frequently than others. Greg was meeting people, connecting and making new friends. We found this comforting and encouraging.

And then there was Megan.

After the holidays and into the new year, a different name became a frequent part of our phone conversations with Greg. He was nonchalant about her. He didn't announce, "I met this great girl. We've been spending time together, and it's just awesome." I wouldn't expect most twenty-eight-year-olds to make such a pronouncement. And Greg was definitely a newcomer to dating and a relationship novice.

We did hear frequent, but low-key, mentions of Megan.

"What did you do this week?" I'd ask.

"I was on call on Saturday, and then Megan and I went to Coopers Rock State Forest Sunday and played around on some boulders," Greg would answer.

Or maybe if I asked how his day had gone, he might reply, "My shift ended at five, but we were super busy, so it was almost eight before my charts were done. Megan fixed some dinner for us."

Megan Webb was a med student at West Virginia University School of Medicine. She lived in the same apartment building. They became friends. They became a couple.

Her name continued to appear in our conversations, and the frequency increased as spring rolled around and the weather turned warmer. I was happy for Greg and, based on his inherited social awkwardness, surprised he hadn't scared this intelligent young lady off after one or two dates.

Greg seemed to change during his first year in Morgantown. He matured, become more confident, and smiled more. I got the sense he felt this residency program was the right place for him. We soon learned that having Megan in his life brought the puzzle pieces that were Greg together to reveal this fascinating new version of him.

In May 2008, when Dorothy (Sue's mom), Kaity, Sue, and I visited Greg, we didn't specifically ask to meet Megan, but we expected to. I had no doubt about Megan, but some of Greg's friends later said they'd even questioned her existence. They were skeptical Greg had changed enough to actually be seeing someone. A couple of friends told me when they met Megan, they thought, "She really exists, and she even seems normal!"

Megan was better than normal. Much better. My first impression was that she was intelligent, friendly, and caring. I remember Greg standing next to her with a great big grin on his face. That's what I immediately appreciated most about Megan, that my son seemed very happy.

During that visit, we were surprised to discover Greg's newfound love of cats. Or at least his love for a cat—Megan's cat, Tevia. We met her too, and she was definitely friendly. Greg had always been a dog person. He and Lady were inseparable. He took her death as a significant personal loss. Now Greg and Tevia got along great and were best buds.

Megan later told us Tevia would typically run into another room when there was a knock on her apartment door or when friends would visit. She was amazed that when Greg arrived for the first time, Tevia actually came sauntering in from the other room, walked up to Greg, rubbed against him, and purred. Megan took it to be a sign that Tevia thought this guy was OK.

A signature move of Greg's was his brisk entrance into the apartment and Tevia's coordinated approach. Greg would drop his books or the mail or anything he was carrying on the table and in the same motion, scoop up Tevia with the other hand. I never saw this happen, but I love the image. It reflects both Greg's exuberance for life and his love for Megan and Tevia.

As we left Morgantown and headed back to Indiana for Hannah's graduation party, the talk in the car centered on Greg. He seemed happy with the location and the opportunities provided in and around Morgantown, with his work and the people, and especially with Megan and their relationship. We all liked her too. Kaity even stated emphatically, "I like that girl!" She made a great impression on us all during our brief visit.

In the weeks and months ahead Sue and I noticed a difference in our phone calls with Greg. He wasn't venting to us as much. There was a time when I hesitated answering Greg's phone calls. He was a very genuine person and expected the same from others. He didn't necessarily call to complain, but eventually during the conversation he would inevitably come down hard on some person or situation. Things still bothered him now, but he took these upsets more in stride. He was happier. He felt very comfortable with Megan. She was now the one who had to listen to his complaints. I was happy, not that I no longer held this role, but that he had met someone to tell his troubles to. For a while I did miss my role in that part of our conversations. It was a very, very short while.

Sue and I didn't return to Morgantown for over a year. By this time Greg was well into his third and final year of residency. The four of us enjoyed a wonderful evening with a great dinner and a few drinks. I grabbed the check and paid the bill without giving it a second thought. After all, Greg was still only a resident living on a resident's salary.

That evening back in his apartment, Greg took me by the arm and led me off where we could talk in private. He told me, "Dad, tomorrow when we go to dinner, would you let me pay the tab? Megan wasn't too happy with me that I let you buy dinner tonight." I promised him I would keep my hands off the check and let him cover it. I did, and he did.

When Christmas 2009 rolled around, Sue and I expected to receive a phone call from Greg announcing their engagement. It didn't come during the holidays, but we got the call in late February after Valentine's Day. The wedding was set for May 2011. We were happy for both of them. It was a very exciting next step in Greg's life. In four short months he would complete residency and become an attending physician. In another year, we'd have a daughter-in-law. Wedding plans quickly became our focus.

When Sue and I attended Greg's residency banquet in Morgantown, things didn't seem quite right. It wasn't that Megan and Greg weren't together or anything that drastic. But there was little talk of wedding plans. And Megan didn't seem as enthusiastic as I expected. I wrote it off to the stress of med school and the changes and added responsibility Greg would face as an attending.

Greg and Chris both flew home to celebrate their grandma's eighty-fifth birthday in Proctor in early November. Greg seemed happy and in good spirits when he arrived. He soon informed us they had decided to postpone the wedding. He wasn't upset. He said the timing wouldn't be right because of where they were in their careers. Megan's med-school graduation was just a couple of weeks before the originally planned date. That was definitely a lot to anticipate.

Thanksgiving evening, we received worse news. Greg called, devastated. The wedding was off. His worst fear had come true. He had nothing to show for his emotional investment. He felt rejected. He blamed himself for the breakup, told us his actions had concerned Megan and caused her to reevaluate their relationship. Greg's distress had us worried.

We talked for a while, but I couldn't calm him down. I tried to listen, but it was difficult because he was irrational. I thought he'd been drinking and was afraid he might do something he would regret. It was one of those times Sue and I wished we weren't a thousand miles from our sons.

Greg was still very upset and depressed during our phone conversations over the next two to three weeks. We offered to come out, but he vehemently refused the offer. We felt caught in the middle. Should we contact Megan? Were she and Greg even talking? Was she angry? All Greg ever replied to our questions was, "I don't know."

Sue and I discussed contacting hospital staff. We didn't know anyone well and had no idea of their knowledge of the situation, but this was a serious issue and they definitely cared about Greg.

Finally, Sue called Megan. The call went to voice mail. Sue left a message expressing our concern for Greg and asked if Megan and Greg were communicating. We never received a reply from Megan. Or so we thought.

In February, when Greg was more in control, we received notification of a new voice mail. To my surprise, it was from Megan, returning Sue's December message shortly after she'd called. I can't explain why there'd been no indication we had a message for ten weeks. We used our cell phone infrequently, but I know we'd checked for messages and never had any.

Megan's message said she was in contact with Greg. They were talking mostly because she was concerned about him. She persuaded him to seek professional help. We'd been unable to get him to agree to this approach. I still regret we didn't connect with Megan and work together to help Greg get through this. Maybe that's how it was meant to be. Maybe too many people in his face might have led to a worse outcome. How ironic that he navigated through his depression and then died a few months later when he thought life was getting back on track again.

Soon after the engagement was called off, Greg gave his notice at work and planned to move west. I was a little surprised he chose to do that. There were reasons for and against staying. He enjoyed the teaching aspect of medicine in an academic setting. But his dream had always been to live in the mountains. Being close to Megan truly was his main reason for staying in West Virginia. Now that she wasn't in the picture, why not follow his lifelong dream?

We noticed Greg's mood improve gradually after the first of the year. Maybe the counseling helped. I think Greg benefited most from just having Megan around, seeing her concern, knowing she cared about him. He still very much wanted her in his life. He eagerly anticipated his move west. In early February 2011, Sue suggested I help Greg prepare for his move, an offer he enthusiastically accepted.

I had dinner with Greg and Megan on my final evening in Morgantown. I was confused about their relationship. The wedding was off, but Greg obviously cared for her. The question in my mind was, "Where does Megan stand on this relationship?" The evening was most enjoyable. I was happy to see Megan, and she seemed happy to visit with me. She and Greg smiled at each other and exchanged occasional touches on the shoulder and arm. I loved my son, and I thought the world of Megan. I wanted them both to be happy, even if it wasn't together. I left the next day with a sense that at least they were on better terms.

When he stopped briefly in Afton on his move west, we asked Greg about his relationship with Megan. "We'll see where we both are in five years and go from there," he answered.

Once in Montana, I don't know how regularly he talked with Megan. He was sincere about waiting for her. He even arranged for them to celebrate in Las Vegas after her med-school graduation. He did a lot of covert planning. Megan only knew she was flying to Vegas. Greg had lined up a limo to pick her up at the airport. We only found out the details of his Vegas plans by looking through Greg's things and his e-mail after his death. We canceled all the reservations we could late in the week of the search. The day his body was recovered would have been the first full day he and Megan would have been in Vegas celebrating.

I occasionally wonder what life would be like if Greg were still alive. Much of that thought focuses on Greg and Megan. Maybe by now they'd be married. Maybe there would be children. Where would they be living? It's all speculation and wishful thinking.

But some things are certain. Greg loved Megan, and she knew it. She told me specifically. Megan was Greg's first and only real love. I'm so happy Greg had an opportunity to love someone like he loved Megan. It made him a better man.

18

MUSIC

*The Big Wu song "Two Person Chair" even came on with my iPod on
shuffle and got me really stoked with the line,
"Tomorrow, go climb the mountain." I was super amped.*

—JUNE 4, 2007,
En Route to Grand Teton National Park to Ski Middle Teton, Wyoming

The third *M* in Greg's life was music. He was actively involved through
high school, but it became the more passive *M* as mountains and
medicine grew in importance. He continued to attend concerts
until the week before he died. For his obituary, I wrote, "His love of
music often led to long road trips to Phish, Yonder, and Widespread
shows"—a short sentence that says a lot about his preference for
jam bands. His huge CD collection accompanied him on many
road trips. I guess he enjoyed listening to music on his way to listen
to music. He'd flash that big smile and rattle off playlists from a
certain venue on a given date at the slightest hint of interest, or
even without anyone's expressed interest. Even now his uncle Rick
hears a new song and wants to share it with Greg, only to remember
that's no longer possible. Yes, Greg loved his music, medicine, and
mountains. His three Ms were intertwined.

Greg's initial involvement with music is a favorite memory of mine. Alto sax was his instrument of choice in the elementary school band. I don't know how or why he chose it. He may have had an opportunity to try different instruments. His music teacher might have suggested sax to Greg. Or maybe he made the decision for no reason at all.

He practiced regularly and worked hard to improve. He became a technically sound saxophonist. His math aptitude was important to his music development. He used that side of his brain to learn to read music and count beats. Musical expression, though, didn't come easily for him. He practiced and complained and got down on himself when a certain piece eluded him. We calmed him and encouraged him to continue to practice. He expected to do well and worked to play each selection perfectly. I feared this exacting approach would lead him to quickly abandon the instrument. Fortunately, that didn't happen. He persevered, but never became less demanding of himself.

Sue recorded Greg's sax rendition of "Happy Birthday" on a cassette and sent it to her brother for his birthday. Uncle Scott appreciated Greg's musical wishes. As a radio personality in northern Minnesota, he kept the recording handy and occasionally played it for listeners who called to wish a friend or family member a happy birthday. Unfortunately, Greg received no royalties from this repeated airplay of his only "released" track.

Greg played well enough through junior high and high school to usually qualify for the best band for which he was eligible. He also played with the jazz band, a small ensemble that performed some very entertaining selections.

Greg was occasionally assigned to play a solo in concerts. He would worry about it, but he always did well. At least it sounded fine to my biased, untrained ear. But improvisation wasn't Greg's forte. Some jazz band solos offered musicians a chance to improvise, but Greg refused. This reluctance—or perhaps inability—meant he was always considered a good musician, but never an exceptional one.

He decided to continue playing sax after high school. Music opportunities became one of the parameters he considered in college selection. He chose St. Olaf College for several reasons, including its excellent music program. The people in admissions encouraged Greg to audition for a spot in the band.

Greg took private sax lessons throughout high school from Don Fieder, a former Stillwater High band director, and continued during the summer of 1998 in the months before he started his first year at St. Olaf. He attended lessons and practiced faithfully. Mr. Fieder focused on audition preparation. He felt Greg was ready and had a very good shot at earning a spot in a band at St. Olaf, maybe one of the better bands.

Greg felt prepared for the audition, but was still nervous going in. He bombed the audition. He didn't make any band, not even the lowest—and there was no second chance. His only option was to play with one of the informal music groups on campus. Greg decided not to. I don't think he ever picked up his saxophone again.

Sue and I were fortunate to attend the lauded St. Olaf Christmas concert all four years Greg was a student and then again in 2002, the year after he graduated. With a student enrolled, parents were just about guaranteed tickets. The concerts were exceptional, but attending them rekindled my disappointment that Greg was no longer involved in a music program.

Greg's introduction to and his subsequent interest in particular music genres happened outside my influence. Greg's good friend and roommate for seven years, Pete Buchholz, remembers it well: "At Olaf, I gravitated toward those in Hoyme [Hall] who had similar music tastes. Greg was part of that group, as were many of the Olaf friends I am still in contact with. We spent a lot of times sitting in dorm rooms listening to music. When Greg and I moved in together, there was always music playing in our Hilleboe dorm room, unless Greg was busy studying in his closet."

During his freshman year, Greg became a big fan of jam bands, which feature "jams," or improvisation, in their performances.

Perhaps Greg's unwillingness to improvise in his own music led him to appreciate this talent and drew him to this genre. Pete remembers the beginning of that passion. "Early college was the 'Golden Age' of the MP3. It was a relatively new technology so, with some digging, it was pretty easy to find classic albums and live tracks from jam band shows. I spent a lot of time amassing a large collection of MP3s, and we would set it to shuffle and just listen. We discovered a lot of music this way." These listening sessions were the catalyst of Greg's large CD collection. It became his most valued possession. Those CDs accompanied him on all his road trips to see and hear Phish, Widespread Panic, String Cheese Incident, Yonder Mountain String Band, and many others.

Pete recalls their first road trip as sophomores:

> The first show Greg and I traveled to was Widespread Panic in Davenport, Iowa, on April 20, 2000. It was a Thursday night, and the next day being Good Friday, there were no classes. Mike, Greg, and I went to the show. Panic's album *'Til the Medicine Takes* had just been released, and it was an album that we listened to at least once a day. I don't remember much from the show—many shows have blended together in my memory. I remember it was a good show, and Panic covered Van Morrison's "And It Stoned Me" because it was April 20, a date that resonates with many fans of jam bands and cannabis. Because we were poor college students or because we preferred flying by the seat of our pants, we didn't have anywhere to stay after the show. We drove an hour or so out of Davenport and found a rest stop and tried to sleep in the car.

Greg was hooked. He and his friends attended numerous shows at many venues. Pete and Greg shared the same opinion of road trips.

Pete said, "Oftentimes, going to shows was as great as getting to the show. I always loved the music and was excited to see my favorite bands, but I was just as excited to hop in a car with a group of friends and drive to Madison, Chicago, Kansas City, Des Moines, Denver, Milwaukee, or just about any city, as long as there was a show."

Phish became a favorite of Greg and his friends. Four consecutive nights early in his junior year at St. Olaf demonstrated Greg's passion for music. He and Pete drove to Chicago for a couple of Phish shows on Friday and Saturday. Their next shows were on Sunday in Minneapolis and on Monday near Kansas City. Pete and Greg took quick action. As Pete tells it,

Greg and I saw Phish together for the first time in 2000. Before their 2000 fall tour, Phish announced that they would be going on indefinite hiatus when the tour ended. Greg, Ben, and I decided that we would go to two shows in Chicago and then Sunday night in Minneapolis. . . . There were five of us crammed into a compact Saturn. Outside of the Dells, we hit stopped traffic on the interstate and did not move for close to an hour. . . . Around the time we hit Chicago, the car . . . started having some sort of problems. . . . We finally got into the show and found out that we had missed the first five songs. I'm not sure why, but we watched the remainder of the first set from behind the stage in the second deck.

I went to the next show in Minneapolis with my girlfriend, Lisa. The next morning, we joked that Phish was playing in Kansas City and that wasn't too far away. It was a beautiful, crisp late September day. We knew that because of the hiatus it may be a while before we could see Phish again. Soon the joke started to become more serious. We looked to see if there were still tickets. It didn't take us long to decide that if we didn't go to this show we may regret it down the line. We convinced Lisa and our friend Liza to also go with us. . . . It was an awesome show and, even though Phish is back, I have never thought that we should have stayed at Olaf and gone to our classes that day. . . . Liza volunteered to drive home, so Greg and I sat in the back seat. In order to stay awake we played the memory game, "I am going to a picnic and I am going to bring . . ." We took turns reciting the list and adding an item starting with each letter of the alphabet. We made it to triple GGG before I messed up and couldn't remember something from earlier in the list. We probably spent two hours playing and years later Greg could still recite the first seven items from the list.

And here's further proof Greg didn't just think or talk about things, he did them! Pete remembers:

Two of our more epic road trips were to Nashville for Bonnaroo and a spring break trip to Denver. We were planning on skiing at Jackson Hole. Shortly thereafter, String Cheese Incident announced a spring tour starting in Denver at the beginning of our spring break. We quickly amended our travel plans to include two nights in Denver in order to see a couple Cheese shows. We then drove to Jackson. We then ended our trip with a Keller Williams show at the Mangy Moose. Following jam bands around the Midwest allowed me to see a large chunk of this country and visit cities that I wouldn't have if my favorite bands weren't playing there.

My own knowledge of jam band music and shows was minimal, except for two incidents involving transportation. The first occurred after college graduation. A group of Greg's friends planned to attend the inaugural Bonnaroo Music Festival in Tennessee. I asked the usual responsible-parent questions: Do you have money? Who's driving? How long will you be gone? Greg detailed well laid-out plans and indicated our involvement would be minimal. The biggest impact on my life would be several friends' vehicles left in our yard. I could deal with that.

Late the evening they were to leave, plans changed. One of the drivers wouldn't be going. Now half the group had no ride. Greg wondered if one of our vehicles was available. Sue and I agreed Greg could take our van. It was our newest vehicle (which was reassuring for a road trip), and it meant the entire group of six could ride together.

The St. Olaf contingent gathered in our yard during the night, loaded the van, and headed out. Sue and I were very nervous. It wasn't that we didn't trust Greg. It just felt like our responsibility to worry. Our philosophy was that if we worried and nothing happened, it was the worrying that kept anything from happening. Pete remembers the trip this way: "Greg arranged for us to take his parents' minivan at the last minute. We pulled into Afton around three in the morning and were off—all six of us in the van. It took us about fourteen hours to get to Nashville and get in line to enter Bonnaroo. We were in traffic for fourteen hours before we were able to park the car and set up our tent."

The trip went fine. Greg reported no car trouble. Everyone had a good time. But once we started driving the van again after Bonnaroo, we had problems. Shortly after Greg returned, the head gasket needed replacement, a fairly common problem in GM cars at that time. I didn't connect the problem to the Bonnaroo trip until one day Greg casually informed me that they'd waited many hours on the interstate and the approach to the venue. The car was running most of that time, idling, going nowhere. He didn't think that was important enough to mention.

When Greg emerged from the wilderness after seven days of solo backpacking in the Bitterroots to discover his car had been vandalized, he was as distressed that his CDs were gone as he was with the loss of his clothes and the damage to his car. Recordings of concerts he'd attended were gone. The music meant a lot to Greg. It represented memories of good times with special people, friends from all over and from many periods of his life. To him, the collection was priceless!

I'm not sure if he ever replaced all the stolen music. I don't know if he even really knew everything he had. Then again, he had an amazing memory for people and things that were important to him. He didn't need an index. He definitely remembered details about his three Ms—because music, medicine, and the mountains were the focus of his life.

The other transportation memory was driving to a Phish show at the Alpine Valley Music Theatre in southeastern Wisconsin during Greg's med-school years. We rode together, just the two of us, on the two-hundred-eighty-mile trip.

Greg put lots of miles on his 1995 Cavalier and his 2002 Rendezvous, many of them to enjoy music with friends. He managed to see interesting places because he wanted to hear the music offered at a particular venue. In addition to Bonnaroo, Denver, and Alpine, he saw shows at the Gorge in Washington and at several venues out east.

Music also provided the setting for gathering with friends. Greg didn't attend shows alone. He always managed to find someone to accompany him or meet at the concert. Music provided a constant backdrop to visit friends and to blend friends from different periods of his life. Greg had that way about him. His uncle Rick accurately describes Greg's gift: "I feel our love of music was a very special bond between us, and I think he instigated that. He had that special quality of finding a common ground with his friends and family and capitalizing on it to grow relationships. He knew what bond worked for each person. I really respected that in him. He could've been a politician if he wasn't so damn honest about how he felt; no bullshit with Greg."

Chris and Greg formed a bond in their selection and enjoyment of music. Chris remembers seeing Leftover Salmon at First Avenue in downtown Minneapolis and String Cheese Incident in Bozeman with his brother. While Chris never accompanied Greg to any Widespread Panic performances, the two brothers saw Phish together a couple of times and at least a half dozen Yonder Mountain String Band shows, including one in Missoula a week before the avalanche in Garnet Canyon. That was Greg's last concert.

I never connected with Greg through the music of particular bands while he was alive. Now I have. Since Greg died, I've listened to more of his favorite music than ever before. I have my own Phish, Yonder, and Widespread favorites. Music from the String Cheese Incident, moe., Railroad Earth, and others remind me of him. Greg and I are now connected on another level. The main reason I subscribe to satellite radio is for the Jam On station. I regret it was only after his death I was able to find this other medium to relate to Greg. He's probably smiling at me, or maybe even laughing and sharing his familiar "sweet" in response.

19

THE FINAL MAJOR EFFORT

. . . we climbed a small hill & suddenly, the whole cirque was laid out in front of us. I turned to Chris & said, "Welcome to heaven." . . .
I was happy how stoked Chris seemed.
He said, "We climbed that!" pointing at Pingora. He did well.

—JULY 23, 2010, Pingora, South Buttress, Wind Rivers, Wyoming

On Saturday the sky is blue, winds light, and visibility good. A large-scale, concerted search will proceed as planned. Thirty-five SAR team members assemble and are shuttled by helicopter into Garnet Canyon shortly after sunrise. Nick Armitage, a ranger and a friend of our son Chris, is assigned as the field operations manager for today's effort.

Jocelyn, David and Linda Francis's daughter, and her children meet us at our motel and we head north to the park. We appreciate their presence; we're relieved not to be alone. We arrive at the Incident Command Post at about ten and introduce Jocelyn to the search-management team and other key people. We're briefed on the status of the day's activities so far and the plans going forward. Jocelyn asks some questions and seems satisfied with the answers she receives. She later tells us the search appears to be very well coordinated and planned. Sue and I also have a few questions. I know the SAR team will primarily probe a large avalanche debris field. Though this is obviously now a recovery operation, somehow I'm still in rescue mode. The plan is explained to me, but survival instincts and parental love won't allow me to accept the facts.

Terry Roper leads us to the heli site on the Teton Park Road. Jocelyn has her first look at the Tetons up close. We describe the route Walker and Greg took from the Taggart Lake trailhead into the canyon. We point out key areas, including the general location of Garnet Canyon and the search area within it, which is hidden from view by the ridgeline.

The morning search produces no sign of Walker or Greg. Terry suggests we get some lunch. Jocelyn, her children, Sue, and I head to Dornan's, which is opening for the season that day. At lunch we talk about the search. Jocelyn reassures us this effort is well organized and in no way resembles the Francis family's search for Jon. Jocelyn's children, Audrey and Charlie, are a nice distraction from our concerns for Greg and the stress of the search.

After lunch, we return to the heli area. There have been no further developments. Another ranger offers me her binoculars. I scan the approach to Garnet Canyon, what's visible of the canyon itself, and the southeast face of the Grand. I decide to walk up the road a ways for a slightly different angle on and possibly an improved view of the canyon. Really I just want time alone. As I walk, I stop every so often to look up at the Tetons. I think about Greg's admiration for these mountains. He gives God credit for their beauty. He and Chris attended church every Sunday as children. I know he believes in God, but doesn't work to know and understand theology better. His relationship with God isn't as intimate as I would like. I wish I'd been a greater influence on his faith development. But I trust God knows Greg is a good person, has a big heart, and is always willing to help others.

My thoughts stay with the searchers, but also with Greg and Walker. I wonder not only where they are, but about their approach into the canyon exactly one week ago. They were probably very focused on their objective, even more so because of the poor conditions and limited visibility that afternoon. They were undoubtedly working hard to make progress. What a sharp contrast to today's beautiful, bluebird day.

I walk about a half mile and stop again. The sun is warm on the left side of my face as I scan the canyon with the binoculars. The Tetons are majestic, blanketed with clean, fresh snow. Little snow has fallen at road level the last two days. Above nine thousand feet, in Garnet Canyon and higher up the Grand, as much as three feet of new snow has accumulated. SAR has their work cut out for them. I pray for their safety and for a positive resolution to this tragedy.

Park admission is free on this comfortable, cool day. There's a lot of foot and bike traffic on the closed portion of the Teton Park Road, which will soon open to vehicles. Today is one of the last days for visitors to leisurely enjoy this stretch of road.

Most of the people enjoying the park today aren't personally concerned with the search for Greg and Walker. There is a high level of awareness of the search in Jackson because many of the locals enjoy playing in the mountains and share a connection with others of a like mind-set, whether local or visitor. The realization that this can happen to anyone is repeated to us many times.

As I stand focusing on the canyon through the binoculars, a group of bikers stops nearby and talks among themselves, speculating about what's going on. I assume they aren't locals. I don't know what compels me to walk over and explain the situation to them, but I do.

The group of four consists of a gentleman my age, a younger man, and two children. It appears to be a family of a grandfather, father, and children. I explain that two mountaineers had planned an overnight trip to summit the Grand and ski out the next day. I continue with a brief summary of their failure to come out and of the search since Monday. The older gentleman comments, "You seem to know a lot about the situation. Are you involved in the search?"

"Not in the way you might expect," I answer. "My son is one of the men missing on the mountain." He's understandably taken aback by that news, and expresses sympathy and concern for our family and Walker's family. We talk for a while, exchanging mainly biographical information. Afterward, I think nothing of it, and I make no effort to try to remember details of anything we discussed. That meeting turns out to be significant in the months ahead, however.

I walk back to the SAR base near the helicopter to rejoin the others. Still no developments, no sign of Greg and Walker. Jocelyn decides to return to Jackson so Audrey and Charlie can swim at the hotel pool. We make plans to meet for dinner. Sue and I stay for a while, talking with Terry and others on the ground. I'm beginning to become puzzled about why there's been no sign of Greg and what may happen next. I don't know if I still don't really understand the details of the situation, or if I'm in denial. I just know that I still think the best-case scenario is that Greg and Walker will be found alive—and the worst case will be finding them dead.

Sue and I decide to head for town at about three o'clock. The warmth of the car's interior meets my face as I enter. I put on my sunglasses and gaze at the majesty of the snow-covered Tetons on my right with eyes wide open. Greg seems so small, insignificant, missing among those massive peaks. I feel helpless looking up toward Garnet Canyon. I feel my helplessness turn to hopelessness as I finally admit to myself that their chance of survival is virtually zero after a week. I recognize that my earlier assessment was wrong. The best thing that can happen is Greg and Walker are found. The worst, they aren't.

My heart will break if Greg is dead, but I can't imagine leaving Grand Teton National Park without him, without knowing his fate. Chris later explains there was a clear point during the week when the effort changed from a rescue to a recovery. I wasn't aware of that change, but I can finally see the shift has occurred. This realization helps me later that same day.

Sue and I return to the Angler Motel. We rest, check e-mails, and make several phone calls. Then we drive to Jocelyn's hotel and meet them for dinner. Just as we enter the restaurant, the cell phone rings. It's operations manager Scott Guenther, calling to let us know the search has come up empty and they're going to shuttle the SAR team out of Garnet Canyon. It's about five thirty p.m.

As we leave the restaurant, I call Terry to let her know we're on our way back to the Incident Command Post for the evening briefing. She doesn't pick up. I leave a message. We drive to the park in two cars, wondering what's next. We find out sooner than I expect.

20

STORYTELLER

*About halfway up I heard some rock fall so I quickly moved to the
center of the couloir & hopefully out of the fall line of anything that might
be coming down the left side. (I had been pretty close to the steep scree &
talus previously.) Some small rocks came tumbling down & then I didn't hear
anything else. I took a few more steps & then heard a large rumble. I took
a few more steps toward the middle of the couloir quickly & then turned to
watch a large rock (150 lb.?) tumbling down near the left side of the couloir,
then bounce into it, continuing to the bottom pretty quickly. It was really cool
to watch, but I am sure it would have been a real day ruiner if I had stayed on
the left side & gotten drilled by it. I believe it was shortly thereafter (I think I
remember being a lot higher in the couloir) that I heard more rock fall. I looked
over to my left & saw the cause, 4 mountain goats. Those things are so badass
& fun to watch. (They could have also easily been the source of the rock fall
that nearly killed me. They were just scampering around on the loose cliffs left
of the couloir.)*

—JULY 14, 2005, Imp Peak, Montana

Greg was a passionate and entertaining storyteller. He could relate
details of a recent, or long-past, rock-climbing road trip—including
partners, weather, terrain, access, routes, and more. The story might
include a list of required equipment and their uses and advantages
in pursuit of an objective. He could captivate his audience, even
those unfamiliar with his subject.

His friend Joel Anderson referred to Greg as "portable talk radio." He said, "Greg was the perfect partner to be with on a climbing adventure because if you were stuck in a tent on a rainy day he could regale you with a nonstop string of stories." Joel described Greg's stories as "crazy, humorous, and endless."

It was an achievement Greg loved to talk as much as he did. Maybe he was still perfecting proper speech after so many years. Before beginning school, children of Greg's generation were tested in several areas, and Greg's speech skills weren't developed to the expectations for his age. He was difficult to understand as a three- and four-year-old. Based on those test results, Greg was recommended for the four-year-old program in the Stillwater School District. He rose early to catch the bus with other elementary school kids. Fortunately, a fourth-grade neighbor took Greg under his wing and helped him along the first few days. Greg was so little. I don't know how he even got on the bus. Maybe that's where he first developed climbing skills! The program helped. By the end of the school year Greg's speech was much clearer and understandable.

Greg possessed a good memory—he easily remembered things he read, did, and was told. That's an important attribute for a doctor. I discovered the vast amount of information he could retain during his med-school years. It amazed me the way Greg could sort through stored knowledge to access information relevant to the issue at hand. It didn't seem to make any difference if the information was recently learned or long archived. Greg could quickly recall what was needed.

His detailed memory extended to other areas of interest, such as music and climbing. This ability to rouse details from the depths of his memory merged with his eloquence and passion for these activities to form the source of his stories.

Greg's storytelling was widespread and well known. In the memorial journal we received from his colleagues at West Virginia University Hospitals, his storytelling is mentioned repeatedly. Greg was a big *South Park* fan, and he watched the episodes multiple times. He remembered lengthy dialogues from his favorites. One of his colleagues wrote that on one trip they all "lived out one of Greg's favorite *South Park* episodes. I think he quoted the whole episode."

Greg kept detailed journals of his road trips in spiral notebooks. The journal entries that begin each chapter are typical of his writing. He was strongly committed to his writing—and if he missed a day, he'd eventually find time to catch up, relying on his memory to record all specific details. I treasure these journals now. I imagine Greg laughing at me because I continue to live vicariously through him, even after his death.

In addition to his journal descriptions, he took tons of pictures on every trip, transitioning from analog to digital photography. (I can't begin to calculate how much Greg spent on film and developing.) He created amazing summit panoramas by taking multiple pictures as he moved slightly clockwise over the entire 360-degree view. At home after his trip, he would assemble the developed pictures in a series, overlapping the common features of adjacent photos, to form the summit view as he experienced it. The first manual panoramas were from his 2003 road trip, the one inspired by his vision of a "constantly changing horizon." Many others followed.

Part of what made Greg a marvelous storyteller was that he was an excellent listener. He heard and remembered what others told him, which helped him learn and made him a compassionate doctor. He took an interest in his patients and tried to understand their concerns and determine their needs based on their input. We have a picture of Greg taken during a residency exercise. Even in the fictional scenario pictured, in which the "patient" is actually another resident or med student, Greg's absorption in his patient's story is obvious. Friends and colleagues also commented on his ability to listen in other circumstances. Fellow resident John D'Angelo wrote in Greg's WVU journal, "When Greg told a story, you were captivated much the same way he was when you told a story." Greg could block out all the room noise, focus on you, the speaker, and listen.

Greg considered knowledge and information something to be shared, not hoarded. If he learned something related to medicine, he made that knowledge available as best he could. The same was true of climbing and mountaineering. Information gained by research or experience was available to anyone who might find it useful. He shared knowledge as if he were telling a story. In fact, he was. The source or method by which he obtained the information was as much a part of the story as the information itself. He taught by storytelling.

Since Greg's death, I find sadness and irony in his stories. One of Greg's most ironic stories was his Grand Rounds lecture on avalanche safety during his senior year of residency. It was based on his experiences and the knowledge he'd gained from avalanche classes and mountaineering colleagues. His residency director, Dr. Hollynn Larrabee, described it as "one of our best lectures of the year."

Sue and I also benefited from Greg's storytelling. He loved to tell us about strange occurrences in his medical education and profession. I call them "dumb-patient stories." It is common to be among family or friends and hear horror stories of medical mix-ups, poor procedures, and incorrect diagnoses. Greg provided the other side of the picture. He never violated doctor-patient privacy, though. His patient stories were always generic and nonspecific.

A gentleman from a small town a fair distance from the hospital visited the ER. Greg inquired, "What brings you in today?"

The patient answered, "Chest pains," a response that always results in prompt action.

"How long has the pain bothered you?" Greg asks.

"Six months or more."

"Why did you decide to come in today? What changed?"

"My wife wanted to do some shopping in town, so it seemed like a good chance to stop in the ER and get checked over."

Greg was a little disturbed with this abuse of an Emergency Department. But he followed protocol and did a blood draw and checked vitals. When he returned to the patient a few minutes later, the man was dressing to leave.

"Where are you going?" Greg asked.

The man said he was feeling better and was headed home. Naturally, Greg had to discharge him against medical advice. The patient didn't care.

The blood work that came back after the patient left indicated the gentleman was having a heart attack. Greg called his cell phone number, gave the patient the results, and instructed him to return to the hospital.

The man refused; he didn't want to drive all the way back.

"No. You don't understand. I want you to hang up, call 911, and come back in an ambulance." The man refused again. Greg learned later this patient had done this multiple times.

Our family didn't have an established tradition of storytelling. Our many trips to visit family when the boys were young were devoid of stories. There was plenty of talking and arguing, but little storytelling. Later, Greg was more likely to share stories as a driver than as a passenger, when he'd usually nap or listen to music. His constant chatter was irritating at times. Now I feel cheated that I didn't hear more of his stories.

We did a lot of hiking with Greg and Chris from the late 1990s on, but we missed out on Greg's storytelling on the trail. Those two young men were generally far ahead of Sue and me. They'd hike ahead, stop, and wait till we came into view, and then move on again. If we were only with Greg, he'd hike with us, but generally he was cheerleading for us rather than telling us stories.

Greg's stories centered on his experiences, adventures, and knowledge. He told them not to build himself up in others' eyes or because he lacked self-confidence. He told them to inform, share what he'd learned, and inspire. "If I can do this, so can you," is what I heard in Greg's voice. His stories were a proclamation of the beauty he saw in nature and in the human body. Greg was all about the experience.

Greg and Chris were just like any other kids, always asking for things in elementary school. I would advise them to focus on experiences, not possessions. Try things, learn things, but don't worry about owning stuff. Stuff is just—well, *stuff* that eventually will wear out, break, and become obsolete. But experiences and memories stay with you. Greg seemed to understand that at a fairly young age. He even called out Chris on his desire for possessions once.

We were driving back from a visit in Duluth. Chris saw a car pulling a boat and said, "We should get a boat."

I ignored him.

A couple of miles later, Chris said, "Why don't we have a four-wheeler?"

This time I attempted to give a reason by saying, "It's just one more thing you have to fix when it breaks."

Two minutes later, Chris declared, "We need a canoe."

This time twelve-year-old Greg laughed out loud. He informed his brother, "Chris, do you realize you spent $30,000 in the last ten miles?"

Greg listened to me about the value of experiences over possessions. Sometimes now I wish he hadn't. Maybe he'd still be alive today, sitting at home, collecting stamps or coins. But then he wouldn't be our Greg, would he?

Greg loved to tell stories, but he wanted to hear yours too. He could connect with anyone, no matter how little they seemed to have in common. He had no interest in people who weren't genuine, though. He didn't have time for someone's BS. If you had a story, an experience to share about a passion in your life, Greg was ready to hear it. You didn't have to share his passions to be a friend, but it helped. You could simply want to tell your story. Greg was OK with that.

His friends and colleagues have shared stories about Greg we hadn't heard from parts of his life that we didn't see. Those stories mean a lot, and I hope we'll continue to hear and share stories that keep Greg alive for all of us. It helps.

21

THANKS

*I love early morning climbs because it means that I get to eat candy
before most people are even out of bed.*

—JUNE 14, 2007, Soloing Middle Teton to the Dike Couloir,
Grand Teton National Park, Wyoming

One of our earliest family rules was saying "Thank you" and writing
thank-you notes for gifts received. This was a firm and ongoing
expectation not only for our sons, but also for Sue and me. Greg
and Chris learned the importance of appreciating what others did for
them and then expressing their gratitude by spoken and written word.

Since Sue's family lives near Duluth, and mine's even farther
away in Detroit, we celebrated birthdays and holidays with only a
few of our family members. Many gifts the boys received came by
mail. That's how the thank-you rule was born. A verbal thanks was
acceptable for a gift received in person. Delivered gifts required a
written thank-you.

The rule was: Write a thank-you or return the gift. This may seem
like an insurmountable challenge to a seven-year-old or an invitation
to an argument with a teenager, but it worked. Not one present was
ever returned.

In the early years their notes were simple, "Thank you" with a few other words or a crayon picture. Sue or I addressed the envelopes and sent them off. Later the system evolved. We provided a list with the name of the giver and the gift. The list would be handed to Greg or Chris with actual thank-you cards or blank paper on which they could write their notes. It didn't always happen smoothly or automatically. There were sometimes discussions, prompts, and even downright nagging. But it did get done. And there were some interesting rewards.

The first unexpected compliment came from a nearby friend, Helen. Chris graduated high school, and we held the traditional open house attended by family and friends from all over. Several weeks after the party I received a phone call from Helen. She and her husband, Burton, weren't able to attend Chris's party. She said they'd given many gifts over the years and been thanked many times, but this was the first time they ever received a thank-you for sending a card. She went on to say how impressed she was and complimented our boys.

Helen and Burton lived on a small lake only three or four miles from us. They were kind enough to invite us to use their rowboat to go fishing when Greg and Chris were in grade school. We accepted only a few times over the years. The boys really enjoyed being on the water. I don't think we ever caught a single fish. It didn't matter. We had fun. Greg and Chris were always grateful for the opportunity, and never forgot their generosity. When Chris sent the thank-you note, he acknowledged their past kindness, in addition to expressing his appreciation for the card.

Then there's the thank-you that spans fifteen years. At the high-school awards assembly, Greg and another student received Palmer-Rathert Medical Scholarships. Sue and I were surprised Greg had been accorded this honor, as was he. In fact, when the award winners were announced, Greg's friends had to nudge him and tell him to go onstage to receive his scholarship. He was probably dreaming about mountains. Greg received a plaque from faculty member Dianne Lawson, who remembered winking at Greg as he stepped onstage. She leaned in and told Greg, "This is for you," as she presented the award. Greg smiled.

In 1996, as a junior in high school, Greg took Integrated Chemistry-Physics taught by Ms. Lawson. She was excellent. Greg did well and respected her as a teacher. She encouraged Greg and watched him grow from an insecure student, unsure if he belonged in this class, to a more confident individual who was eager to help others. Sue and I weren't aware she played a role in Greg's selection for this award until years later.

Fast-forward to 2003. Greg had completed his undergraduate studies at St. Olaf and taken a year to prepare for the MCAT and navigate the med-school application process. During that time, he was accepted at the University of Minnesota Medical School. He understood he hadn't accomplished it on his own, and the thank-you rule was now ingrained in him. He took the time to thank one person he felt had been an important contributor to reaching this goal in his life, Dianne Lawson. At the time, Sue and I knew nothing about it.

Now jump ahead to the tragic days of April 2011. When we returned home from Jackson after Greg's and Walker's bodies had been recovered from Garnet Canyon, sympathy cards had already arrived. Phone messages accumulated on the answering machine. The cards and calls continued before the funeral and for a long time after, and we appreciated the support. It was meaningful to hear from people we didn't know, people we'd never met, people who were part of Greg's life at every stage of his education and career. Among them were teachers from junior high and high school. This was a pleasant surprise to us. Greg was a good student, but he wasn't one to consider teachers as friends or entertain conversations on nonacademic subjects. At least that's what we thought.

A short while after Greg's funeral, we received a sympathy card with a letter from Dianne Lawson. In the card, she referred to Greg as a "unique and wonderful young man." She went on to write, "I have included the letter he sent me in 2003. It meant so much to me and is an example of what a special child he was."

Dear Ms. Lawson,

I am writing to thank you for the help you gave me in reaching the point that I am at today. I was accepted into the U of Minnesota (Twin Cities) Medical School for this coming fall. The strong science background which I received from numerous teachers and professors was obviously necessary for medicine. However, your support was invaluable in giving me the strength and belief in myself to push on through the tougher times. I never really believed that I could get into medical school. Being a doctor was what I wanted, but it was also an easy answer to the "What do you want to be when you grow up" question. The odds are against everyone who tries to be a doctor, from high school students to people who have interview offers at schools. At no point in the process do you have a greater than 50% chance of getting in. Getting the Palmer-Rathert scholarship was invaluable for my confidence in allowing me to get into school. My parents had always encouraged me to go for medicine, but that is their job. They would encourage me in whatever I wanted to go into. Your support was the first real encouragement I got from someone who did not have "unconditional support for Greg" in their job description. When I realized that you believed in me, that did a lot for getting me to believe in myself. So, I hope things have been going as well for you in your life as they have been for me. (I have spent the last year in Bozeman, MT, working as little as possible and playing in the mountains as much as possible.) Thank you for your help in building the necessary science background to get through college as a biology major and your support in helping me get the confidence to pursue medicine.

Greg Seftick

There it was, proof Greg abided by the thank-you rule even when the gift wasn't tangible or immediate. And the evidence continued to show up after his death. Sue and I were touched that Dianne had kept the letter and then thought to share it with us. Greg couldn't have foreseen the lasting impact of his letter when he sat down to write it in 2003.

Sue and I laughed at Greg's reference to unconditional support. We tried to supply that for both boys. And Sue was an ever-present cheerleader for Greg from early childhood through residency. I remember often hearing her provide praise and encouragement over the phone with a "You can do this, Greg!"

Greg said thanks often. Anyone who knew him well, saw him frequently, or spent a stretch of continuous time with him knows this. He said it so often it would be easy to think it was just automatic rather than genuine—but he meant it every time he said it. He was conscious that someone was doing something for him. Often it was just a simple act of courtesy, doing something that wasn't necessary but was kind. Other times it was a requirement, maybe part of the job being done in partnership with him. Didn't matter. He was grateful.

Maybe he said thanks too much. It could even be funny. When Greg moved to Columbia Falls, he spent a lot of time at the apartment of Joel and Angie Menssen. He was probably there more than he should have been. It might have caused problems if it had continued too much longer. But after the avalanche in Garnet Canyon, the visits seemed too few. Angie told me how fortunate she and Joel were to spend so much time with Greg those last few weeks of his life.

Angie had fun with Greg and his propensity to thank people for any small thing. During one visit to their apartment, Angie decided to try to do something for Greg without him thanking her. She describes:

> I turned on the light. Greg said, "Thanks!"
>
> I handed him the salt. Greg said, "Thanks!"
>
> I gave Greg a glass of water. Greg said, "Thanks!"
>
> I shut off the light. Greg said, "Thanks!"
>
> I couldn't trip him up!

It wouldn't be right to talk about Greg's gratitude without expressing my own. After all, what kind of a father would I be if I violated my own rule?

So, Greg, thanks for being my son. You were a very good one. You made me a dad. Your arrival made us a family. Thanks for making me proud to be your father so many times. And thanks for the few times I wasn't so proud of that. You gave me the opportunity to learn to be a better dad and a better man. Maybe I should throw in an "I'm sorry" here because I know there were many times I didn't step up and respond like I should have. Those were probably times you weren't very happy to be my son.

Thanks for turning a city boy into a man who appreciates and loves the outdoors. In that respect, I pale next to you and Chris, but my love increased because of you. Your interest in the mountains led me onto many trails I would never have pursued of my own initiative. Thanks to you, Mom and I explored Glacier National Park. Your encouragement led us to visit Grand Teton National Park for the first time in 2003. I would never have made it to the summit of Hyalite Peak if you hadn't been cheering me on. Mom and I may not have visited Yosemite for our thirty-fifth wedding anniversary if we hadn't had so many wonderful experiences and seen so much beauty at other national parks—and heard your high praise for Yosemite. We would've missed an opportunity to see Glacier Point at Yosemite if I hadn't wondered, "What would the kids do?" as we left the park.

Thanks for having good friends. We never had to encourage you in your studies because the young men and women you associated with in elementary, junior high, and high school were all motivated and provided positive peer pressure. They not only stuck by you in your success, but were there for you when you were down.

Thanks for being an amazing friend to a wide variety of people in many different walks of life. Your ability to make and keep friends is an inspiration. We heard many stories about you as a friend at your funeral. I wish I'd known these things while you were alive.

Thanks for sharing your friends. The friends you made in different parts of your life became friends to each other. I don't know anyone who did that as well as you.

I was most impressed that not only your male friends grieved at your death, but so did many of their wives and girlfriends. That is the true measure of a man. If he can earn the admiration of a friend and the respect of his friend's spouse, there is an example of real friendship.

Thanks for loving your family. Not just Mom, Chris, and me, but also your extended family, people you didn't see on a regular basis. You never tired of our annual trips to Duluth or Detroit for Christmas. Sometimes you were the impetus behind our decision to make another drive through questionable weather. Mom and I thought at some point you and Chris would insist we stay home for the holidays so you could be with your friends, but that never happened. And it wasn't just Christmas. You looked forward to visits with uncles, aunts, and cousins during your travels—even if just for dinner, a beer, or a place to sleep for the night.

You were a gracious host too, always willing to let family and friends bunk in your apartment. Accommodations were not luxurious or spacious, but there was always room. Thank you!

Thanks for being a good teacher. You started on the slopes at Afton Alps as a ski instructor for those snotty-nosed five-year-olds.

You finished, by all accounts, as a great teacher to med students and younger residents. In between, you encouraged many old friends and made new friends by sharing your climbing and skiing knowledge.

Thanks for being a good brother. You and Chris had many spats growing up, and I often wondered if you two would ever be close. I scolded you and told you how important it was for you to get along as brothers. Somehow, together, you figured out how to do that. It's no exaggeration to say you became best friends, and it hurts to think what still might have been for you two brothers.

Thanks for teaching me to smile. That big grin of yours dominates our house now. Even though you're gone, I can't help but smile back at your picture. Many people characterized you as "the happiest person" they knew. Wow! What a testimonial to a life well lived.

Thanks for remembering to send cards—birthday cards, Father's Day cards, Mother's Day cards, all kinds of cards. Thanks for the last two cards you planned to give Mom and me, cards we found among your things after you died.

And, finally, thanks for showing me how to enjoy life. You, more than anyone I know, could prioritize demands on your time, get done what needed to be done, then enjoy the rest of your time doing what you loved and valued. The other stuff I so often got hung up on was just that—stuff. You let the stuff slide as well as anyone I know.

Thanks, Greg.

22

SCATTERBRAIN

The bear spray, which had been inadvertently left in the window, exploded in the car, creating a 4" wide & 4" deep divot in the speaker board, coating the inside w/ pepper oil, but, surprisingly, did not break the rear window. The cleanup made both of my arms burn all the way to Billings & also delayed my departure about 1 hour.

—AUGUST 22, 2005, Bozeman, Montana

Intelligence, wisdom, and common sense aren't identical and aren't possessed in equal measure. Greg was intelligent. You don't get through med school on luck and good looks. He also seemed to have common sense, most of the time. But he could be a bit of a scatterbrain. Some of the foolish things he did were legendary.

Several incidents involved cars, mostly his Cavalier. At various times he ran out of gas, locked the keys inside, left the car running, and got lost. I helped resolve most of these to some extent. I don't recall any scatterbrained medical screw-ups. If there were any, maybe he didn't tell me because I couldn't help. At the time, Greg's mishaps were inconvenient and irritating. After a while, they were humorous. Now, after his death, they're precious pieces of the interesting individual he became.

How could someone as intelligent as Greg be so prone to simple mistakes? I think Greg, in preparing for a climbing adventure or heading to a music venue, became so focused on the upcoming event that he couldn't be bothered with peripheral concerns. He never learned from the inconveniences caused by his occasional mistakes.

Greg ran out of gas for the first time early in his driving career. He left home in the Cavalier one cold, snowy evening. He wasn't gone ten minutes and the phone rang. The car died. He didn't have a cell phone at that time. Fortunately, someone had stopped to check on him parked on the shoulder and let Greg use his. I brought out a can of gas, added some to the tank, and had him start the car. It turned right over. In fairness, even though the car was only three years old, the gas gauge wasn't very reliable. I was partly to blame too. I drove the car on occasion and could have filled the tank.

I wasn't aware of any other instances of running out of gas until I read Greg's journals after his death. He chronicled leaving home for Montana in the evening after dinner for a not atypical all-night road trip. He mentioned his travel progress and included a comment "I would have made better time except I ran out of gas." He lucked out again—someone stopped and drove him to a gas station and back. I can picture the anticipation on Greg's face as he set out to leave the drudgery of everyday life for another adventure in the mountains. Getting there was just a necessary evil and keeping his car gassed up was an afterthought.

One of Greg's Colorado road trips included a day of skiing at Arapahoe Basin. Greg learned skiers were allowed to camp overnight in the parking lot. We didn't know Greg's exact itinerary, only his approximate schedule. One evening, the phone rang. A representative from AAA Road Service (which we carried for all four drivers in the family) called to verify I had a vehicle that needed a door unlocked in the A-Basin parking lot in Colorado. "My son is driving my car somewhere in that area, so the call is legitimate," I replied. Greg called later that evening to tell us about the incident. He'd been in the car, listening to music, and got out for some reason. It was very windy and the door blew closed behind him. He was locked out. I told him about the phone call, and we just laughed. Greg realized the problem as soon as he stepped out of the car, but the wind blew the door shut before he could catch it.

During his senior year of high school in January 1998, Greg called me at work on a day when the temperature was barely above zero. "I locked the keys in the car after school," he announced. I told him I'd be there in twenty minutes. I quickly located the car in the parking lot, and noticed the car was running as I walked over to unlock the doors. It had been running for a while because the car was warm inside, and the exhaust pipe was covered with ice. So much so, that not much exhaust was even coming out of the tail pipe. I knocked a little ice off before I got back in my car and we both drove away. I was concerned that there could be some serious engine damage if the exhaust was completely frozen shut. Everyone made it home safely, and the car suffered no permanent ill effects.

Greg had three passengers with him that day, including Chris. No one ever explained what happened. It seemed unreasonable for four people to get locked out of a car. Maybe Greg had gone out first, started the car, got out to scrape windows, and locked the keys in before the others arrived. Or maybe the story is more exciting. Perhaps the car had been left running the entire school day.

Many of Greg's other scatterbrain instances involved road trips. I enjoy vacations and the opportunity to travel. I also enjoy hearing the details of other people's trips—destination, accommodations, miles driven, and route. Greg and Chris discovered my interest after being barraged with questions after their trips. They were feeding my wanderlust. Ultimately, though, my interest created a problem for me.

Often when Greg set out on a road trip we'd eventually get a call from him. "What are you doing?" would be his initial question, followed by, "Can you get on the computer and look something up for me?" A route request would follow.

"Where are you, and where are you going?" I'd ask as I accessed MapQuest or pulled out the atlas. After I provided a route, Greg repeated the sequence of highway numbers several times to make sure he had it right. If I asked why he hadn't checked a map before leaving, he'd have some lame reason that might make sense for an inexperienced driver with less than a med-school education.

Most of the route requests came after Greg moved to West Virginia for his residency. This was newer territory to him than Montana and Wyoming, so he needed to check a map before starting out. Fewer roads out west present fewer choices heading through the mountains.

The first time Greg called for directions he was near Bishop, California, during his major road trip of 2003. He was checking in, as we'd asked. But he also needed some help determining which routes were open since some roads in the area aren't maintained in the winter and are still closed in March. He may have checked before departing, but his travels weren't fixed. He was making choices and adjustments as he went, based on information he received along the way. I tried to help, but I could tell he was frustrated by his situation. It looked like he had a lot of miles to drive just to get somewhere only a fraction of the distance away. In his journal Greg mentioned someone at a gas station told him a road would be open, but it wasn't, which added to his frustration.

Early in his intern year of residency, Greg again called for directions. I was watching a television program I didn't want to miss. Sue handed me the phone, and I somewhat tersely helped him select the optimum route from among some choices he provided. He thanked me, and I went back to watching the show. I later regretted being so abrupt with him.

During a subsequent conversation, Sue mentioned to Greg, "Dad wasn't happy you interrupted the program."

Greg replied, "I thought he liked looking for directions."

He knew I took these road trips vicariously through both him and Chris. He was correct. I liked to hear about his trips and know the details, but I guess I wanted to do it on my schedule. I was pleased when Sue told me Greg thought I liked to be asked for help. I tried to be more receptive to his requests after that. The truth is, he stopped calling routinely and only called for route help if he really needed it. I should never have put off my son for a TV show.

Greg's final call for directions came in December 2010. He was on I-78 in eastern Pennsylvania headed for New Jersey to spend Christmas with friends Greg and Melissa. He told me his destination and current location. I told him to take I-287 to the southbound Garden State Parkway. He called again later and said, "I suppose the Garden State Parkway and the New Jersey Turnpike are two different roads." He'd exited too soon and was headed south on the wrong road.

After consulting the map, I advised, "Looks like the best thing to do is get off at the first exit and turn around, drive north on the turnpike, and then rejoin the interstate eastbound for just a short distance to the parkway." He thanked me and was on his way. He soon called again stating sarcastically, "You would think if you could exit off a road one direction, you would be able to get back on that road." Turns out he could not go east on I-287 from the turnpike, only west. So he not only backtracked on the parkway, but also on the interstate. He wasn't happy. In all fairness, this trip was happening after Greg and Megan broke up, so he had other things on his mind. I was surprised he'd agreed to drive to New Jersey to spend Christmas with friends. Sue and I were pleased he didn't stay home alone, which would have been more difficult.

Greg had one transportation mix-up involving a bus. His first med-school apartment was just off campus. He often rode the bus to class because parking was scarce and expensive and the bus stop was only a few houses away. The first day he took the bus, he arrived on campus without incident. But he somehow got on the wrong bus to come home. The route was U shaped, so eastbound and westbound designations were meaningless—on either route, the buses traveled east and west at some point. He arrived at the wrong end of the route, walked three miles home in the dark through some questionable neighborhoods, and immediately called us to complain about living in the city. Sometimes it seemed as if he screwed things up just so he could complain.

Greg didn't limit his scatterbrained events to ground transportation. He flew to Pittsburgh for a residency interview and called us while he waited for his luggage at the carousel. "Here's my bag, so I'm going to head out," he said. Two minutes later the phone rang again. It was Greg's name on caller ID, but not him calling. A woman said hello and asked if I had just talked to someone on this number. She found the phone on the edge of the baggage carousel. I thanked her, but didn't know what else to tell her. She asked for Greg's description, which I provided. Greg called five minutes later, laughing and relieved. As he had approached the carousel looking for his misplaced phone, this kind woman asked, "Greg?" So he had his phone back.

His voice mail recording was priceless. It was funny in college, but I thought it was a little ridiculous not to change it in med school or during residency. He kept it on his phone till the day he died. I can still hear his voice: "This here's Wildcat. My 20 makes me 64. So leave your 37 after the beep and I'll 16 ya. And remember, keep your nose between the ditches and the Smokey out of your britches."

Then there was the income-tax blunder. Sue and I did the boys' taxes for a few years, including Greg's for 2002 when he was in Montana. The completed forms went in a large envelope for mailing. Sue attached some sticky notes with instructions for Greg. I said, "You don't need to show him where to sign and date. He's a college graduate." Two months later, Greg informed us his tax forms were returned. They hadn't been signed. From Sue, I deservedly heard, "I told you so."

Even Greg's last trip from Minnesota to Montana in March 2011 included a small scatterbrained moment. I called Greg on the road to ask when he'd left his friend Ryan's place in Minneapolis to begin his drive. "The first time or the second time?" he quipped. He'd left, realized he forgot his cell-phone charger, and returned for it. Typical!

What treasured memories! They make me smile—and they make me proud because they reflect some maturation in my son. Greg had difficulty accepting defeat and rejection as a child and young adult.

But later, he was able to ignore his lapses, his errors and omissions. He was unforgiving of himself to the end about the important things, relationships gone wrong and such. But these inconvenient, but relatively trivial, issues seemed quickly forgotten. He was growing in wisdom, heading in the right direction. And then . . .

23

RESURRECTION

17 people . . . were trapped high on the Grand Teton by multiple lightning strikes at 11:50 a.m. One person, from Iowa, was roped in & on the belly crawl section of the Owen-Spalding when lightning apparently melted the rope & tossed him to his death at the bottom of the Black Ice Couloir.

—JULY 27, 2010, Climbing near Bozeman, Montana

Sue and I are in the lead as we turn into the park's administration area. Jocelyn, Audrey, and Charlie follow in their car. It is exactly seven p.m. on that bright, sunny Saturday evening, April 23, 2011. The sun has dropped behind the Tetons. The mountains' features are diminished in their backlit natural radiance.

We drive back to the Incident Command Post entrance and are surprised to see Terry Roper and Chris Harder waiting in the parking lot.

"I wonder why Chris and Terry are in the parking lot," I say to Sue.

"Maybe search and rescue isn't done with their debriefing, and they don't want us in there yet," she replies. That isn't it at all.

We get out of the rental car. Terry and Chris approach. Jocelyn makes her way to us. Chris begins speaking to us in a calm, hushed, solemn voice.

"SAR personnel were being shuttled off the mountain when Nick Armitage, today's field operations chief, decided to make a final sweep of the canyon. Only two groups remained on the mountain. On his way from the upper landing area to the lower, Nick switched his transceiver to receive mode and skied passes across the width of the canyon. He picked up a beacon signal. He radioed the remaining SAR personnel at the landing site, and they joined him. Nick rechecked and was now receiving two signals. The searchers probed the area without a positive hit. They started digging. There was little time left before the helicopter would need to shuttle them off the mountain if it was to return to the landing field to meet regulations. After digging down about five feet, they probed again. This time they got a hit. Probe placement indicated the presence of two bodies. This was as far as Nick and the others could proceed. They had to get off the mountain before the helicopter was grounded by darkness."

Sue and I are numb. How else can you feel at a time like this? A parent doesn't prepare for such a moment, for a situation where you receive the most unwanted, terrible news possible about a child.

"How sure are you this is Greg and Walker?" I ask.

"Ninety-five percent, based on shape of the outlines from the probe and the presence of beacon signals."

My immediate thought is, "Who else could it be?" I don't ask any more questions in the parking lot. Sue and I hold each other as we're overwhelmed with sorrow, relief, confusion, and much more. We enter the Incident Command Post meeting room with Terry, Chris, Jocelyn, and the kids.

The conference room is quiet when we enter. Many of the SAR personnel are present, most with heads downcast. Everyone is certainly extremely tired, but I feel they are equally disappointed with the outcome of the search. I look at the room full of people, relieved hardly anyone is looking at me, because I can't look anyone in the eye at this moment without transferring my great sorrow to them. These men and women are already disheartened.

Chris Harder gives a summary of the day's efforts. We know these people have worked extremely hard. We tell them we appreciate their efforts and thank them for finding Greg and Walker. The summary centers on the final hour after Nick picked up the beacon signals. It's difficult being this close to having Greg back, but it wouldn't have been wise to continue the recovery in the fading light and risk injury to anyone. There is so little to gain. Nothing will change by waiting until tomorrow for Greg and Walker to come off the mountain. We know our son is dead.

Chris explains how the recovery will be completed. It seems appropriate for the boys to be dug out the next day. Tomorrow is Easter Sunday, Resurrection Day. It is also my birthday. I had looked forward to this day because it is the first time in my lifetime my birthday falls on Easter. What an ironic twist of fate. The combination of those two events will now be overshadowed by this tragedy. My birthday will never have the same meaning.

After the debriefing, we're led into an office. I'm not sure whose cubicle it is, but Sue and I meet there with Chris and Terry. We talk for a while, and they offer us the use of the phone on the desk. Cell service in and around the Incident Command Post is spotty because of the low elevation of the office and the lay of the land around the building. We make calls to family. We choose our words carefully. There is solid evidence two bodies lie below the snow, but we don't actually have proof of Greg's death. We talk to Chris, Megan, Sue's mom, my brother, and maybe others. I don't remember. The reactions are predictable. I feel the worst when we tell Megan. She takes it the hardest. What a tremendous loss for all of us. It seems so wrong, such a waste of a promising life.

Nick Armitage kindly and respectfully asks to talk with us. He looks physically exhausted and emotionally drained. We thank him for finding Walker and Greg. He explains the day's search in greater detail. Nick tells us he worked the crew hard all day. They know this is the final day of intense searching and everyone wants resolution for both families. Nick tells us every SAR team member is tired and frustrated by the end of the day when it is time to quit.

"What inspired you to make that final, productive sweep of the canyon after all the searching already done?" I ask him.

He explains, "As I became more experienced with search operations, I moved up the chain of command. While the crew had worked physically hard all day, I hadn't. When the groups were being shuttled out of the canyon, I felt I still had more to do. I wanted to physically contribute to the effort, so I decided to make that final search."

Nick further explains that when he informed the remaining people of his intentions, they questioned why he'd bother checking an area already covered. He insisted on making the sweep and instructed the remaining crew members to ski down to the lower chopper pickup site. He thought he was mistaken when he heard the first beacon signal. He radioed for the others to return. They asked if he was sure. Nick replied, "Pretty sure." He checked again for transmitter signals while the others returned. Now he picked up two. The searchers started probing without a positive hit. They dug through five feet of snow and ice and probed again. The probes definitely hit something. Using the spacing techniques they'd learned, the search crew was able to determine two separate objects that resembled human shapes.

The sun had settled behind the Teton Range in the cloudless sky, and a definite chill in the air indicated the day was drawing to a close. The chopper had to get them off the mountain and back to base. Nick and the others reluctantly left Garnet Canyon. Although he is repeating information I already know, I feel it is important to hear it again, as if the repetition will convince me this nightmare is reality, that my recent revelation was accurate. Greg and Walker have been found, and this is a good thing. This truth goes against anything I ever considered. I am not comforted.

We again thank Nick for his effort, leadership, and for that all-important final sweep. He says this was personal for him. He knew Greg, but not well. But he and our son Chris are friends, having been fellow patrollers at Big Sky Resort the previous season. Nick wanted to get this done in every way possible.

It's almost ten p.m. when we're told a small crew will return to the site early Sunday to complete the recovery. The bodies will be off the mountain by noon. I know I need to be present when Greg and Walker are brought out of Garnet Canyon.

Jocelyn suggests we follow her back to Jackson. We accept her offer. I am in no frame of mind to navigate the drive to Jackson in the dark with elk along the road and an image of Greg buried in the snow searing in my brain and tearing at my heart.

Greg was always ready for a road trip—from age one onward.
Getting in some early climbing practice too!

Greg with his new baby brother, Chris, January 1982.

We couldn't keep Greg off the ladder.
He wanted to climb even at twenty months.

Greg's first summit? On the monkey
bars in our yard, July 1983.

We put him in this tree, and he
liked the atmosphere up there,
September 1983.

Greg rock climbing at Whiskey Gulch near Whitehall, Montana, in 2007.

Greg climbing the Bearcrack with Joel
Anderson in East Rosebud Valley near
Red Lodge Montana, June 2006.

Ice climbing on Jeff's Right in Hyalite Canyon, near Bozeman, Montana, in 2010.

Summit shot of Greg, Grand Teton, July 2005.

The smile on Greg's face proclaimed the joy he experienced after a back-country ski in Grand Teton National Park, July 2005.

Chris and Greg with Grandpa and Grandma Seftick and Grandma and Grandpa Drazich, summer 1983.

Here's one of our favorite early pictures of Greg. He looks very contemplative at age four, leaning against a birch tree in our front yard, almost looking into the future.

Greg and Chris in Sue's handmade Superman and doctor costumes, Halloween 1983.

Greg in the process of making donuts with his mom and Chris, 1985.

Greg's first day of kindergarten, as he gets on the bus with our neighbor Joanna King, fall 1984.

Greg and Dan after returning home from Game 7 of the
1987 World Series.

Greg's backyard quinzee, 1991.

Role reversal—Chris on the sax while Greg plays Chris's trumpet, 1994.

Sue, Chris, Lady, Greg, and Dan at a party celebrating our twentieth wedding anniversary, August 1995.

Greg with his proud parents at the Stillwater Area High School Awards Ceremony, where he was awarded the Palmer-Rathert Medical Scholarship, 1998.

Chris and Greg during the open house to celebrate Greg's
graduation from high school, 1998.

Our family hike to Harney Peak in the Black Hills,
the highest point in South Dakota, August 1998.

Greg with his Grandma and Grandpa Drazich at his
St. Olaf graduation, May 2002.

Greg and his friend Pete Buchholz,
St. Olaf College graduation, May 2002.

Greg and Chris playing around near Beartooth Pass, Montana, 2004.

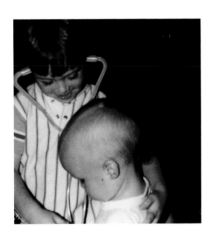

Four-year-old Dr. Greg and his first patient, his little brother Chris.

(Below) Greg receives his white coat at the University of Minnesota Medical School, October 2003.

Greg with Aunt Jan, Sue, Uncle Scott, and Grandma Drazich after the White Coat Ceremony at the University of Minnesota Medical School, October 2003.

Sue, Greg, and Dan at his graduation from the University of Minnesota Medical School, May 2007.

Greg feeling very comfortable at his med-school graduation, May 2007.

Pete Buchholz, Greg, Brian Junnila, Nick St. Ores, and Mike
Danaher after Greg's med-school graduation, May 2007.

Greg's reaction to performing the supposedly impossible intubation at Sim Lab, October 2009. After which he was told, "You realize you've ruined the entire morning's exercise!"

Greg receiving his residency diploma from Dr. Joseph Minardi and Dr. Hollynn Larrabee, Morgantown, West Virginia, June 2010.

Megan, Greg, John Hanowell, and Lisa Kreutz at the
residency banquet, June 2010.

Greg and Chris skiing over spring break at Bridger Bowl,
Montana, March 2001.

Our family trip to Alaska, August 2002.

Greg (taking the picture) with his friends Jason Cline and Joel Menssen at the Northwest String Summit, Horning's Hideout in North Plains, Oregon, July 2005.

Sue and Greg on the trail to Mirror Lake, Montana, 2004.

(Below) Greg climbing in the Beartooth Mountains, Montana, 2006.

Greg visiting with Aunt Sally, Detroit, December 2006.

Route finding in his favorite place, the Tetons, June 2007.

Chris, Greg, and Joel Menssen on the Cowen Summit,
Montana, August 30, 2007.

A more challenging summit—Greg and Sue on Hyalite Peak,
September 5, 2007.

Cousin Kaity,
Greg, and Megan
at Coopers Rock,
near Morgantown,
West Virginia,
May 2008.

Greg and Sue at Coopers Rock, near Morgantown,
West Virginia, September 28, 2009.

Greg and Megan in Winchester, Virginia,
at Apple Blossom Festival, May 2, 2010.

(Below) Greg and Chris on the summit of
Mount Rainier, May 2010.

Our last family photo, after Grandma Drazich's eighty-fifth birthday party, Proctor, Minnesota, November 2010.

A reproduction of Allison McGree's tribute painting *Wildcat*, framed for the Gregory E. Seftick, MD, Resident Lounge, at the West Virginia University Department of Emergency Medicine.

Residents' lounge plaque, Department of Emergency Medicine,
West Virginia University Hospitals.

Candles lit for the first Greg's Night of Light at home in Afton,
April 16, 2012.

Greg's friends from the St. Olaf class of 2002 gather on campus for their ten-year reunion and the dedication of a bench and tree in honor of Greg, June 2, 2012.

At the sacred ground—our first hike to Garnet Canyon, Grand Teton National Park, August 2011. Left to right: Chris Harder, Allison Armitage, Nick Armitage, Chris, Jesse, and Sue.

At the sacred ground—our second hike to Garnet Canyon, Grand Teton National Park, July 2012. Front row: Sue. Middle row: Luke Oltrogge, Kendra Kuhl (Walker's sister), Pete Buchholz, Mitch Diers, Kees Van de Wege, and Joel Menssen. Top row: Joel Anderson and Anya Fiechtl.

At the sacred ground—another hike to Garnet Canyon, Grand Teton National Park, August 5, 2013. Left to right: John Hanowell, Megan Webb, Rick Seftick, Chris, and Megan Hamilton.

24

ONE ON ONE WITH GREG

WOW! All done with residency. It sure feels weird, and really scary. This may be the last time for a very long time that I journal. There will be some big changes in my life coming in the next year or two.

—JULY 1, 2010, Afton, Minnesota

Memories of family and friends are treasures. Memories of deceased loved ones are priceless. We hold tight to them because they're all we have left. The very personal memories, the one-on-ones, hold special meaning because of their intimate nature. Those belong to only two of us, and now one of us is gone. I regret there were too few occasions Greg and I spent alone together, but the handful of memories keep him present. They occupy the highest place in my heart.

Some fathers and sons take regular camping, fishing, or hunting trips or have some other time-sharing ritual. Greg and I didn't have a tradition like that. Our infrequent camping weekends were family events. Greg and Chris weren't crazy about camping as young children. Maybe our state park visits were too tame for them. We stopped camping when they became active in sports and our schedules filled with practices and games. It was difficult to find time for things beyond planned activities, traditional visits to family, and the occasional special vacation.

Some things Greg and I did together, just the two of us, were pretty amazing, special events while others were ordinary things that have become extraordinary since Greg died—the 1987 World Series Game 7, a day spent painting, a ride, an exhibit, and packing for a move. These can't be repeated.

It's a little strange to talk about attending Game 7 of a World Series as something Greg and I did alone. The Metrodome was packed on October 25, 1987, for the final game of the Minnesota Twins World Series with the St. Louis Cardinals. We had two tickets for all four home games. Since I'd attended the 1968 World Series in Detroit, Sue and Greg went to the first game. We gave the tickets for the next game to friends who also had a son very interested in baseball. Although Chris came to regular season games with us, at age five he was more interested in the food than the action on the field. So Greg and I attended the sixth game, which the Twins won to force a climactic final contest. Then our family had a decision to make. Even though Greg was only eight years old, Sue thought he and I should be the ones to use that last pair of tickets.

Greg watched Twins baseball with me almost from birth. We sat in front of the TV, freeing Sue up to do other things. It was my way of babysitting. Sue often sang "Take Me Out to the Ballgame" to baby Greg. It was his favorite lullaby.

He was a good T-ball player because he understood the game. He wasn't faster, stronger, or more talented than other kids his age, but if he was told to play second base, he knew to go to the position, not to the bag.

I remember one good play he made at age eight. Playing second base, he ranged to his left to field a grounder, allowed his momentum to carry him into right field and turn him completely around, and made a perfect toss to first for the out. It wasn't something I or a coach taught him at that age. He'd seen it on TV, understood the mechanics, and adopted it for future use.

Greg listened to and watched Twins games, learned strategy, followed the standings and statistics, and collected and traded baseball cards with Ryan Pederson. He wanted to play well and improve. When he didn't, he got discouraged. It was the same for him as a spectator. He loved to see the Twins win and hated to see them lose. He was so excited when the team won their division title in 1987 and went on to beat the Detroit Tigers to advance to the 1987 World Series.

As hard as it was to believe, there we were in the Metrodome's upper deck in left-field seats for Game 7 of the World Series! It was a close, exciting game. Greg and I cheered until we were hoarse. There were some anxious moments, during which Greg was every bit as nervous as I was. The Twins took the field in the top of the ninth with a 4–2 lead. The place was rocking! We were laughing, smiling, cheering, and sweating out every pitch. I can still see the ground ball to third, Gary Gaetti scooping it up, and making a perfect throw across the diamond to Kent Hrbek at first base for the third out. The Twins had won the World Series—and Greg and I were there.

Greg was jumping up and down like a madman. I had tears in my eyes. I don't know if I was happy the Twins won or overjoyed to see my son so ecstatic. We stayed there in our seats for a long time. Well, we never sat down, just stood there. The players came back out and made a lap around the field, waving and cheering with the fans. What a night for an eight-year-old! I think Greg found out that night how it feels to have your heroes succeed.

We finally made our way out of the stadium and into the cool, fall evening air. There was no hurry to get to the car. The streets were lined with cars essentially parked in the road. Drivers and passengers leaned out car windows screaming and waving Homer Hankies and pennants. Soon we were in our car and stopped in the street with everyone else. It was very slow going, but we didn't care.

I looked over at Greg. If ever there was a picture of joy, it was there in the front passenger seat. I'm not sure what inspired me to say it, but I told Greg he'd remember this night for the rest of his life. Maybe it was because I still remembered attending Games 3 and 5 of the 1968 World Series between Detroit and St. Louis. He just smiled.

"You know, Greg, there's only one thing better than seeing your team win Game 7 of a World Series."

"What?" he asked, still smiling.

"Seeing your team win Game 7 with your eight-year-old son."

He beamed.

I meant it, and I still cherish that night. If I was right, and he did remember that game for the rest of his life, he didn't have enough years to do so.

A later one-on-one day with Greg wasn't nearly as significant, exciting, or even fun, but it did mark a different stage of our father-son relationship. When Greg was a senior at St. Olaf, after living in dorms his first three years, he and four other guys planned to live off campus in a house. Some of their St. Olaf friends had lived in the same house the year before. In fact, there was a tradition of continuity among the residents of this rental unit. Friends of seniors living at the house would spend time there during their junior year and sort of inherit the house for the next year. The owner lived out of state, and it probably made life simpler for her not to have to advertise for renters every summer. Of course, the house had something of a reputation. As we helped Greg move in, Sue asked to use the bathroom. Greg suggested, "Mom, you may want to drive down to the gas station on the corner and use the one there." Even this bat-infested, inefficiently heated rental was fine with him.

During September, Greg mentioned that it would be nice to paint his room. I asked if he was allowed to paint the place. "It's OK," he told me. "The landlady will knock money off the rent for any supplies purchased for improvements." I offered to buy the paint and supplies and come down to help him. He looked surprised and asked, "Are you serious?" I assured him I was. We scheduled our day of painting for a Saturday in late September.

It was a big job. We painted the ceilings, the walls, and even the trim. Everything was painted white. But it made a big difference. The room was much brighter, and the new coat of paint made everything look cleaner. Well, everything except the carpet.

We worked all day, starting with Greg's second-floor bedroom, then moving on to an adjacent sitting room that included the stairway. As evening set in, we continued painting the walls of the unlit stairway in an attempt to finish off the paint. Finally, Greg decided we should use every last drop and paint the steps.

When the paint ran out, I was tired. I had bought cheap brushes and roller covers, so we just gathered everything as trash and didn't worry about cleanup. We collapsed on the couch, and Greg brought out beers. We had some pizza and another beer. Greg thanked me and gave me a hug, and I left for home.

We worked hard to get everything done in a single long day. But we worked side by side and had a chance to be together and talk. It was probably the longest conversation I ever had alone with Greg. No rush, no agenda, no arguing. It was just a really great day, and I knew it. I left with a good feeling, thinking about how there would be many more such days spent together working on projects. My dad and I had shared days like that, and now I'd begun sharing some with my son. There wouldn't be as many in our future as I imagined driving home from Northfield that September night in 2001.

I had another opportunity to do something unexpected for Greg in June 2004. He purchased tickets for two days of music—I don't remember what bands—at Alpine Valley Music Theatre in southeastern Wisconsin. Greg had a med-school final the morning of the first day of the concert, but his friends and brother, Chris, were leaving early. He didn't want to drive alone after studying most of the night and then taking the exam. So I offered him a ride.

I had plans to go to Michigan to help my aunt in Detroit anyway, so I adjusted my schedule and welcomed Greg's company for part of the trip. Greg was ready to sleep when he got in the car on campus. After his nap, Greg caught me up on his first year of med school. I could tell he was relieved it was over and was looking forward to a break. We exited I-90 southeast of Madison, then proceeded on state highways and county roads.

Greg had been to a concert at Alpine once before, so I didn't plot a specific route to the venue. I was counting on him for directions. Bad assumption! We drove past it, doubled back when we hit I-43, then turned on an unmarked road because Greg was "pretty sure" it was the right way. Several miles later, traffic volume increased and we found an Alpine sign. I dropped Greg at the parking lot road, and we said our good-byes. It was a more complicated drive than I'd expected.

I hadn't gone very far when I glanced down at the floor between the front seats in the van and spotted a spiral notebook, Greg's journal. I couldn't really backtrack at that point and became concerned Greg might be disappointed with himself that he'd left it behind. That was the sort of minor oversight that a few years earlier would have bothered him. I needn't have worried. I wasn't giving my son enough credit. Greg never was upset he left the notebook in the van, which told me he was maturing. Med school was helping him prove to himself that he had what it took to succeed.

Looking through Greg's things after his death, I came across his journal entries about this road trip. He wrote that he had a great time and appreciated the ride to Alpine. His ticket stub from the show and a recording of the performance were with his possessions. When I listen to the recording, I enjoy the playlist—and I feel more connected with Greg, knowing I was a small part of his experience at Alpine.

In 2006, an exhibit titled *Body Worlds* was on display at the Science Museum of Minnesota in St. Paul. Sue and I attended during the summer, and it was impressive. A German doctor developed a process called plastination to preserve entire human bodies, sections of the body, or parts of the body for display and study. The preserved specimens were displayed in various poses to depict a certain body system, such as the muscular system, in action. The observer could see the muscles involved in the action. It was fascinating even to someone with limited anatomical knowledge.

Sue and I were intrigued by the individual displays. During the last few weeks of the extended exhibit, she suggested I invite Greg to attend with me. He enthusiastically accepted. We met at the museum and made our way to the exhibit. I assumed Greg wouldn't be overly impressed, given his knowledge of anatomy. He was well into his fourth year of med school, and had seen and studied most aspects of the human body.

I was wrong. Greg was impressed with the number and quality of the displays. He was intrigued by the variously configured bodies. We looked causally at the first few displays and thoroughly read the descriptions. He pointed out minor features too obscure for me to observe. From time to time, I'd look at him rather than the display. I could tell he was intrigued, taking it all in. More than once he uttered his familiar "hmm," which was my cue to ask what he'd noticed. He'd carefully explain the interesting feature in simple terms, followed with "I didn't realize it looked like that" or "So that's how that works."

Most of the displays were set up for attendees to view the body from every side. But some required a concerted effort to observe from a particular angle. Several times I found Greg crouched behind a display observing from a contorted position at an angle of interest only to him. I had to smile. I was pleased Greg was finding this informative.

Initially we moved from display to display together. Suddenly, Greg would be gone. I might have drifted on, or Greg might have become engrossed in a particular feature, not unexpected considering the considerable discrepancy in our levels of knowledge.

Greg observed various contracting and flexing muscles. He mimicked the action with one side of his body, maybe in a rock-climbing mode, and then checked his own muscle response with his opposite hand. I realized how much he already knew about the body.

I asked him questions along the way. He answered each one patiently and plainly, making sure I understood. I did, but often required further explanation to really get it. Most times he provided way more information than required. I was impressed.

Apparently others near us were impressed too. Following one of Greg's explanations, a woman interrupted and asked Greg a question. She apologized, saying she hoped Greg didn't mind. He answered to her satisfaction. I was proud of him, not for knowing the answer, but in the way he handled the situation. He was happy to share his knowledge.

He also handled himself with humility. After Greg answered a question from another exhibit attendee, the woman asked Greg if he was a doctor. He replied, "No, just a med student." This was a true statement. But it was delivered in a way to indicate he felt he had accomplished nothing and was nobody special. That wasn't how I saw it as I looked at the displays with him as a proud father.

Greg was approached multiple times during our tour. At one display, he was explaining something to me and I noticed several bystanders leaning in to listen. The hall was crowded and noisy. It was difficult to hear even the person right next to you. I wondered if others in the crowd thought tour guides were available to explain displays.

Among this small crowd of interested people, someone asked Greg about a previous display and invited him to go back for a more complete verbal and visual explanation. Greg gladly went back to the other body. I think he was enjoying himself. He soon returned, and we continued on as if nothing happened.

Greg thanked me as we parted company that evening and headed home—Greg to his apartment in the Uptown neighborhood of Minneapolis, me back to Afton. When I asked if he enjoyed the exhibit, he replied, "That was really cool, Dad. Thanks." Always the "thanks."

My final and longest one-on-one with Greg occurred just a couple of months before he died. He was preparing to move to Montana, and Sue suggested that I ask Greg if he'd like help packing and cleaning his apartment. He accepted.

Sue and I planned to drive to Detroit in mid-February 2011, for my aunt's ninetieth birthday. She offered to fly back to Minnesota, so I dropped her at the Detroit airport and drove southeast to West Virginia.

I arrived about four in the afternoon, but had to wake Greg to get into his apartment. He greeted me with pleasant words and a big hug, then asked if I minded if he caught another hour of sleep before work. I sprawled on his futon and napped too. It had been an early morning, and I was beat after an almost four-hundred-mile drive.

Greg needed to eat before work. He loved Buddy's Pizza from Detroit, so I brought one for dinner. Greg messed around in the kitchen as I sat on the futon. We talked. He was in good spirits, looking forward to his move west to fulfill his lifelong dream.

After a couple of minutes, I smelled smoke in the apartment. Greg opened the oven door and said, "Oh, I suppose you should take the pizza out of the box before you put it in the oven." We laughed, and I commented that it would be safer. It was another of his scatterbrain moments. He eventually warmed up the pizza without burning down the apartment. He later headed down to Megan's apartment and soon returned laughing. Megan had opened the door, sniffed, and asked, "Greg, why do you smell like a campfire?"

Greg left for work just before six. It was a warm evening, so I took a long walk through a residential neighborhood east of the apartment. I walked briskly in the fading light through this unfamiliar area, reminiscing about our visits during Greg's time here in Morgantown and recalling all that had changed for him.

I was awake when Greg returned home after his shift the next morning. He wanted a few hours of sleep, so he sent me in search of moving boxes and a lock for his rented storage unit. I was happy to have an assignment.

The storage facility was next to the apartment complex. We didn't worry about efficiency and often transported half-full carloads. We piled things in his Rendezvous, drove out of the apartment complex onto Collins Ferry Road, drove a hundred feet, and turned into the storage facility.

We made good progress. Greg packed the things from the kitchen, bedroom, and living room he wouldn't take with him, including random furniture items. We disassembled his bed and moved it to storage. He planned to sleep on a small mattress in Montana until he was more settled with a job and an apartment.

The most unique feature of his apartment was Greg's self-installed climbing grips, a row of lumber bolted to the apartment beam and walls. Holes of various shapes and depths had been drilled and carved into the boards to serve as finger grips. Greg would jump up and get a grab, then maneuver across the boards without release until he navigated the entire span. He practiced climbing and gained strength, but mostly relieved the stress of the day doing something he loved.

It was well into evening before we called it a day. Most of the dishes, glasses, pots and pans, silverware, and nonperishable food were packed. The kitchen cabinets were nearly empty. The bedroom and living room were a shambles. The items that weren't packed and moved already were in boxes or in sorting piles on the floor.

Greg took me out for dinner, a couple of beers, and good conversation. I cautioned him about moving toward a goal, not running away from something. Only he could say which he was doing in this move. He almost too casually brushed off my concerns.

The next day was much the same, but with an earlier start. Shortly after noon, Greg suggested we run an errand and get some lunch. We stopped at a little hot-dog shop for a quick lunch. He was excited to take me there. We each enjoyed a couple of dogs. I thought about how Greg was satisfied with this lunch when he could have afforded to eat anything he wanted. That was Greg. He praised the simple lunch as he inhaled his coneys and repeatedly commented, "Tasty!"

We got back to packing and moving boxes to storage. When Greg ran an errand, I decided to clean his bathroom. There was a lot of mold in the tub. I found some bleach in the apartment and went at the mold. It cleaned up really well. The exhaust fan was running, but the fumes were overwhelming. I felt a definite sense of accomplishment when I looked over the clean bathroom. Greg returned and was impressed. He thanked me repeatedly for my effort.

We knocked off earlier than the day before to have dinner with Megan. It was great to see her again. She talked about her final year of med school, her residency interviews, and the selection process. Her anticipation was growing as Match Day, the day she'd know where she'd spend her residency, approached. Megan told stories about Tevia, who knew me from previous visits and from the month Sue and I cat-sat in July 2010. That dinner reassured me Greg was leaving on good terms with Megan, even though their relationship had changed. Maybe he was moving toward something instead of running away after all.

Greg needed to get up early the next morning for work, his final day at St. Joseph's. It made sense for me to get up and head home as he left for work. It would give me an early start on the long drive. Given our morning plan, we didn't stay up late after our dinner with Megan. We were both tired. There was still a lot to do before the apartment was emptied; I thought we should have done more. Greg told me how much he appreciated my visit and all we'd accomplished, but I felt guilty leaving.

As we were leaving, I realized I hadn't taken a picture of Greg. I had taken a few pictures of his apartment as a remembrance, but Greg was gone each time I did. He reluctantly agreed. He wasn't happy about it. His usual big smile was missing. It's the last picture of him we have. I wish it was a better one. I treasure it nonetheless.

We got in our cars and drove off, Greg to Buckhannon and me to Minnesota. I thought it would be the last time I would be in Morgantown. The place was special to us. Greg had matured as a man and as a doctor here. Sue and I met some fantastic people. The entire experience at West Virginia University Hospitals seemed to have been so positive for Greg. He had become part of their family. We had all discovered some beautiful places to enjoy hiking, climbing, and relaxing in the area.

But Sue and I did return, in eight months, to attend the dedication of the residents' lounge and to empty out the same storage unit Greg and I had started filling.

As I drove away from Greg's apartment in Morgantown on February 17, 2011, I had no idea that in two months, Greg would be dead. The packing we'd done in those two days was our final project together, my final one-on-one with my son.

25

WORKING TOGETHER

My story here continues on to what was the greatest accomplishment for me for the summer, soloing the Middle Teton Glacier to the Dike Couloir.

—JUNE 14, 2007, Grand Teton National Park, Wyoming

I've always thought young people should have one job they hate so much it inspires them to get more training and education. My first job in a Chevrolet factory was manual labor, working with heavy, forged parts on grinders and conveyor belts near heat-treat furnaces. After my summer at the factory, I knew I'd finish college.

Most young people today don't need the encouragement I did fifty years ago. Greg didn't. But his first job in a supermarket certainly didn't discourage him from higher education. He lamented, "I clean bathrooms on warm, sunny days and retrieve carts in the parking lot on rainy days." His working life had started in high school as a ski instructor at Afton Alps. After graduation from high school, he worked on a boat, at a marina, in a chemical laboratory, and in a nursing home. He also had a lab stint at Imation, my employer. We didn't work on the same projects or in the same department, but we were physically in the same building and our paths occasionally crossed.

We rode to work together and sometimes ate lunch together. We had daily opportunities to discuss new commonalities—mutual colleagues, and technology and chemistry on an applied basis rather than a theoretical one. I got to know Greg and shared life with him in a totally new relationship, as equals.

Early in 2000, I had asked Greg if he'd be interested in working at Imation. I wasn't sure how he'd respond. He looked at me like I was insane. "Why wouldn't I want to work with you?"

I offered to investigate if anything was available. My knowledge of our intern program was limited. Things had changed since the company spun off from 3M. As a new, smaller company, programs and procedures were still evolving. I visited the human-resources person supporting our group and asked about a summer job for my son. Fortunately, at that time, the procedure was simple and relatively unstructured. Internships were available, I was told. In fact, a new request had just come in from Len Swanson in the chemical stockroom. Len was a friend, a colleague I enjoyed working with.

I told Greg about the job and answered his questions as best I could. I stressed that his potential supervisor was a great guy, and that I believed Greg would enjoy working for him. Greg filled out the application and provided the requested résumé.

I also visited Len and said, "I heard you're looking for a summer intern."

"How did you know?" he asked. "I just submitted the request a few days ago."

I told him about Greg and mentioned that HR had his application. Throughout our careers, we often talked about our children. Len felt he already knew Greg. Other pieces of the puzzle fell into place, and soon Greg had the job.

Greg's hiring at Imation completed a circle in my life. My dad helped me land a summer job at Chevy the year I graduated from high school. Now I'd done the same for Greg. I had carried on the tradition, done my parental duty, just as my own father did for me.

Greg was hired to conduct a chemical inventory in our labs. There was a system in place to check out chemicals from the stock room and track them. After a while, things weren't where the system indicated. Greg would visit each lab and collect data to rectify the accounting with current reality. It was a project that could easily be completed in a summer.

Greg fit right in. What else should I have expected? He got to know colleagues with whom I'd spent a good part of my career—chemists, physicists, and engineers. He was genuinely interested in their backgrounds and research. He became more interested in my work and asked many questions during the summer to better understand my responsibilities.

We had a number of younger technical people on staff. They were new to Imation, not part of the 3M spinoff. Greg got to know them. Since they were closer to his age, they had more in common, more to discuss beyond shoptalk. This benefited me because, through Greg, I got to know them better than if he hadn't been there. Knowing these young colleagues definitely helped me in the years ahead, though the number of those years were fewer than expected. Imation eliminated my job only three years later and sent me packing at age fifty-six.

Greg got right into the inventory project, scanning bar codes on each container and transferring data to a computer file. In no time he was looking for other things to do. He connected with a chemist working on organic compounds used in our products. This gentleman became a mentor to Greg, not only that summer, but for another two years. The job was going well. Greg had a great opportunity to make money for tuition, gain some experience in a corporate lab, and work with experienced scientists. I learned my son was a very capable employee and a diligent worker. I was proud of him.

Most importantly, I was happy for Greg. Knowing his work was appreciated had to be a tremendous boost to his self-confidence. He came into a work environment as an unknown and proved he could do the job. I know my colleagues had expectations because they knew me. Then again, because they knew me, maybe they didn't expect much from Greg! Anyway—he exceeded expectations.

Greg's first summer at Imation was passing quickly, and he still hadn't inventoried the lab where I did most of my work. Driving to work one Monday, he informed me, "I'll be in your lab this week."

"I'll organize things for you," I offered.

"That isn't necessary," he said.

He showed up in the lab one afternoon while I was running an experiment. I expected he would get started and complete the process the next morning. I showed him the various cabinets containing chemicals, and he briskly got to work while I returned to my experiment.

Greg moved through the lab quickly. Some items didn't scan properly. Others weren't coded. He noted these inconsistencies and continued the process.

A couple of hours later, he announced, "That's it!"

"You're done already?" I asked, surprised.

"It isn't that complicated, and you didn't have that much to go through."

Greg headed back to his desk on the first floor. I completed my work in the lab for the day and returned to my desk. Greg showed up at four thirty, ready to go home. He was always very punctual about quitting time, especially that first summer. We talked about his inventory work in my lab as I wrapped up the day. Greg was very matter-of-fact about carrying out his duties and getting the project completed. But for me, working professionally side by side that brief part of one day was special.

In addition to completing his inventory project, Greg established a good working relationship with Stan in the organic chemistry lab and was invited back the next summer. Greg's skills and confidence grew even more in his second summer at Imation. He was gaining an understanding of the chemistry and a feel for working in research. He appreciated this opportunity to experience a corporate setting, and he was earning good money toward his college tuition—but he knew his future was in medicine.

Stan received approval for Greg to work up to ten hours a week through the end of 2001, and Greg's class schedule provided a day free of classes. He left campus after his last class of the day and either drove directly to work to put in two or three hours or home for dinner and access to free laundry equipment. In either case, Greg would spend a night at home and then go to work the next day. After a full day in the lab, he had the option of dinner at home or heading back to campus. He followed this routine during spring semester as well. Greg benefited in several ways. He earned extra money and built strong connections with talented people at Imation. This strengthened his résumé, added to his work history, and provided another source for letters of recommendation for med-school applications. Not to mention, Sue and I enjoyed extra days with Greg we otherwise would have missed.

After graduation from St. Olaf, Greg was hired again for the summer of 2002. He worked for three months and studied in preparation for the MCAT. It was the only time Greg was OK with staying in Minnesota, delaying his move to the mountains. After he took the MCAT in August, he quit his job at Imation, as planned. Then the house emptied out quickly. We went from having both sons at home to an empty nest. Greg and Chris moved into a four-bedroom apartment in Bozeman with two other guys. It was a great arrangement and the beginning of a closer and stronger brotherly bond for our sons.

Since Greg's death, I treasure the extra time we spent together on the work commute, casual lunches at my desk, and the brief interaction in the lab that afternoon. I never expected our careers would follow similar paths, overlap, or even cross after those summers Greg worked at Imation. But I liked the idea of sharing our memories of those days in the years to come. Now I won't have the pleasure of learning how Greg's perception of those summers would have changed as he matured and grew in his chosen field.

26

THE FINAL DESCENT

I hate how much pressure I put on myself to produce on these trips,
but I can relax when I am old.

—MAY 14, 2007, Disappointment Peak, Grand Teton National Park, Wyoming

And somehow the sun is rising in the east this Sunday morning, April 24, 2011. Today is my sixty-third birthday. Christians around the globe gather to celebrate the Rising of the Son, for it is Easter Sunday. Today my son and his friend Walker will be raised from their snowy graves. From this day forward, Resurrection Day will have new meaning for me.

Sue and other family console me, regretting that Greg's body will be recovered on my birthday. Under the circumstances, I think it is the best gift I can be given. I realize my birthday will never be celebrated or remembered in the same way. This isn't my birthday anymore. April 24 has become Greg's Resurrection Day.

I'm torn that morning between attending mass and being in the park to witness the transport of Greg's body off the mountain. Sue supports either choice. Initially my inclination is to go to church. There I'll be able to pray in union with others. There is nothing I can do in Grand Teton National Park. We intentionally arrive at church early. At first I feel called to be here, at a church named Our Lady of the Mountains. I kneel in prayer and contemplation knowing life has changed. As others arrive, I feel out of place. There is too much joy here. Families are dressed in their best new clothes in a celebratory mood. I know I don't belong here. My place is with Greg, as close as I can be, at least. Today the Tetons will be my cathedral, the Grand will be my cross, Garnet Canyon the tomb of resurrection.

We drive the short distance back to the motel, change clothes, and head to the park's Incident Command Post to meet Terry Roper. The crew in Garnet Canyon has dug through the remaining eight feet of snow and reached the bodies. The recovery is about to happen.

Terry drives us farther into the park and turns and stops at the end of the road to the American Alpine Club Climbers' Ranch, today's helicopter landing site. Chris Harder had informed us that the weight of the snow and ice might have caused some distortion of Greg's face as it froze. It might not look natural. We accept his advice to keep our distance, despite how badly I want to see my son and hold him, even though I'd only be holding his lifeless body.

As soon as we stop, we see the chopper rise above the ridgeline in Garnet Canyon. Then, ever so slowly and reverently, the sling hanging at the end of the fixed-length line suspended from the helicopter comes into view. Walker and Greg will be descending the mountain in a way they never wanted and certainly hadn't foreseen last week. If all had gone well, they would've been nearing the summit of the Grand at about this exact time a week earlier. My stomach knots.

The chopper heads north and northeast, and then disappears briefly behind the peaks beyond the canyon. I impatiently wait for it to return into view. After it emerges on the northeast side of the Grand, it banks south, and heads toward us with the precious cargo. I don't know why it returns by this circuitous route. I reason that the pilot, Nicole Ludwig, and the SAR team want to give Walker and Greg a final tour of their original objective. But there's probably a logistical reason. The entire flight takes maybe ten minutes. It seems like an eternity.

The chopper hovers above the landing site and slowly and gently decreases altitude. The sling line goes slack. We know Greg and Walker are on the ground. They have completed their final descent. Nicole lands briefly to release the fixed-length line, then guides the helicopter away from the drop zone and heads off for a final flight to Garnet Canyon for the remaining SAR members, the last group left to shuttle off the mountain. Nicole has brought Greg home to us. She flew numerous runs shuttling men, women, dogs, and equipment during the search. There were no issues, no injuries. Everyone on the SAR team worked hard, and they're safe. This is an important part of the search, one we take very seriously and for which we are most grateful.

I want to be at Greg's side so badly, but I stay with Sue and Terry in the vehicle and wait. Soon Chris Harder arrives at the car. He says, "The bodies have been successfully recovered from the campsite in Garnet Canyon. The coroner is performing his initial investigation and making observations. Nick Armitage will be by shortly to speak with you. The coroner will also stop on his way back to town to discuss the schedule for the rest of the day."

After Chris leaves, Nick approaches the car. We owe him so much. He performed heroically and selflessly yesterday, as has the entire SAR team. He briefly tells us a little more about the recovery and his part in it, how important this effort is to him, how determined he has been to find Walker and Greg during this main search effort so we don't leave Jackson without knowing Greg's fate. We know his words are sincere. What do you say to someone who led the effort in the field to find your son? We don't have to say anything. Nick knows what this means and senses our pain and relief. I realize then that Nick, Chris, Terry, Scott, Elizabeth, Bonnie, and the others are now a permanent part of my life. They are my friends, my Teton family. I will see them again.

The coroner arrives. He stops by Terry's car to tell us Greg and Walker will be transported to Valley Mortuary in Jackson. He asks to meet at two thirty, then leaves down the road by which we entered. Terry backs out and follows. We stop at the Incident Command Post and go to our rental car. I feel numb. My thoughts are not logical. I don't thank anyone. I don't think it is required now, even though we won't be back in the park again this trip. We arrived with hope and fear. We leave with only heartache. Sue and I drive to Jackson.

Chris and Jesse are waiting in the Angler Motel parking lot. Chris looks as numb as I feel. He says nothing, just stares blankly at the ground. We hug and cry. Walker's family is also here. They'll meet with the coroner at the mortuary at one thirty. It is already after one, so they'll be leaving soon. We make plans to reconnect at the motel after we return from our meetings with the coroner. We also introduce everyone to Jocelyn and her kids.

Soon it's just Chris, Jesse, Sue, and me. Our family. Right now, this is our family. It doesn't feel right. Someone is missing. How can this be? Why should it be like this? What did I do wrong? So many questions without answers. We sit here together and yet it feels like each of us is alone. Just alone.

The four of us arrive at Valley Mortuary at two thirty to meet with Sheriff Dave Hodges, deputy coroner for Teton County. A female deputy is also present. Sheriff Hodges reviews his findings. Greg and Walker were found in their tent in a sleeping position. There was no sign of struggle, no anxiety or fear on their faces. It appears they died instantly, or very nearly instantly. This is corroborated by the fact there was no "ice mask" around either Greg or Walker's mouths. Ice masks form as warm, moist exhaled air is cooled by ambient air (for example, the frost that forms on a scarf covering a mouth and nose). No ice mask indicates Greg wasn't breathing after being buried in the avalanche.

Sheriff Hodges then reviews his findings as they will appear on Greg's death certificate. The manner of death is "accidental." The cause of death is "asphyxiation." We ask what will be listed as Greg's date of death. Sheriff Hodges indicates they'll write "April 24, 2011 (found)," since the actual date of death is undetermined. There's no way to know if Walker and Greg died on April 16, before midnight, or April 17, after midnight. Sue doesn't like the thought of my birth date also being the date on Greg's death certificate. I tell her I have no objection. Getting Greg back is all that matters to me now.

As the coroner reviews these details, I keep wondering who he's talking about and why we're here. Greg can't be dead. This is all wrong. So much just never sinks in. I'm somewhere else, because I certainly shouldn't be here. But I am. Greg is dead. There must be a way to make me understand, to make me accept it, to prove it to me. That will come shortly.

After the official paperwork is discussed and completed, we talk less formally about the accident. Sheriff Hodges assures us Greg and Walker did nothing wrong. They used good judgment, but sometimes that isn't enough. The other officer tells us she had camped at the exact spot where Greg and Walker died only two weeks ago. She says she always considered that area, Garnet Canyon, to be safe. She'll never feel that way again. Why did Greg and Walker have to be the ones to change people's opinions of that area?

Chris has been quiet throughout the entire meeting. I worry about him. I'm dealing with all this official stuff only because I feel obligated to do it. I certainly don't want to be doing it.

Sheriff Hodges asks if we'd like to see Greg. I say yes, but immediately realize if I see him, I'll know he is dead. I won't be seeing Greg, only his body, the shell of who Greg was. My heart breaks.

We walk through the door into the adjoining room. Greg is lying there, covered with a sheet except for his head and face. My son! How can this be? He was so gifted. He had so much to offer. He could have helped so many people. He worked so hard to get to this point. It makes no sense for him to die here, to die now. Others have less to contribute to society, to the world, to the betterment of mankind.

Sue and I walk up to Greg. Chris and Jesse stay back. Now I can see Greg is dead. Or is he? After all, he's frozen. Maybe if we just let him thaw out, he'll be good as new. I know it isn't possible, but I still want him to wake up, to flash his big grin at us and ask us why we're all crying.

There are no signs of trauma, just as we'd been told. His head and face aren't deformed or unnatural at all. Now I wish I'd been at the heli landing site after all. But he is cold. We gently roll back the sheet covering him to reveal his arms and chest. His arms look muscular and solid, just as I remember them. His hands are cracked. There are numerous small cut-like cracks on the backs of his hands and on several fingers, probably the result of the freezing and drying out of his body. It is terrifying to see Greg lying here. But he looks to be at peace. That provides only small consolation.

Sue and I look at Greg, talk to him, touch him, hug him, and kiss him. Then we move from our dead son to our living son. Chris is still silent. He and Jesse walk up to Greg. I can't begin to understand how Chris feels, but I know I feel immense sadness and fear for him, even through my own pangs of hurt and loss. His only brother is dead. His future is as uncertain as ours. In some ways, Chris's future is more changed than mine. He planned on many years with his brother, many good times, many adventures in the coming years and in the more distant future after Sue and I would be dead. Now he's alone in this journey. Chris, like us, has lost part of his future.

After a while, Jesse moves back to join us. Chris, alone with his brother, bends over and whispers something to Greg. I don't know what he said. I don't want to know what he told his dead brother. But after that, Chris speaks to us. It isn't much, but it's something, more than he has said since arriving back in Jackson. I'm glad for that, and proud of Chris.

We leave the funeral home after another brief discussion with the two deputies. Later that evening we meet again to go through some of Greg's things, the items inside the tent that were retrieved when Greg's and Walker's bodies were recovered.

Life can change in a heartbeat. The future is uncertain. Those lessons were brought home to me that week in April 2011—like a two-by-four between the eyes. My life had changed with a phone call.

27

HOME, TEMPORARILY

*It was kind of cool getting to play around on the glacier,
picking our way through the crevasses, probing snow bridges with
my ski poles and having it poke through with ease (oops, don't
take that snow bridge) or not (well, I guess let's see if this bridge
holds me). The whole time I was aware, but confident.*

—MAY 28, 2007, Lower Nisqually Glacier, Mount Rainier, Washington

The death of a child delivers a brutal, cruel blow to parents both emotionally and physically. The unimaginable has just happened. In the case of an accident such as Greg and Walker's, there's no warning. What lies ahead is suddenly undefined. Writers and psychologists talk about the stages of grief, but in those first few days after Greg's death, all stages are present in fleeting moments. It's not possible to recognize them, let alone deal with them. For a time after the call notifying us Greg was late out there was uncertainty about his status. My thoughts were "What might have happened?" and "Where could they be?" The possibility of death was always present in my mind, but it didn't dominate my thoughts. Many scenarios could have played out. I focused on positive outcomes. I don't know why. Denial? Most of us were hopeful. Initially it's impossible to make an accurate assessment of the situation because so little is known. So we hoped. As more information became available, a clearer picture of the chance of survival was revealed. I see it more clearly in retrospect, but not as events unfolded.

As the search continued, the possibility of finding Greg and Walker alive was obviously diminishing. There was no moment of revelation when I absolutely knew all hope was lost. My perception of the situation slowly shifted from the best-case scenario to the worst, not in some linear fashion, but more accurately described as reality overwhelming hope in my mind and heart.

This shift in probability led me to think about what would follow. Sue and I made minimal funeral plans while in Jackson during the search. I was afraid to talk about it. Yet at times, I thought wistfully that perhaps expending thought, planning, and energy on this negative outcome might somehow magically result in the guys walking off the mountain. This is exactly what Chris and I talked about when Greg's car was towed to have the locks rekeyed on Thursday. "Let's do this because maybe if we do, Greg will show up and get confused and think someone stole his car."

Everything changed Saturday when Nick Armitage picked up the transceiver signals as the search team was ending the day's operations. Then it changed again in the coroner's office with our first look at our Greg's frozen body. It was real!

Now we can notify family and friends of the tragic news. The funeral-planning process begins. Sue and I make phone calls to discuss preliminary plans for the visitation and funeral.

Planning for Greg's funeral is complicated by the fact he died in a distant state. We must make arrangements for the transport of his body. Since Greg had only recently moved to Montana and we feel his connection to Minnesota is stronger than to West Virginia, where he'd most recently lived, we make arrangements for the services to be held where Greg was born and raised—where we, at least, consider him to be home.

Sue and I meet with Tyson, the funeral director at Valley Mortuary in Jackson, on Monday morning. The coroner has provided all the required documents to return Greg to Minnesota. Bradshaw Funeral and Cremation Services in Stillwater will coordinate things on that end. Greg will be flown to the Minneapolis–St. Paul Airport, we will have a visitation one day, a memorial prayer service the next, and Greg will be cremated. I want a viewing with Greg's body present. This is important to me. His face had come through the avalanche with little trauma. I would have forgone the open casket under different circumstances.

Tyson verifies all is in order. We had found Greg's suit and dress clothes in his car, there for the third phase of his trip, his meeting with Megan in Vegas. This eliminates the need to shop for clothes or to send someone to Greg's apartment in Columbia Falls for them. Tyson agrees to ship them with Greg to save us the trouble of trying to pack them with our clothes on our return flight later Monday.

Once all the plans required in Jackson are complete, we have a few minutes to spend with Greg at the mortuary before flying home. I am angry with myself. I don't feel as sad as the first time I saw him yesterday. Have I already begun adjusting to the fact that my son is dead?

It's an emotional shock to return home later that evening and realize how much has changed. Our world has been completely devastated. How ironic to step into the house almost exactly to the minute a week after receiving the first phone call from Elizabeth Maki.

Tuesday afternoon we meet Michael Sorrell at the Bradshaw Celebration of Life Center in Stillwater, close to the high school. I don't recall why we selected this particular funeral home. We have no connection with them, but we're familiar with their services. It proves to be a good choice. The staff was and continues to be cooperative and supportive. They're very professional and help make the process as meaningful as possible.

Sue and I select a simple memorial pamphlet for Greg's visitors. I'm willing to forgo the more traditional Catholic holy card that includes pictures of Jesus, Mary, or saints on one side and the name of the deceased and a prayer on the other. Greg wasn't a practicing Catholic or very religious. Browsing through catalogs, I come across one option of several pictures including the Sacred Heart of Jesus. My brother, Rick, has a deep devotion to the Sacred Heart. Michael advises we can order two versions, opting for a limited number of holy cards to give to select family and friends. He shows us possible verses. My eyes light up when I read one that seems perfect. To me, the words from Psalm 104 tell the story of Greg's death and life:

> Thou coveredst it with the deep as with a garment;
>
> the waters stood above the mountains.
>
> They go up by the mountains;
>
> they go down by the valleys unto the place which thou hast founded for them.

As we finish the planning, Michael mentions he has the impression I want to be involved in things, in the details. I confirm his observation. He informs us Greg will be arriving later that evening from Jackson. The shipping office closes before Greg will arrive, so his body will have to wait until Wednesday morning for pickup. I accept his invitation to ride along.

Michael and I meet at the Bradshaw chapel on Snelling Avenue in St. Paul at five thirty on Wednesday morning, April 27. I ride with him in the mortuary van to the freight terminal at the Minneapolis–St. Paul Airport. Michael tends to the necessary paperwork, and then we're directed to loading dock four to pick up Greg.

The box is smaller than I expect. I thought it would be about the size of a standard coffin. The length and width are similar, but it isn't nearly as high. The words "Human Remains," scrawled in large black letters on the top, knock the breath out of me.

We transfer the box to the van and return to the mortuary chapel. Michael asks me to wait in another area as he returns to Greg to open the box for a brief inspection. He wants to protect me from any transfer issues that might make the sight of my son unpleasant. That doesn't occur with Greg.

Michael offers me some time alone with my son. I apologize to Greg for dragging him back to Minnesota when I know he wants to remain in the mountains. I tell him he is only home temporarily, that he will soon be back where he really wants to be for all time. That promise is important to me because I know I am fulfilling my son's final wish. It is all part of the deal I made with Greg on Saturday: "If you let us find you, Greg, I'll take you back to Minnesota. But I promise to bring you back to the mountains."

Later Wednesday morning Sue and I meet with Sister Dorothy Mrock, Father Bill Martin, and others from Guardian Angels Catholic Church, where the funeral service will be held. Pastor Jan Mehlhoff from Lutheran Church of Peace, Sue's church, was asked to be part of the service and is also in attendance. Music and readings are selected. We decide to have a luncheon following the funeral in Peter O'Neill Hall, the parish hall on the lower level.

Sue has kept her Lutheran faith throughout our marriage. I continue to practice my Catholic faith. Our dual-faith marriage created minor problems over the years, but we've always been able to work through them. Greg and Chris were baptized in the Catholic Church. Sue wanted them educated and confirmed in the Lutheran faith. I agreed. Both boys spent more time in church with Sue. We would have had the funeral at her church except for one issue, size. We expect a large turnout for Greg's funeral. It makes sense to hold the service in my larger church. All involved are supportive. We appreciate that.

Sue and I go to Rose Floral in Stillwater to purchase flowers. We're given a number of books to browse through and make our selections. We purchase an arrangement for ourselves and also another from Greg's grandmother. This takes longer than I expect. The process is unpleasant. I try to focus on the task, but I keep thinking I really don't want to be doing this, I shouldn't have to be doing this. This just isn't supposed to happen. This isn't my plan—

this doesn't match my vision of the future. Greg is in my future, and now he won't be.

Family and friends begin arriving on Thursday. Michael from Bradshaw calls to ask if any family would like the opportunity to see Greg in a quieter setting, before the family and general viewing on Sunday. Megan, Greg's girlfriend, immediately accepts. She would appreciate a chance to see Greg, to talk to him alone. My brother Rick agrees to come along to support both of us.

The three of us drive to the Bradshaw Chapel on Snelling Avenue in St. Paul on Friday afternoon. We're greeted as we enter and directed to a side area, where Greg awaits us. I have already seen Greg's lifeless body three times. It isn't any easier the fourth time. It's a much greater shock to Megan and Rick. I feel I should have better prepared them for the initial encounter.

We stand together and talk among ourselves and with Greg. I ask Megan if she would like some time alone with him. She would. Rick and I leave her and walk silently into the main chapel to wait.

We hear Megan talking, but can't make out her words. Soon we hear her crying. She leaves Greg's side and walks toward us. It is almost too much for her to bear. My heart is breaking. She sobs, slowly collects herself, and then returns to Greg. I'm grateful she has this time to tell him what's on her mind. Greg died with things left unsaid between them. The same is true for him and me. I feel this quiet time with him is a valuable part of all of our good-byes.

Soon Megan invites us back to the side chapel to join her. Rick, Megan, and I spend a few more minutes with Greg before we hesitantly leave. It is hard to desert Greg. It seems like the wrong thing to do.

We appreciate this special opportunity offered by Bradshaw. I never thought to ask if a private visit was possible. Being in the mourning business, they're much more aware of what people need than those going through such a tragic experience for the first time.

On Saturday we meet with Pastor Jan Mehlhoff from Lutheran Church of Peace. We had asked her to deliver the eulogy. She comes to our home to talk, collect information, and hear stories about Greg. Megan speaks of Greg's love for her cat, Tevia, of the special relationship those two shared. Chris shares stories of climbing together and about Greg's "sphere of influence" philosophy—we're only in control of what's within our reach, so why concern ourselves with what's outside that reach. She does an excellent job of making the discussion an opportunity to share precious, happy memories of our deceased son, brother, and beloved friend. I'm grateful she'll be part of the service.

The plans are complete. Are we prepared for the funeral? Not really. Yes, the logistics are in place, but I'm not emotionally prepared for what is to come.

28

MOMENTS OF COMFORT

*This is a beautiful basin, but all I really want is to get on the summit of
Kintla. I am sick & tired of failing on that peak.
I would give almost anything for good weather & climbing tomorrow.*

—JULY 11, 2010, Glacier National Park, Montana

Being a deeply emotional person, I can be sympathetic and
empathetic. But I have no sympathy for stupidity. I get angry and am
short-tempered. Greg was like that too. I'm also a logical, analytical
person. So was Greg. We were intrigued by how things work. We
possessed many of the same personality traits, yet I felt we were very
different. Our differences sometimes overwhelmed our similarities.

When Greg died, I was placed in a position unlike any I had
ever experienced before. I had nothing to compare it to. And yet,
thinking back to those days in Jackson and at home for the funeral,
I didn't react as I would have expected. I cried, but not as much as
I expected. I felt little compassion for others. I became very selfish.
I felt the worst blow possible had just been dealt me and now it
was the world's turn to show me some sympathy. I became short-
tempered and angry when I didn't get the sympathy I expected.

Once the initial shock had worn off and the constant intense grief subsided, the analytical side of me was activated. Something like this isn't supposed to happen. Well, it does happen, accidents happen all the time. But they aren't supposed to happen to me, and they aren't supposed to be fatal, to inflict the finality of death. There had to be a reason for Greg's and Walker's deaths.

At times I was comforted knowing Greg didn't die alone. There are many stories of deaths that happen in the company of a friend, or even a stranger. The common thinking is that it's a mercy the person didn't die alone. Greg's death was different. He and Walker died together, but they didn't know they were dying. There was no slow entrance into eternity. This was instantaneous, and neither knew what was happening to them; they didn't have time to think about what was happening to their friend or feel comforted because someone was with them. But I'm still glad Greg wasn't alone when he died. I think his death would have been more difficult for me to handle if he'd been somewhere solo when this happened.

But why did Greg die? Why did Walker die? What purpose do their deaths serve?

The entire episode is beyond explanation. There is a physical reason for their deaths. At least the evidence provides the most probable scenario. But why did that avalanche occur in that brief time Walker and Greg were in Garnet Canyon, in the very area they were camped, and at night? It doesn't add up. It is illogical that Greg should go through college, med school, and residency to practice medicine for eight months and then die. It's a waste.

This reasoning falls under the category "Why do bad things happen to good people?" But it goes deeper than that. I think Greg was a good person, a good man. Maybe others don't agree. Maybe they saw a different side of him or had a bad experience with him. That wouldn't surprise me. Greg wasn't a saint. He had his faults, bad habits, prejudices, and biases. I won't argue those points. But he was a good person. More than being good, he had the potential to do good. That's where I get hung up. The studying, work, and effort to become a doctor—and so little opportunity to apply his skills. He could have helped so many people. It's what he wanted. That's what he told his mentor in Morgantown, Dr. Larrabee: "I just want to help people."

In my grief I was left to struggle with the feeble explanation that all things happen for a purpose. Even if I accept that premise, I can't convince myself there's any good or useful purpose for Greg's death. In my humanness, I can't understand God's plan.

Another chain of thought involves punishment. Did Greg die as punishment for something he did, for something I did? This second option is a great place to go to inflict severe guilt on oneself. I don't really believe either, but if somehow that is the case, it really worked. Greg's death punishes me every day.

My attempts to rationalize this tragedy continue. I don't think about it constantly, but occasionally it crosses my mind. As time has passed, I've produced absurd scenarios. My favorite has made others shake their heads. What if Greg had been in the ER one day and a patient was brought in. This was a terrible person, bent on the destruction of the human race. Greg was the only person capable of saving this person's life. So, in order to save the human race, Greg had to die so he wouldn't be available to save this person. Grief can be so consuming, so devastating, so mind altering. I confess that this imagined scenario has brought me comfort more than once.

I haven't come up with a reason, logical or illogical, for Greg's death at age thirty-one when he had the potential to do so much good in his life, to heal so many people, to help many more with his knowledge, friendship, and laughter. Maybe I'm not intelligent enough to understand. Maybe the human mind can't comprehend why things like this happen. Or maybe there's no reason for this tragedy. Things happen in nature, and sometimes people just get in the way.

Sue and I have dealt with our grief in many ways. We prayed, tried individual therapy, attended support groups, created a centerpiece in Greg's memory, and read many books about grief, especially grief dealing with the death of a child. We've also read a number of books dealing with near-death experiences, which have helped me, at least.

One concern I wrestled with after Greg died was how he felt when he realized he was dead. I worried that when the realization hit him, his first reaction was anger. He was in Grand Teton National Park, a place he thought was among the most beautiful on earth. He had mountains to climb, not just this next day, but for years ahead. He wanted a family. He wanted to practice medicine and help people. And he was dead before he was able to realize those dreams. My brother reminded me anger is a human emotion. Greg was now beyond human emotions, failings, and shortcomings.

Accounts of near-death experiences discuss a sense of calm overwhelming the individual as they prepare to leave their bodies and enter the next phase of their existence. The names don't matter. Call it eternity, a heightened state of awareness, heaven, or the next phase. I personally believe there is a Creator, and we continue to exist after death. If I'm wrong and there's nothing, it doesn't really matter, does it? We're dead and gone and have moved on into nothingness. But if the afterlife is real, the accounts are overwhelmingly positive. Near-death survivors often report they're reluctant to return to earth, to their life with family and loved ones. After returning, they no longer fear death because they've experienced the goodness and beauty of what comes next.

Running through this rationalization many times over the years has brought me moments of comfort. I no longer continually ponder how Greg felt when he realized he was dead. But this comfort is only a visitor. It isn't my prevailing state. And then I force myself to work through the thought process to again find peace. But I can find it now, occasionally.

Maybe we're all put on this earth for a reason. We each have an assignment. Perhaps Greg already completed his. Perhaps he accomplished everything he was assigned in his life, but it only took him thirty-one years. We just don't know. Sometimes I can accept this; sometimes I struggle to understand.

If I can honestly and finally reach the point of admitting there's no logic to Greg's and Walker's deaths, where does that leave me? I admit Greg is gone. Or is he? In a sense, he's still alive in me because he changed me and inspired me. He continues to exist in me, in his mother, in his brother, and in his friends by making an impact on our lives. Though Greg died, that part of him living on in us continues to exist. There is hope in that. Even though I find myself asking why Greg died, as Father Bill said in his funeral homily, the right question is "Why did Greg live?" That's where I find the logic.

Thank you, Greg and Walker. We miss you and love you. This whole thing sucks. I struggle to understand and accept your deaths. I believe you're better off than I, and that we'll be together again. It will make sense when the spiritual truth is revealed, a truth beyond human logic and intellect. That's what really matters.

29

Beginning another journal! I wonder what will be written in here over the next 10 weeks. It feels damn good to be done w/ boards. I am pretty sure I passed (I hope).

—JUNE 17, 2005, Minneapolis, Minnesota

Greg's storytelling came in written as well as spoken forms. He journaled, not about your basic day-to-day events, but about road trips and adventures. His oral stories were shared with friends in the ER, while mountaineering, or socially over a beer or five. His journals, on the other hand, were personal, private. I knew he kept them but he never talked about them, never read entries to me, never explained anything. His purpose for writing the journals is unknown. His brother and friends knew he journaled because he wrote in their presence at campsites, but he never shared his writings with them either.

I didn't realize the quantity of his journal entries until after his death. Among his belongings we found plastic bags containing hundreds of pictures with one or more spiral notebooks, the journal associated with those pictures.

His record keeping was sketchy. The entries usually included a partial date, but little location info. They're further complicated because Greg often journaled when time permitted, so the dates on the entries don't always correspond with the activity dates. It is difficult for me to track his adventures with my minimal knowledge of climbing and back-country ski areas, but the places he writes about were deeply familiar to Greg.

Spanning from 2003 to 2010, the journals contain thousands of words. I thought about publishing his journal writing. Aside from the excerpts I'm using in this volume, that won't happen. His historical accounts and musings are personal, not for the general public. I even considered omitting the journal excerpts here completely, but that would be a disservice. Those notebooks help complete the picture of my son, present another aspect of Greg the storyteller, and display his passions in another form. While primarily consisting of technical climbing descriptions, he also lays bare his loves, hopes, dreams, and philosophical thoughts as in no other place I know.

Each chapter in this book begins with an excerpt from Greg's journals. Selecting appropriate quotes was difficult because it was painful to read his remarks. I would often begin a day's entry and by the end I was no longer reading it—I was hearing Greg tell the story. Perhaps you'll have the same experience.

> Back at the ranch on my birthday! Yesterday we summited the Grand via the Owen-Spalding route. It was a lot more difficult than I expected. Our day started at 4:50 & we summited at 10:00–10:20 (me last). We left at about 5:30 & got to the black dike in relatively good time. We began climbing steep snow. We passed up the Exum guide & his client in the couloir. I asked the guide how many times he had climbed the Grand. He paused, thought, & said, "I dunno, a lot. But not as many as some." When I passed his client, I made a comment about how nice of a day it was. . . .

We took the 5.6 chimney up accidentally. It was hard to get into & I did slip when I was cleaning Joel's gear. Otherwise, the chimney was an intriguing intro to mixed alpine climbing. It was also very strange running around unroped while this guide was belaying his client everywhere. . . . After climbing the chimney, I came up to the belay station & Joel says, "Okay, how do you feel about soloing that chimney?" I was already exhausted & I was looking at a solid 100 ft. of mixed Class 4 climbing. . . . I had no mixed experience before then, so it was difficult trusting my equipment on rock. Joel talked me into it & I soloed it. I don't think I have ever been so scared in my life. We got past that & easier snow & mixed terrain led to the summit. I had to drag myself there. I was exhausted. When I was descending I came across the guide. He was sitting in the snow belaying his client up. I asked "should I go up & around, or should I step carefully over the rope. I am not sure what's kosher here." He said, "Not falling is what's kosher here. Just step over the rope."

When we were leaving we saw helicopters flying in. We must have seen 6 different flights. I thought that they maybe were practicing. It turns out that a 34-year-old Jackson resident & experienced climber had fallen off descending the East Ridge of Cloudveil peak. She fell about 300 ft. & they recovered her body about 4:50. It was a very real & sobering reminder of why you can't make mistakes in the mountains, as if the enormous cliffs & slick ice & snow wasn't enough of a reminder.

As I sit here writing this, w/ Jeff & Joel napping & Anya outside writing postcards before dinner, I have some time to reflect on my time here. Climbing the Grand was an incredible experience. I am lucky to have a friend like

Joel. As I said yesterday to him, I don't need someone to hold my hand, just to lead those icy & mixed 5.6 chimneys & set me up a solid top rope anchor. It feels so good walking around here & being able to look at the Grand & think I was on top of that. The view was incredible, & the climbing was much more difficult than anything I had ever done before. Too bad I couldn't enjoy the summit view more. When I got to the top I said, "Well, 20% of the way there," as 80% of the accidents happen in descent. It was definitely a big boost to my mountaineering confidence.

—July 2, 2005, Climbers' Ranch, Grand Teton National Park, Wyoming

Greg used a little trick in his journals that I was slow to recognize. He had two good friends named Joel, Minnesota friend Joel Anderson, and Montana friend Joel Menssen. He distinguished them in his journals by using "Joel" for Anderson and "Jol" for Menssen. I wonder if that missing letter was just a shorthand device, or if Greg had a story about how and why he started using Jol.

Greg was practical and honest. He felt good about his accomplishments, but recognized others had done much more. He had unsuccessful summit attempts, aborted attempts, and missions abandoned in deference to safety. Greg never summited Kintla Peak in Glacier National Park—thwarted three times by my count. It nagged at him. He really wanted to bag that summit. It was one regret I know he took to his grave.

I grabbed a branch in my left hand & had my axe as a cane in my right. I took a few steps, laying back against the branch (apparently not enough), as my feet suddenly & unexpectedly came out from under me. I slammed my head into the rock, bending my glasses (still wearable though), knocking my hat off (I would have forgot it, I was so stunned, but Jol picked it up for me), & causing a cut on the lateral edge of the orbit of my eye, which began to bleed immediately. I asked Jol how bad I was cut (not too bad) & began to evaluate things. A head injury where I was was a death sentence. I told Jol, "Well, I may only have a half hour (the lucid interval), so if I go down around 10 a.m. (accident time was 9:30), just remember where I am so my parents can retrieve my body so they have something to bury." 10 came & went & other than a slight headache & sore spot, I was okay.

We gained the ridge & began to follow it up toward the summit. Jol knew we had to traverse around onto the west side, but apparently we began that too late as we ended up about 200 vertical ft. (80 ft. moderate fifth class) short of the summit by some spires & chimneys. If it were good rock, I might have said let's solo it to the top and find a way (the normal route) down. But I knew it wasn't trustworthy rock & if one hold broke, we were looking at a fall of 2,000 or so ft. We downclimbed, dejected, shocked that we could be thwarted by Kintla again.

—August 22, 2005, Glacier National Park, Montana

The next excerpt, from the same year, occurred between these two climbing accounts. Greg was at the Wilderness Medicine Conference in Colorado, where he had the privilege to hear and meet people he admired. He wrote glowingly about the experience. He envied Dr. Freer, Aron Ralston, Tashi Tenzing, and others like them for their accomplishments and their careers. He hoped to follow in their footsteps to some degree in his own medical and mountaineering pursuits.

I think Luanne Freer gave the 1st talk. It was about working on Everest. She lives in Bozeman & works in Yellowstone the other 9 months. She showed a slide of Alex Lowe's memorial on Everest. Found out that my shirt was a replica of that. . . .

So there I am, talking to Aron Ralston. I began the conversation with "Aron, congratulations on finishing all 54 14ers in CO." He said he was surprised I knew about that. I told him I saw it on the Hot Flashes page on climbing.com. He said, "Oh, wow, I'm always surprised when the climbing industry takes an interest in a hack like me." I asked him about current projects (he said he wanted to do the 50 high points in 50 days) & we talked for a while. I asked him about his prosthetic ice axe & how that was attached & we talked about back-country skiing. He even asked my name (I'd been considering offering it, but I figured he didn't care) & shook my hand. I told him I enjoyed the Phish and SCI quotes in his book & he thanked me. We parted ways & then I called everyone I could to tell them: "I just met Aron Ralston!" Definitely the coolest person I've ever gotten to meet.

. . . then they let us in to hear Tashi Tenzing speak for free. I sat down . . . & listened to his talk about Sherpas. It was pretty cool. Me . . . & some other students went to get some drinks. We sat down & what do you know, Tashi Tenzing sits down next to me. I talked w/ him about climbing for a while, & I think I impressed him when I correctly asked if it was Ama Dablam in the background of many of the pictures he had. I asked about his kids, & he asked where I was in school, & we had a good conversation. A very nice guy.

—July 31, 2005, Snowmass Village, Colorado

I learned something about my son from these journals, sensed a shift in the seven years of their creation, which surprised me. Maybe I would be more surprised if he hadn't changed. More importantly, Greg showed me newfound maturity because he realized he had changed, and accepted and welcomed that change. In his final journal entry in 2010, he writes as I never heard him speak. He was living his dream.

> Bachelor month left me feeling completely exhausted. It felt weird to shave my beard but good nonetheless. I learned that I'm not as young as I used to be. A month seemed like it dragged on too long. 2 weeks seems like a better amount of time to be away from home. I still really miss Megan a lot & can't wait to see her in 10 days. I know I still feel the same way about her that I did before I left (probably love her even more) & I hope the same thing is true for her. I really do feel like I am ready to move onto another chapter of my life, one, as I told Megan, more focused on the home & possibly children in the not-too-distant future. . . . It has been kind of funny over the last few days because I have actually felt bored at times, kind of almost wishing I had some household projects to tinker with. I just can't wait to see Megan. I don't really understand why, but the last month has confirmed that I want to spend the rest of my life with her & that I want to do everything in my power to make her happy & comfortable.

> —August 6, 2010, Morgantown, West Virginia

30

THE FUNERAL

It was again nice basking in the happiness & fulfillment that the mountains had provided. I have yet to find any greater joy in life than completing a challenge w/ physical danger that nature has designed.

—JULY 19, 2005, Hilgard Basin, Montana

Preparations, guests, and expressions of sympathy take my mind off the tragedy as Sunday, May 1, arrives. I'm exhausted. Any chance to stop and rest is welcome, necessary. But those pauses are like a dam bursting, allowing a flood of sorrow to pour into my heart. It's still unreal. With all these people around, Greg must be among them. He wouldn't want to miss this gathering.

Family is invited to the Bradshaw chapel in Stillwater at two thirty. Sue's family drives directly to the funeral home from northern Minnesota and arrives before we do. Among them is Dorothy, Sue's mom. This has to be unimaginably difficult for her. Greg was her first grandson.

Chris gets busy with staff to set up the memorial video display. I appreciate all his effort to put the video together. He rounded up many pictures of Greg. Sue and I went through our photo albums and pulled others from Greg's childhood to include. Greg's friends from residency at WVU, climbing, skiing, and mountaineering sent pictures to Chris. Also included are two videos, one from the successful summit of Mount Rainier in May 2010 and another in the Wind River Range in June of the same year. The entire slide show runs about seventy-five minutes. I think that's a bit long, but it's difficult to boil down Greg's short, action-filled life into a brief slide show.

The initial family time isn't as reverent or low-key as I hoped. Our first glimpse of Greg in the casket is upsetting. His face looks unnatural, too gray. The funeral director, Michael Sorrell, works feverishly with makeup to create a more acceptable appearance. He is very responsive to our requests, and his adjustments are complete before the general viewing at four p.m.

The visitation is a blur. We expected a lot of people and aren't disappointed. A line forms at four and a continuous stream of people console us without a break until after six thirty. I discover afterward when looking through the guest register that many people bypass the line. They sign in, say good-bye to Greg, and maybe visit with others they know. At first, the greeting line consists of Sue, me, Megan, Chris, and Jesse. After the first hour, the young adults are drawn away, leaving only Sue and me to greet those entering, a likely reason we miss some visitors.

After the line ends, I mingle randomly with people. It is heartwarming to see many of Greg's friends from Stillwater High School and St. Olaf College, an affirmation of the way he was able to keep friends. It is especially rewarding to see his soccer and ski teammates. I later think how sad, and yet how meaningful, it is for these young people to gather when someone they care about dies. I wonder if, for some, this is their first experience dealing with the death of a peer. I appreciate this chance to visit with special friends. Then I realize I haven't spent much time at Greg's side, which I regret.

Before we know it, the clock has raced past nine o'clock. We say our good-byes. There will only be tomorrow remaining. How can Greg be gone at such a young age? Life isn't fair, but this is the most unfair outcome there could be. We leave the funeral home and walk out to a very cold and damp evening. There have even been a few flurries from time to time during the day.

I don't sleep much that night. I'm surprised I sleep at all. There is such a tremendous sense of loss. Tomorrow I'll say good-bye to the person, the body, I know to be my son for the last time. I'll never look upon his face again, even if this final image will be merely of the lifeless container for the Greg we knew and loved.

For the hundredth time I agonize over what I could have done differently. What one thing could I have changed? What one decision could I have made to prevent Greg from dying? As I understand it, this foolish exercise is a fairly common reaction. For some reason, Greg was supposed to die on that night in that place and nothing could be done about it. How egotistical am I to think I have control over life and death? Tomorrow we'll all gather for his funeral and then my son will be cremated. The Greg we all knew will cease to exist, will walk the earth in his body no more.

The day of the funeral is much like the day before, cool, cloudy, and windy, an appropriate day for a funeral. As we prepare to go to church, every action and emotion seems incorrect. The sadness is a sharp contrast to Greg's laughter and big smile. Silence seems disrespectful compared to Greg's constant talk and storytelling. Yet every word spoken rings hollow.

We arrive at Guardian Angels Catholic Church at nine thirty for our family's final gathering time with Greg. Friends and colleagues are invited to join us at ten o'clock, before the funeral at eleven.

Other family members are present at the church when Chris, Jesse, Megan, Sue, and I arrive. Some had been at the funeral home the day before. Others have just arrived in town this morning. There are more hugs, expressions of sympathy, and shared memories.

Chris again coordinates the video slide show for viewing on the church's overhead screen. Other final details of the service are attended to. Greg's cousin Chelsea meets with the music director, Roger Stratton, for her song. My brother, brother-in-law, and cousin are directed to the church's funeral coordinator and receive instructions for their readings. We make sure everything else is as we want and try to be respectful to Greg as he lies there in the coffin in church. It's easy to be distracted by the preparations. But today I want to just be with Greg, just him and me alone. I hadn't spent enough time with him in life. Why do I want everyone else to stay away and have him to myself now? I regret all the things I haven't done with him. I thought there would always be time next year, but there will be no next year for us.

People begin arriving a little before ten—another large crowd to honor Greg and support us. Sue and I stand near the casket and greet friends for forty-five minutes. Sue is pleased so many of her colleagues from the Nutrition Coordinating Center attend to support us. Her coworkers don't know Greg personally, but probably feel they do from hearing stories, accomplishments, and concerns from Sue over her thirty-year career in dietary research studies. Some friends stop only to pay their respects, but most stay for the funeral service.

Just before eleven we're given the opportunity to say our final good-byes. Father Bill Martin begins the service with prayer, and the casket is closed. What I thought would be my last vision of my son isn't what I had ever dreamed it would be.

As we walk into church behind Greg's casket, every eye is on us. I feel exposed, yet invisible. It seems my feet are not touching the floor, and yet my legs are leaden with this tremendous burden. I resist moving forward as if this will somehow eliminate the reason we're here. Despite my resistance, I sense I am carried on a cloud or on the wings of angels and delivered to the front of church. I don't want to be here. I know who sits in the front pew at a funeral.

The music of "How Great Thou Art" accompanies us. I hear the organ and the voices of our family and friends, but the sound comes from very far away. I've heard this song many times at other funerals. Its message is different now—ominous and final.

The readings and music for Greg's funeral have a mountain theme. The first reading from the twenty-fifth chapter of Isaiah, read by my brother, Rick, talks about a wondrous feast on Mount Zion. The image produced by these words is anything but a wondrous feast. I recall hikes with Greg and Chris. At the destination of our hike, we'd stop to rest and to replenish our energy with fruit, granola bars, jerky, and water. We had reached a place of great beauty, a place where "God did some of his best work," as Greg would describe it. This is how Greg thought of Garnet Canyon, the Grand, and the Teton Range. Now I'm listening to the words of the Bible reading hoping, trying to believe, he is in a place even more beautiful.

Sue's brother, Scott, reads next from the fifth chapter of First Thessalonians. These verses are more a description of Greg's death. They speak about death coming "like a thief in the night." The reading delivers a warning to "be on guard and not asleep." But I don't know if being awake would have made a difference for Greg and Walker.

For the gospel we select the Sermon on the Mount, which begins, "One day Jesus went up the hillside with his disciples and sat down and taught them there." This wonderful image reminds me of Greg as he taught young residents and med students. He followed a similar approach to the mountains when he shared experiences with friends not as accomplished as himself. More often in this situation, I picture Greg as the student, eager to learn more and advance his skills to increase his confidence.

Father Bill delivers the homily. He speaks about the beauty and value of Greg's life, even if that life was shorter than we wanted it to be. I am most moved when Father says Greg's family and friends asked him, "Why did Greg have to die?" Father admits that's a good question, even though it's impossible to answer—but, he tells us, it's the wrong question. The more important question is "Why did Greg live?" He points out that the large number of people in attendance indicates there are obviously a lot of reasons for Greg's life. We each have a reason Greg is important to us. I continue to find comfort in that thought.

Next, Chelsea sings the Michael Joncas song "On Eagle's Wings" that's often heard at funerals. It seems especially appropriate today. Her powerful voice blends with Roger Stratton's organ music to offer a ray of comfort in the darkness of this tragedy. I can almost picture Greg being raised up by angels, but not to heaven, to the summit of the Grand Teton. I smile, and cry.

Greg's cousin Kathleen reads the prayers of the faithful. Kathleen has always had a special place in my heart as my first godchild. I was a young man when my cousins asked me to be her godfather. I was honored. My faith was very much in the developmental stage at that point in my life. I didn't think I had what it took to be someone's godfather. Maybe I still don't. I do know that Kathleen and I have been very close. She's been a blessing. Kathleen's good friend Jeff died less than two years before Greg. They'd been together for many years. She's been able to support me in a most special way on this tragic journey of grief because she has traveled her own.

Pastor Jan Mehlhoff offers a very moving eulogy that covers specific aspects of Greg's short life—his love of the mountains and of climbing rock and ice, among others. Pastor Jan does a beautiful job.

The prayers of commendation are read. We say our farewells by singing "The Hand of God Shall Hold You" by Marty Haugen. Greg's friends form an honor guard from the front of church to the outside doors. We process behind the casket singing "Jerusalem, My Destiny," a song that holds special meaning for me. I fell in love with the music and the lyrics the first time I heard it. I told Sue to include it at my funeral. The words seem more appropriate for Greg's. "I have fixed my eyes on your hills" is an accurate description of Greg's focus on life. The song continues, "I cannot see the end for me," a fitting reflection of the circumstances of Greg's death. The chorus refers to the journey of life, a journey together that makes us one. Our family and friends are perfect examples Greg didn't travel through life alone.

We pause at the back of the church, where Father reads the final prayers. Megan stands with Sue and me, holding a rose. As we conclude and Greg is being taken to the hearse, Megan cries. One of my omissions comes to light here. I hadn't explained the service completely to her beforehand. She holds the rose because she wants Greg to have it in the casket. She thinks there will be additional time with him; she didn't know that the casket is closed for good. Michael takes the rose from Megan and hands it to another staff member to place in Greg's hands before he is cremated. This confusion and Megan's tears lead me to a decision.

Michael had invited me to be present at the crematorium when Greg's body was placed into the furnace. I considered it, but declined. Several family and friends discouraged me from accepting this offer because of the final image of Greg with which I would be left. I could see their point. Now, though, I know I must be there to assure Megan that Greg holds her rose to the end.

I tell Megan I'll go to the crematorium to verify Greg has the flower in his hands. She accepts my offer. Some of her fears are allayed. Rick hears this conversation and says he'll go with me. He doesn't want to see Greg that way either, but he feels he can't allow me to go alone. I'm grateful.

Then it begins to snow! How perfect! Some in attendance may be disappointed by the blustery conditions for May 2, but I'm comforted by this sign from Greg. I can almost hear him laughing.

We look out through the falling flurries and watch as Greg is placed in the hearse. And Greg left.

During the luncheon in the church hall that follows the funeral, nearly three hundred friends, colleagues, and family members gather to share and hear memories of Greg. The range of stories speaks to the diverse ways he impacted everyone in the room— tales of studying at night in the dorm closet with the door closed and the light on, detours to visit friends, and compassionate care in the hospital. It's a special time that brings together people from all parts of Greg's life to share in celebrating and grieving a life ended too soon.

It's difficult for me to make the emotional transition from the solemnity of the funeral to the celebratory feeling of the luncheon. Afterward, there are only a few minutes to visit personally with friends and family, especially those who traveled many miles to say good-bye and honor our son. Sue and I have just begun to greet guests individually when Rick takes me by the arm and reminds me that it's time to leave for the crematorium.

Rick and I drive to Forest Lawn Cemetery and Crematorium on Edgerton Street in St. Paul. We talk during the entire twenty-minute drive, but avoid discussing the purpose of our mission. I have only an idea of where to go, but my instincts are right. We arrive at precisely three p.m.

A young woman opens the front door as Rick and I approach. I can't remember if she was from the crematorium or the funeral home. She leads us into the front lobby and explains what we'll see. We're taken into the next room where the access to the furnace chamber is located. Two workers stand beside Greg lying in a shallow tray, on a cart that isn't quite waist-high off the floor. He looks like he did in the casket, but with Megan's rose clasped in his hands. I have seen what I came to see.

The entire process is explained to us in a nearby control room. I listen, but hear very little of what is said. This seems too impossible to believe. I'm offered the option of pushing Greg into the furnace and pushing buttons to begin the cremation process. Six days ago Michael explained this during funeral arrangements, and I considered participating. Now, with the options staring me in the face, I want nothing to do with it.

We walk back to the front of the chamber for a final look at Greg. I bend down, kiss his forehead, and say good-bye to my son for the last time.

Just thinking about these events and writing about them weighs heavily on my heart. I can't imagine how I held up through it all. A definite numbness must have encased me during the days of the search, preparation, and funeral. There were things to do, people visiting, and many distractions. But after, when there's time alone to consider what has happened, the reality hits hard and deep. The sorrow is relentless, but there's no way to go back. Greg showed me any day could be our last on earth and we should live life knowing it. He approached the final part of his thirty-one years with that attitude. I'm so very grateful he did.

Chris returns to Bozeman with the difficult task of emptying Greg's apartment. I had always imagined Greg would someday have a house. It didn't happen and, in light of the circumstances, I'm relieved he didn't. Greg had few possessions when he died. His modest apartment is nearly empty. (Most of his things are in storage in Morgantown.) He slept on a mattress on the floor. The only cars Greg ever drove were a 1995 Chevy Cavalier he got from us and drove for 240,000 miles (he was disappointed it didn't make a quarter million miles) and a 2002 Buick Rendezvous with 140,000 miles purchased from our neighbor. He said, "I want everyone to know which car in the doctors' parking area is mine. Let's see: Cadillac, BMW, Lexus, Greg's car." Everything Greg has in his apartment he moved to Columbia Falls in that Rendezvous. Greg had adopted and lived by my "experiences-over-possessions" philosophy far better than I do.

Sue and I have a difficult time selecting a local site for Greg's remains. It takes two years before we decide on Evergreen Cemetery, a small, local cemetery in Afton. In August 2013, a group of fifteen family and friends gather to commit Greg's ashes to the earth, the nature he loved so much. Sister Dorothy Mrock, my friend and unofficial grief counselor, joins us by phone from Ohio and offers a prayer. Greg's grave marker reads:

An Inspired Life
Gregory Eric Seftick, MD
July 2, 1979 ____ April 16, 2011
Beloved Son – Brother – Friend

Chris refers to his brother's life as inspired. We choose to include that as an accurate description. The outline of a mountain is engraved between the dates. Mountains were my son's life.

31

FIREFLIES

Sweet views of Mts. St. Helens and Adams to the south with the sun setting on it. It was beautiful and I was content to just be back in the mountains.

—MAY 28, 2007, Mount Rainier, Washington

We look for signs. Superstition? Tradition? Spiritual? Whatever the force behind the sign, we seek reassurance that our loved one is all right after death.

In the weeks after Greg's death, I looked for a sign. I received none after his snowy funeral. Maybe I missed it. Maybe he wasn't ready to make contact. Or, my worst fear, maybe he wasn't OK. No sign from Greg. No message from him. No dream about him.

Then in late June, more than two months after the avalanche that took his life, I got a sign. A firefly approached and flashed near our open bedroom window screen. It stayed for a minute or two as Sue and I watched. We even made conversation, as if Greg were present in that illuminated insect. We honestly felt the spirit of Greg make contact. Greg was OK. He'd provided a sign.

Why fireflies? Greg's birthday, July 2, was usually celebrated with a Fourth of July picnic. We grilled hamburgers, hot dogs, and brats. Sue would bake a special cake in the form of some requested shape. One year Greg asked for a space shuttle, another year a garbage truck, and once a gum-ball machine.

His grandparents were always eager to visit for his birthday. Grandpa Seftick was still working when Greg and Chris were born. It was convenient for him to take vacation and drive with Grandma from Michigan to visit and stay with us over the holiday. My in-laws would also come down from Duluth. The kids and grandparents would spend several full days together. Once his younger brother went to sleep for the night, Greg had his grandparents to himself— and he loved it. One of the few sources of consolation for me now is knowing Greg is with his grandparents who have passed away. He surely must be smiling to be in their company again.

At the back of our one-and-a-quarter-acre lot is a usually dry gully where snowmelt and heavy rains run. The wild-grown sides of the creek bed slope gently down from our yard. The fifty feet at that part of our yard wasn't cut when we bought the house, and we've continued to let it grow wild. We always called it the high grass.

One summer when Greg was three or four, my parents were here to celebrate his birthday. As night fell and Chris went to sleep, Grandpa, Greg, and I wandered into the yard toward the high grass. We were lured in that direction by the flickering light of many fireflies. We'd seen them before, but Greg was now just the right age to want to investigate.

"Come on, Greg. Let's see what's back there," Grandpa urged.

And so Greg's first adventure began.

We caught fireflies, depositing several of our captures in a covered jar. Greg was fascinated! He wanted to catch more and more. Soon it was difficult to put another in the jar without some escaping. Grandpa and I were losing interest because, although there were plenty of fireflies, there were more mosquitoes. Finally, Greg decided we had enough fireflies, and we adjourned for the evening.

Greg carried the jar into the house, proudly showing it to his mother and other grandparents, and immediately put the jar in his room for the night. The flickering lights on the nightstand next to his bed captivated him.

But disappointment showed on Greg's face the next morning when he woke to find the fireflies were no longer flickering—instead they were actually dying. He felt badly, but had definitely enjoyed this backyard adventure with Grandpa.

Fireflies have been in our yard almost every summer since. Each time I see them I think of Greg as a young child watching the fireflies and trying to guess where their light would shine next.

We had another firefly experience with Greg in 2010 in Morgantown, West Virginia, when Sue and I were there for his residency banquet. While that was the main attraction for this trip, there was time for hiking a few of our favorite trails and checking out anything new Greg might suggest. We were most familiar with the trail along the Monongahela River, a trail Sue and I found on our first trip to Morgantown while helping Greg move.

One day during our banquet visit we somehow got on the subject of moonshine. Greg later mentioned he wanted to show us something, but we'd have to wait until after sunset. Sue surmised we were going to see something connected with stills and voiced her concern about the wisdom of taking this little walk in the dark. Greg smiled, but made no attempt to clarify what he planned to show us.

That evening we headed out from his apartment up Collins Ferry Road, to the dirt path, and finally onto the Mon Trail. It was getting dark when we reached the dirt path. Our headlamps were on before we set foot on the trail.

Sue's concern increased as we walked. Greg kept saying there was nothing to worry about. As we walked in the dark we saw an occasional firefly alongside the trail. Their numbers increased as the last waning light of day disappeared. Greg remained silent about our hike's objective.

About a mile in, we rounded a bend, came out of the forest into a meadow, and reached Greg's objective. Thousands of fireflies filled the entire scene! Lights flickered to our right and left, high overhead and just above the grassy floor. The moist woodland air of the warm June evening was fragrant with the scent of wildflowers and pine. We took it all in. Sue was relieved we wouldn't be sneaking up on someone's still. Greg said he'd come upon this beautiful sight while running and biking on the trail after work. As thrilled as we were with the sight in front of us, Greg said he didn't think there were quite as many fireflies this evening as other times.

These two fleeting incidents—small parts of otherwise ordinary days—almost thirty years apart make me associate fireflies with Greg. I thought of Greg when I saw fireflies before his death. I think I always will.

Fireflies pass only fleetingly through our days. Greg hadn't lived at home for thirteen years. We saw him on visits or as he passed through on his way somewhere. The fireflies are only here in summer, only at night. But each grab our attention, bursting on the scene with the unexpected. They add light to the darkness of our world. They leave an impression on our minds and our hearts. They create memories.

Greg's flashes of brightness came from his smile, his laugh, and his love of life. He's gone and will pulse with flashes of light no more. But he created memories too, memories that bring a smile to our faces, make us laugh, and help us to love life.

Greg and fireflies. Shine bright, Greg. Shine often, Greg. Shine forever, Greg.

I finally did dream of Greg in January 2012, a full nine months after his death. Sue and I were in Bozeman for Chris's thirtieth birthday. In my dream Greg didn't speak to me, but simply turned and walked away. I awoke with a smile on my face. I told Sue about the dream and a look of amazement appeared on her face. She too had dreamed of Greg that night for the first time. I felt goose bumps on my neck, shoulders, and arms. What are the odds? We decided it was fitting to dream of Greg in Montana and not in Minnesota. Greg's spirit was there in the mountains.

I received my sign that Greg is all right. In my dream, he was going home.

Sue and I, Chris, Megan, Greg's family and his friends continue to journey, to enjoy this road trip of life, to make new memories in a "constantly changing horizon," and to tell our long and detailed stories. If only Greg could again journal: We set out at the appointed time on a cool, cloudy day, and Dad was lagging behind soon after we left the trailhead . . .

AFTERWORD: A FUTURE WITHOUT GREG

I feel like a completely different person journaling now than the person journaling in my 1st one about 8.5 years ago. Much less energy. In some respects, the boundless energy that characterized "Wildcat" is gone. I don't know the next time I will journal again. If things work out like I want them to at this point, it very well may be when I am retired. It has been an interesting journey over the last 8.5 years, but at this point I am tired & ready to settle down. Life sure is a "long, strange trip."

—AUGUST 6, 2010, Morgantown, West Virginia

The search and funeral preparations were exhausting. I thought it was the most emotionally draining time of my life, until everything was over. Greg's body had been recovered, we remembered him during a visitation and a funeral, family and friends had gathered to support Sue, me, Chris, and Megan. Then those overwhelming and busy days were over. I had time to think. Reality set in. That's when it got really hard, when it got real. My son was dead and what I could see of the life ahead of me was unlike anything I had considered. I was lost.

What do you do after the death of a child? The death of a child is not something I considered possible. It's something no one should have to face, so why prepare for it? Anything can happen in life. We hope for the unexpectedly good and try to avoid the unexpectedly bad. Sometimes we have no choice.

Immediately after Greg's death, I was emotionally incoherent. As time passed, the grief changed and my mind attempted to assess the present and future losses. I allowed myself to consider what Greg might be doing if he were still alive, but tried not to dwell on it. That would have been detrimental to the healing process. But thinking about Greg's development after his death allows me to speculate on the impact he could have made in others' lives. I naturally focus on only the positive.

Greg's death threw me the ultimate curve. I wasn't expecting it or planning for it. My vision of the future probably meshed with others of my generation: children who would provide grandchildren and expand my lineage and legacy, not a legacy of fame, but a legacy of family. I watch others' legacies develop with envy, knowing mine won't match theirs. Sue and I may have grandchildren, or we may not. But it will be a linear legacy. There will be no breadth to it. Chris faces the future as an only child—yet worse, for he is an only child with a void in his heart. Who expects that when they have siblings? The same happened to Walker's sister, Kendra. She made that comment after the bodies were recovered. "I never expected to be an only child." It still gives me chills to think about it.

Not a day passes without thinking of my firstborn son. Greg will always hold that special place in my heart. I have all this love designated for Greg and Chris. Some of that love has a receptor, a place to go, the remainder does not. What happens to the rest? Part of grieving is the search to find a place for the unclaimed love. There are family and friends, of course, but they've always been there. My love for them has already been assigned. How to apportion the unclaimed love?

The grief from the death of a child is the greatest grief. Nothing can match it. Sometimes it seems it would be simpler if we didn't have to grieve. But not grieving means not being invested in another person, in relationships. The more love in a relationship, the greater the loss after a death, the greater the grief. It's far better to feel a loss, to grieve intensely, because the gift of the person and the love for that person was indeed special. What is the value of a life without love? How much more worthwhile is a life filled with love for many? How blessed to have loved during one's life so intensely and deeply that the death of that person leaves a tremendous void in your heart and life and leaves behind pain and the emptiness of inconsolable grief. It is the magnitude of loss from death that measures the depth of the love.

So I choose to deal with this grief, to face this real mountain in my life's journey. It's not an option to not grieve because Greg died. The option was not to have loved. And that's no option at all if we honestly want to be truly human and experience and enjoy the emotions that come with our humanity.

The trick is to move through the grief and not remain stuck. This is a monumental task for an individual to face. The truth is this task does not have to be faced alone. I have appreciated the sympathy and support of family and friends. There's that "love" thing again. The price we pay for being supported in grief is leaving ourselves vulnerable and open to grief when another person dies. There are also professional options to dealing with grief—support groups and counseling. They're useful tools to consider.

It quickly becomes apparent after a tragedy like Greg's death that there are many others traveling a similar grief journey, people in similar situations all around us. It helps to have company on the grief journey. It also becomes apparent we may travel that journey together, but we make progress in our own individual ways. No two people make their ways through the minefield of grief on the same path. Sue is more private in her grief. I am very public in mine. As individuals, we don't advance along the path of grief in the same way on different days. The key is to be observant, willing to admit our pain, and humble enough to accept the help necessary to continue to move through the grief.

Sometimes support and compassion come from the least expected sources, while others close to us fail to show up. After Greg's funeral Sue and I received a package from Rigby, Idaho, that contained an inspirational DVD, CD, and note. It was from Rob Crowley, the gentleman I met biking with his son and grandkids on the road in Grand Teton National Park the day Greg's and Walker's beacon signals were picked up. He followed the search after he returned home, made the effort to find our name and address, and sent this package. He wrote that he'd been touched by our conversation and felt a desire to extend his sympathy when he learned of the final outcome. What a beautiful message and powerful expression of sympathy and concern from a man I didn't even know. Rob and his wife, Tauna, continue to remember us at Christmas and the anniversary of Greg's death. In July 2015, we met Rob in Rigby and shared our sadness together.

As a grieving parent, I've become more aware of tragedy involving young people. It seems as if more young people have died since Greg than before. This is probably not statistically valid, but it's true that I now notice news of this kind. The death of a child is now a significant news event for me that triggers an emotional response as well. It's like buying a car in a color that you think isn't very common. After that it seems every car of that model is the same color as yours. Now I have an emotional connection to tragic events that were possible to ignore before because they weren't personal.

Sue and I have also read books on loss and grief—especially the grief of the death of a child—shared by friends or that we've found ourselves. Some are more helpful than others. But every book I have read has helped because each has provided at least one insight that applied to my grief and helped me identify, categorize, rationalize, or deal with it.

Despite my faith, there has also been a lot of doubt and questioning accompanying me on this grief journey. This was especially true initially, but has diminished in frequency and intensity as the months have passed. I've searched for reassurance that there's more to Greg's life than his thirty-one years on earth produced. I find some in the stories and memories shared by his friends. My family has provided comfort and strength for me. I can see Greg's influence in them and know he made an impact on their lives. But doubt lingers.

I had the issue of anger to resolve soon after Greg's death. Not my anger—his. I wondered if Greg was angry when he realized he was dead since he died in a place he considered among the most beautiful on earth. He died while doing something he enjoyed as much as anything. Was he disappointed he couldn't finish what he'd started that day, what he had planned for the rest of his life?

To help resolve this issue Sue and I have read several books about near-death experiences. What do people remember from their journeys into death? The descriptions are never the same but always contain similar elements. One of those is a sense of calm, peace, and love. I trust now that Greg also was greeted with similar feelings as his essence left his earthly body. He was wrapped in love in a place far better than any on earth. He wasn't angry.

Our grief journey has been an attempt for us to find our places in a changed world. It's a search for normal, but a new normal. To try to return to and fit into the world that existed before Greg died is pointless. The world has changed. Greg is no longer physically present in this new world. The former world no longer exists, and wanting to return to it is a fantasy. But I find myself going back and forth between what was and what is. I spent more time in the old, nonexistent world at first, but less now. That's progress.

Change is difficult. When change is thrust upon us suddenly and without warning, it can be extremely challenging. But the change has happened, and we have no choice but to face it.

In her book *Scarred by Struggle, Transformed by Hope* Sister Joan Chittister talks about change—the challenges it creates and the opportunities it presents. She says change happens whether or not we want it. We don't have a choice. But we have a choice in our response to change. She sums it up so eloquently by observing: "You cannot not change. But you can choose to be converted." The change has happened. Will I now be converted to fit into the new normal, the new reality that is life without Greg? The answer has to be yes. To answer otherwise is to be stuck in the past, in a world that no longer exists. The attempt to re-create a nonexistent world can lead to isolation, depression, anger, and subsequent false solutions like alcohol and drugs. I believe Greg wouldn't want me, or any of us, to make that choice. We go on without him, but with him encouraging us, leading us, and cajoling us into a future that's still bright, even in his absence.

In my journey through grief, I've chosen to work to build Greg's legacy. This book is part of that effort. At first, writing was therapeutic. Later it became a burden, and I wanted to quit. But there was so much I still remembered and wanted others to know that I continued, ever so slowly, to document my memories—and I'm happy I did. Now I'm enthusiastically approaching the end of this phase of my grief journey, and I'm experiencing the excitement I imagine Greg felt when he attended a Phish performance with his friends, completed an impossible intubation, or summited Mount Rainier. Maybe I'll never fit into the new normal as comfortably as I did in the old, but I won't stop trying.

In my darkest hour, on my lowest day, when my hope was drained, I never, ever pictured a life without both of my sons. They were always present in my imagined future, no matter the circumstances. But that isn't the future I have before me. It disappoints, upsets, and saddens me. But it doesn't mean I quit. I won't give up or succumb to hopelessness—not because I'm better than others, more resolute in the face of adversity, or better able to overcome sorrow. I'll proceed and live each day forward because I know that's the best way to honor Greg. Greg is dead. But I will enjoy the beauty of nature, be compassionate to my family and friends, and push myself to do things I didn't think I could accomplish. He expects no less of Megan, Chris, Sue, me, and the rest of his family and friends. It will be a lonelier, different journey without Greg, but that's the road now before us.

TIMELINE

July 2, 1979 — Greg is born

January 21, 1982 — Chris is born

June 1998 — Greg graduates from Stillwater High School

May 2002 — Greg graduates from St. Olaf College

September 2002–July 2003 — Greg lives in Bozeman, Montana

May 2007 — Greg graduates from U of MN Medical School

June 2007 — Greg moves to Morgantown, West Virginia, for medical residency

May 2008 — Dan and Sue travel to Indiana for Hannah's high-school graduation; extend the trip to include a visit to Greg and bring along Sue's mom, Dorothy, and their niece Kaity

March 2010 — Greg and Megan are engaged

June 2010 – Greg finishes his residency at West Virginia University Hospitals; Sue and Dan attend residency banquet

August 2010 – Greg begins working at St. Joseph's Hospital in Buckhannon, West Virginia

November 2010 – Greg and Chris return to Minnesota for Sue's mom's eighty-fifth birthday—the last time Sue, Dan, Greg, and Chris are together as a family; Greg and Megan break off their engagement; Greg resigns his position at St. Joe's

March 2011 – Greg's last visit to Minnesota (during his move to Montana)

Wednesday, April 13, 2011 – Greg's interview at hospital in Libby, Montana; clothes shopping in Kalispell, Montana; last phone conversation with Sue and Dan

Thursday, April 14, 2011 – Greg drives to Bozeman, Montana

Friday, April 15, 2011 – Greg drives to Jackson, Wyoming, to meet up with Walker Kuhl

Saturday, April 16, 2011 – Greg and Walker check in at the Grand Teton National Park (GTNP) Visitor Center in Moose to get a backcountry permit; they enter GTNP and camp in Garnet Canyon

Sunday, April 17, 2011 – Greg and Walker's anticipated return

Monday, April 18, 2011 – Walker's girlfriend calls GTNP staff when Walker doesn't show up at work; rangers ski into the canyon to look for signs of Walker and Greg; Dan and Sue receive a call from Elizabeth Maki that Greg is overdue

Tuesday, April 19, 2011 — Search continues; Dan and Sue make calls to family; Dan talks with David Francis; updates from Elizabeth Maki

Wednesday, April 20, 2011 — Search continues; Dan and Sue fly to Jackson, Wyoming, and meet up with Chris; Walker's family arrives at GTNP

Thursday, April 21, 2011 — Snow prevents search; Greg's and Walker's vehicles moved from the parking lot

Friday, April 22, 2011 — No search again; Chris, Jesse, Brandon, and Walker's family depart Jackson

Saturday, April 23, 2011 — Search resumes; Jocelyn Plass arrives with her children; SAR team locates Walker and Greg

Sunday, April 24, 2011 — Walker's and Greg's bodies are flown out of Garnet Canyon; Chris, Jesse, and Walker's parents return to Jackson; the coroner meets with the families

Monday, April 25, 2011 — Arrangements are made to transport Greg to Minnesota; funeral plans are made; Dan and Sue fly home

Tuesday, April 26, 2011 — Funeral plans are finalized at Bradshaw Funeral Home in Stillwater

Wednesday, April 27, 2011 — Dan accompanies Michael Sorrel to Minneapolis–St. Paul Airport to pick up Greg's remains; Sue and Dan meet with clergy to plan the funeral service

Thursday, April 28, 2011 — Out-of-town family begin to arrive

Friday, April 29, 2011 — Megan, Rick, and Dan have a private viewing at Bradshaw

Saturday, April 30, 2011 — Greg's family meets with the Pastor Jan Mehlhoff to share memories as she prepares the eulogy

Sunday, May 1, 2011 — Visitation

Monday, May 2, 2011 — Greg's funeral; cremation

August 2011 — Dan, Sue, Chris, and Jesse return to GTNP to hike to Garnet Canyon

August 2013 — Committal Service at Evergreen Cemetery in Afton

ACKNOWLEDGMENTS

This tribute to Greg could not have happened without the support of many people.

Thanks to my wife, Sue, for your encouragement, love, and simple presence during these months of intense sorrow. Thank you for allowing me to grieve in my own way. I hope I've supported you as you expected since our son's death. You always have been an amazing lady. I love you.

Thanks, Chris, for answering my questions and being there to help and support Mom and me and for connecting when you needed support too. I'm sorry you are without your brother, friend, and mentor.

Megan, thank you for loving Greg and giving him someone special to love. You made him a better person. Thank you for your continued presence in our lives.

To our families, Greg's family, your prayers, calls, and visits mean so much as we continue to grieve and face the future. Grandma, aunts, uncles, cousins, we've been drawn closer in our grief. Just as he did in life, Greg's death has pulled us together.

A most special thanks to Greg's friends, our friends now, who continue to remember their partner in crime and share our sadness: John and Lisa, John, Cindy and Jeremy, Steve, Marcy, Matt, Sara, Andy, Pete, Mike, Mitch and Kelly, Jason and Brianna, Tony, Brian, Mirza, Rich, Andy and Hilary, Joel and Anya, Joel and Angie, Ryan and Stephanie, Nick and Kristel, and Matt.

And thanks to Chris's friends for their love and support for him and Sue and me; to Josie, Rob and Tara, Kees, Ryan, Jesse, Megan, and countless others. Thanks to Allison McGree for sharing her talents to create *Wildcat*, the amazing painting of Garnet Canyon and the Grand. Thank you, Brandon, for your presence in Jackson during the search and for your gift of the beautiful etched metal Grand Teton.

A special thanks to Greg's WVU family. He definitely matured and grew in confidence under your tutelage. Hollynn Larrabee, Todd Crocco, Jack Ditty, and especially Judy Kraycar, you shaped an awkward, uncertain med-school graduate into a competent, caring doctor.

Thanks to our dear neighbors and friends Helen and Eldo Thielfoldt. I was inspired to continue this project by the persistence you showed in restoring your Corvette, Eldo. To all our friends and neighbors, too numerous to mention, who have listened to our laments, been patient with us in our grief, and haven't told us to "get over it." To all who have continued to support us over these five years with cards and caring words, thank you.

Sue and I could not have traveled this grief journey without our trust in God. Our faith communities, Guardian Angels Catholic Church and Lutheran Church of Peace, supported us and walked with us throughout. A very special thanks to Sister Dorothy Mrock. Your unofficial counseling allowed me to navigate dark areas of my soul; because you were guiding me, I was unafraid that I would falter. Grief counselor Tony Del Percio and all the folks at Bradshaw have been professional and compassionate.

It's been said that every author needs a writing community. That was especially true for me as a first-time author. Thanks to the wonderful people at Beaver's Pond Press not only for taking a chance on me, but for your encouragement and very professional support. To Lily Coyle, Alicia Ester, and Dan Pitts, thank you. *Real Mountains* is infinitely improved because of my editor, Wendy Weckwerth. Thank you, Angela Foster, for teaching me about memoir, finding value in Greg's story, and improving those early drafts. Chuck Campbell, Alvin Handelman, David Francis, Kaity Drazich, Chelsea Skone, and Rick Seftick provided advice and encouragement via edits, e-mails, and phone calls. And a great big, most special thank-you to my writing group, the PEAs—Arlys, Donna, Lois, Lola, Maryah, and Sharon—for your suggestions, encouragement, and tears shared in appropriate monthly doses. Your hearts and skills reside within the pages of this book.

Thank you to our Teton family. To the family advocates who lovingly guided us through the tragic days in April 2011, Elizabeth Maki, Terry Roper, and Bonnie Whitman, thank you from the bottom of our hearts. You were beacons in those dark days as we searched together for Walker and Greg. Thanks to Jackie Skaggs, park spokesperson, and to Scott Guenther and Chris Harder for professional, yet compassionate leadership. And Nick Armitage. I can't imagine how we could have left Jackson without knowing Greg's fate. Thank you for your persistence and for making Greg and Walker's recovery personal.

Thanks to the people of Jackson, Wyoming, and surrounding areas. You cared enough to provide convenient accommodations, a free dessert, a hasty meal to go, sleeping-bag dry cleaning gratis, and much more. Unknown to us, many of you changed plans so as not to interfere with SAR. I would be remiss if I didn't mention Steve Romeo, a prominent local mountaineer and blogger who wrote supportively and compassionately about Walker and Greg after their deaths. Sadly, Steve and a friend died less than a year later in an avalanche in another section of Grand Teton National Park. Thanks to Brendan Hughes and his group, the last people to see Walker and Greg alive, for taking time to contact the park rangers and share your important information with the search team.

The Jon Francis Foundation has been a valuable resource for us, providing answers and advice we needed during the search. Sue and I will be forever grateful for the presence of Jocelyn Francis Plass while we were in Wyoming. And David and Linda—thank you for so much. For your friendship, for speaking to the media during our time in Jackson, and for recognizing that there was a story to tell about Greg's short life.

Thank you to all parents of the same heart, those who have suffered the death of a child, for your presence and support. Our sincere sympathy to all, no matter the circumstances of your personal tragedy.

Richard Kuhl and Marylane Pannel, what can be said? I'm sorry. Thank you. I truly wish I had known Walker. He was a good man. We had confidence in him and respected him as much as any of our sons' friends.

Special recognition to Gayle Cragoe and again to David and Linda Francis. I smile and cry as I picture our sons—Jared, Jon, and Chris—playing soccer during their elementary-school days. Thanks also to Lindsay Cragoe for your support and love since your brother Jared's death.

Thank you to everyone who ever has or ever will participate in Greg's Night of Light. I have joked that April 16 should be a national holiday, or at least important enough to merit a section in Hallmark stores for Night of Light cards. Even if neither happens, because of you, it has become a worldwide event and a source of light on an otherwise dark day. As Greg would say, "Pretty sweet."

NONPROFITS—
GIVING IN HONOR OF GREG

All proceeds from *Real Mountains* support programs aimed at preserving and building Greg's legacy and supporting the ongoing work of those who helped bring him and Walker back to their families. Please make a tax-deductible contribution to one or more of the following important organizations—noting "Greg Seftick" in the memo line of your check.

Access Fund
PO Box 17010
Boulder, CO 80308
303.545.6772
accessfund.org

The Access Fund works to keep climbing areas open and conserves the climbing environment.

Grand Teton Association
PO Box 170
Moose, WY 83012
307.739.3406
grandtetonpark.org

The mission of the Grand Teton Association is to increase public understanding, appreciation, and enjoyment of Grand Teton National Park and the surrounding public lands through aid to interpretive, educational, and research programs.

St. Croix Valley Foundation
516 Second Street, Suite 214
Hudson, WI 54016
715.386.9490
scvfoundation.org

The mission of the St. Croix Valley Foundation (SCVF) is enhancing the quality of life in the St. Croix Valley Region by helping people leave a financial legacy to forever support the places and programs they love; wisely investing individual, family, and organizational funds entrusted to its care; awarding grants to support the work of charitable organizations; and convening individuals and organizations to find solutions to community concerns.

The Dr. Greg Seftick Wilderness Scholarship Fund was established with SCVF in 2013 in memory of Greg, an avid outdoorsman who loved the mountains. Each year, a scholarship is awarded in Greg's honor to a member of the alpine ski team at Stillwater High School.

WVU Foundation
Greg Seftick Wilderness Medicine Fund
PO Box 9008
Morgantown, WV 26506
304.293.3980
mountaineerconnection.com/givetoEmergencyMedicine

The West Virginia University School of Medicine improves the lives of the people of West Virginia and beyond through excellence in patient care, education, research, and service. Funds will support the Dr. Gregory Seftick Wilderness Medicine Fund, which promotes and enhances wilderness medicine education, research, outreach, and care in honor of Gregory Seftick.